SEÁN MURRAY

SEÁN MURRAY

Marxist-Leninist and Irish Socialist Republican

Seán Byers

IRISH ACADEMIC PRESS

First published in 2015 by Irish Academic Press
8 Chapel Lane
Sallins
Co. Kildare

© 2015 Seán Byers

British Library Cataloguing in Publication Data
An entry can be found on request

978-07165-3297-2 (paper)
978-07165-3296-5 (cloth)
978-07165-3298-9 (PDF)

Library of Congress Cataloging in Publication Data
An entry can be found on request

Printed in Ireland by SPRINT-print Ltd

Contents

Acknowledgements

Though sustained by activists, independent researchers and academic adherents, the study of Irish labour history endures difficult conditions and faces an uncertain future. Likewise, the institutions tasked with preserving historical sources continue to provide vital services in the most demanding circumstances. For this reason, I am especially grateful for the assistance of staff at various libraries and archives: the University of Ulster at Jordanstown; Queen's University Belfast Special Collections; University College Dublin; the Linen Hall Library, Belfast; the Public Record Office of Northern Ireland (PRONI), the Marx Memorial Library, London; the Irish Military Archives, Cathal Brugha Barracks, Dublin; the National Library of Ireland; Dublin City Library & Archive; and the National Archives of Ireland, Dublin.

I am fortunate to have benefitted from the unique and valuable recollections of Seán Murray's contemporaries: Anthony Coughlan, Wilson John Haire, Roy Johnston, Seán Morrissey, Eoin Ó Murchú, the late Bill Somerset, Edwina Stewart and the late Jimmy Stewart. I am also indebted to colleagues and friends for their encouragement and advice, which have shaped and strengthened the book from its conception: Máire Braniff, David Convery, Erik Cownie, Pat Devine junior, Aaron Edwards, Richard English, Kerry Fleck, Adrian Grant, David Granville, Chris Hazzard, David Howell, Chris Loughlin, Rayner Lysaght, Conor McCabe, Stephen McCloskey, Fionntán McElheran, Cillian McGrattan, Jim Monaghan, Emmet O'Connor, Antaine Ó Donnaile, Connal Parr, Michael Pierse, Michael Quinn, Lynda Walker and Stephen White. The ways in which they have helped are too numerous to mention, though special thanks go to Henry Patterson for his critical insights, acerbic wit, and for nurturing my interest in various aspects of socialist history and politics.

Acknowledgements

My comrades at Trademark – Urko Beitia, Mel Corry, Tomas Gorman, Joe Law, Ali McLarnon, Stevie Nolan, Kellie O'Dowd and Ellie Perrin – have proved a source of knowledge and inspiration, offering fresh perspectives and ensuring that my worldview is subject to critical appraisal on a daily basis. They are incorrigible advocates of progressive politics and shining examples of good practice in their respective fields. More broadly, the labour movement of which I am part is presently engaged in struggles reminiscent of those witnessed throughout Murray's era. As an active trade unionist and member of Unite, I have been sustained and indeed enthused by the actions of comrades in Britain and particularly across the island of Ireland. They have further driven home the importance of recovering aspects of working-class history for the benefit of posterity and doing justice to the efforts of previous generations of labour activists.

The support of Conor Graham and Lisa Hyde has been crucial in ensuring that this monograph has seen the light of day. They have not only given me the opportunity to follow in the footsteps of a number of great historians but have devoted considerable time and effort to aid the research and writing process, particularly in its final stages. They deserve special credit for encouraging young authors towards publication and broadening the scope of Irish historiography as a result.

Finally, I am ever grateful to my friends and family, not least for keeping my feet firmly on the ground. Thanks to my parents, Brendan and Teresa, without whose humour, endless support and unquestioning faith in my ability I would never have even started writing, and my brothers, Brendan and Rory, who are at once a source of irritation and entertainment. This book is as much their achievement as mine, though the faults and errors contained herein are, of course, all my own.

List of Abbreviations

ACA	Army Comrades' Association
AEU	Amalgamated Engineering Union
AOH	Ancient Order of Hibernians
APL	Anti-Partition League
ARCOS	All-Russian Co-operative Society
ATGWU	Amalgamated Transport and General Workers' Union
CEU	Commercial Employees Union
CIU	Congress of Irish Unions
CLC	Central Labour College
CLP	Commonwealth Labour Party
Comintern	Communist International
CNT	Confederación Nacional del Trabajo (National Confederation of Labour, Spain)
CPGB	Communist Party of Great Britain
CPI	Communist Party of Ireland
CPNI	Communist Party (Northern Ireland)
CPSU	Communist Party of the Soviet Union
CPUSA	Communist Party of the United States of America
CYMS	Catholic Young Men's Society
DUTC	Dublin United Tramways Company
ECCI	Executive Committee of the Communist International

List of Abbreviations

EEC	European Economic Community
ICA	Irish Citizen Army
ICF	Irish Christian Front
ICTU	Irish Congress of Trade Unions
ICWPA	International Class War Prisoners' Aid
IDA	Industrial Development Authority
ILDL	Irish Labour Defence League
ILP	Independent Labour Party
INUM	Irish National Unemployed Movement
IRA	Irish Republican Army
IrLP	Irish Labour Party (North)
ITGWU	Irish Transport and General Workers' Union
ITUC	Irish Trade Union Congress
IWFC	Irish Working Farmers' Committee
IWL	Irish Worker League/Irish Workers' League
IWP	Irish Workers' Party
IWW	Industrial Workers of the World
LAI	League Against Imperialism
NATO	North Atlantic Treaty Organization
NCCL	National Council for Civil Liberties
NIC	Northern Ireland Committee of the ITUC
NICRA	Northern Ireland Civil Rights Association
NILP	Northern Ireland Labour Party
NISP	Northern Ireland Socialist Party
NUR	National Union of Railwaymen
NUDAW	National Union of Distributive and Allied Workers
PCF	Parti Communiste Français (French Communist Party)

POUM	Partido Obrero de Unificación Marxista (Workers' Party of Marxist Unification, Spain)
PUO	Provisional United Trade Union Organisation
RIC	Royal Irish Constabulary
ROP	Russian Oil Products
RUC	Royal Ulster Constabulary
RWG	Revolutionary Workers' Groups
RWP	Revolutionary Workers' Party
SYL	Socialist Youth League
UPL	Ulster Protestant League
UULA	Ulster Unionist Labour Association
UVF	Ulster Volunteer Force
VKP/b	Vsesoyuznaya Kommunisticheskaya Partiya (Bolshevikov) (All-Union Communist Party (Bolsheviks))
WPI	Workers' Party of Ireland
WUI	Workers' Union of Ireland
YWL	Young Workers' League

List of Plates

1. Pupils of Glenaan National School with Master MacNamee, 1906. Murray is in the front row, standing on the right of the picture. His sisters, Kate and Mary, are also in the photo (Fionntán McElheran).

2. Members of the IRA Antrim Brigade at the Curragh Camp, Kildare, Autumn 1922 (Fionntán McElheran).

3. National Builders', Labourers' and Constructional Workers' Society, London District branch contribution card, 1925 (CPI/PRONI).

4. Electrical Trades Union, Belfast Central branch contribution card, 1948 (CPI/PRONI).

5. Seán Murray's autobiography for the Comintern, 11 August 1932 (RGASPI).

6. Front page of Murray's letter to Mingulin, a Comintern functionary, re his Russian wife, c. 1930 (RGASPI).

7. *Ireland's Path to Freedom* (1933) (Conor McCabe).

8. Irish Labour Defence League poster, May Day 1934 (NAI, Department of Justice, 2008/117/38).

9. Comintern profile photo (RGASPI, courtesy of Emmet O'Connor).

10. Bill Rust (CPGB and *Daily Worker*), Billy McCullough and Murray at the Hippodrome, London, for the twenty-seventh anniversary of the Bolshevik Revolution, 12 November 1944 (CPI/PRONI).

11. With Margaret outside the farmhouse at Ballybrack, 1956 (Fionntán McElheran).

12. At Nikolai Bukharin's house, Crimea, for the fortieth anniversary of the Bolshevik Revolution, 1957 (CPI/PRONI).

13. 'This is Your Life' 60th birthday celebrations at the ASW Hall, Belfast, 1958. Presentation made by Andy Barr (CPI/PRONI).

14. Visiting a factory in Bratislava, Czechoslovakia, February 1959 (CPI/PRONI).

15. Margaret Murray outside Finche's pub, London, August 1960. She is accompanied by Bill Gannon (centre left) and Jim Prendergast (centre right) (Fionntán McElheran & Jack Gannon).

16. *Irish Socialist*, June 1961 (CPI/PRONI).

17. *Ireland's Path to Socialism* (1962).

Introduction

On 5 July 2013, a year carrying great significance for the Irish working class, members of the Communist Party of Ireland (CPI) assembled at a plot in Belfast's Dundonald Cemetery which was bequeathed to the party by Davey Scarborough, a popular communist shop steward whose efforts to combat sectarianism in the shipyards are dramatised in Sam Thompson's unflinching play, *Over the Bridge* (1960). On this occasion, the party faithful had gathered to scatter the ashes of Jimmy Stewart, a recently departed party member of sixty years, over the grave of his mentor, Seán Murray, War of Independence veteran and general secretary of the CPI from its foundation in 1933 to 1941. Communists and trade unionists from across the island joined Jimmy's wife, Edwina in honouring the three men, whose lives had intersected and who had contributed to various Irish labour, republican and international socialist struggles in their own different ways. This was followed by a social, where those in attendance shared stories about Murray and his fellow deceased comrades as well as their considerable legacies.

In one sense, things had come full circle for the party. Fifty years earlier, in 1963, the labour and republican movements had cause to commemorate a number of significant anniversaries. It was the bi-centenary of the birth of Wolfe Tone, founder of the United Irishmen and one of the fathers of Irish republicanism. It marked fifty years since the Lock-out and formation of the Irish Citizen Army (ICA), a year of class warfare and temporary defeat for the Irish Transport and General Workers' Union (ITGWU) and industrial trade unionism in Ireland. It also marked the thirtieth anniversary of the re-formation of the CPI and the second anniversary of Seán Murray's death. Comrades from Dublin and Belfast were there to witness William Gallacher, the former communist MP for West Fife, unveiling a memorial stone over Murray's grave. Later in the day, a meeting was held to celebrate the work of the CPI during its thirty-year existence. Billy

McCullough outlined the main struggles of the party over the years and led the tributes to Murray for his efforts in building a united Irish communist movement.[1]

A history of the CPI that appraises its contribution in terms of electoral success would be very narrow. The left in Ireland has had a negligible political presence and the communist movement even less. But despite its failure to make inroads in parliamentary politics, the party has, through a series of different incarnations, influenced the trajectory of the labour and republican movements and left a significant imprint on Irish cultural and intellectual life. The efforts of the CPI and its members to change society in unfavourable conditions are documented in the official *Outline History* edited by Seán Nolan, Mike Milotte's *Communism in Modern Ireland*,[2] Emmet O'Connor's *Reds and the Green*[3] and, more recently, Matt Treacy's *The Communist Party of Ireland* (2013).[4] They also feature prominently in studies of the IRA and the phenomenon of socialist republicanism,[5] general histories of Irish involvement in the Spanish Civil War,[6] and (auto)biographies of the Irish left. We still await the door-stopping, comprehensive history the party deserves, but our understanding of the communist movement's overall contribution is growing richer for the scholarly attention it continues to attract.

The genre of political biography remains a popular explanatory tool, a method of exploring the micro-level impact of macro-level processes and providing a nexus between events of international significance and local or national contexts. Appraising the current state of Irish labour historiography, O'Connor and fellow historian Conor McCabe warn against the trappings of hagiography and producing a history from above:

> Few studies connect their subject adequately to his or her context and interrogate their record in the light of the forces at their disposal or the options that were open to them. In consequence, such work has little to say on the concept of leadership or about power relations within the Labour movement, and contributes little to the wider debate on the trajectory of Labour. An upbeat approach, identifying with and presenting the subject in the best way possible, seems *de rigueur*.[7]

In other words, the value of a political biography must lie in its ability to address wider social, economic and political questions along with the individual and personal details that make it unique. They must approach their subjects with an appropriate level of 'imaginative understanding' rather than sympathy, and demonstrate awareness of how they interact with, and are shaped by, the social structures around them.[8]

There are whole biographical industries around certain iconic figures, no more so than James Connolly, whose life and politics is the focus of over three hundred monographs, articles and pamphlets. This body of literature contains its fair share of hagiographies, on the one hand, and incessantly revisionist works, on the other. Aptly, Seán Murray's death in 1961 coincided with the publication of what remains the most thorough biography of Connolly.[9] The author, British communist historian Desmond Greaves, also penned biographies of Liam Mellows and Seán O'Casey as well as a history of the ITGWU in its infancy.[10] One interesting detail about Greaves' research is that he had, in the 1970s, planned a five-instalment series of political biographies of the Irish left, culminating in a prosopography of the working class. He shelved a project on Frank Ryan owing to a lack of new sources before turning his attention to Murray. After amassing considerable material from Murray's wife, Margaret, contemporaries such as Michael McInerney and Peadar O'Donnell, and archivists in Belfast and Dublin, he decided that a monograph based on limited documentary evidence would leave too many questions unanswered, thus falling well short of the 'full story'.[11]

Greaves had every reason to be pessimistic at the time. However, Irish left/working class historiography has since witnessed a proliferation of studies documenting the lives of incorrigible labour, communist and socialist republican activists including Jim Larkin, William O'Brien, Jack White, Seán McLoughlin, Rosamond Jacob, Hanna Sheehy Skeffington, Charlotte Despard, Jim Larkin junior, Harry Midgley, Betty Sinclair, Andy Barr, Roddy Connolly and Peadar O'Donnell. Incidentally, the tragically short life of Frank Ryan is the subject of three biographies, one celebratory, one personal, and the other deeply critical.[12] O'Donnell, a tireless agitator and a central figure in early attempts to develop the IRA's politics, was, unlike Ryan, a prolific writer and left considerable memoirs for the benefit of posterity.[13] His much longer life and more extensive political career is the subject of four full-length monographs.[14] What all of these left-wing thinkers and activists have in common is their personal and political relationships with Murray, who worked with and directly influenced them in one way or another.

Records of Murray's political activities are dispersed across the growing corpus of texts in the field of Irish labour history, including the (auto)biographies of the aforementioned individuals. Yet he has received limited attention in his own right. Setting out to deliver a 'systematic analysis' of Irish communism, Milotte succeeds in rescuing 'from an undeserved obscurity some redoubtable working-class activists and their heroic struggles'. Murray is among the activists whose efforts are rescued. However, he is portrayed as representative of a movement that failed to achieve its objectives because of 'its entanglement with Stalinist Russia and its constant need to reflect the foreign policy requirements of the Soviet state'.[15] Thorough and impressive in its research, Milotte's pioneering work uses CPI documents to attribute the party's twists and turns to the internal politics of the Soviet Union and what is disparagingly referred to as 'Stalinism', even when they are often of dubious relevance to the Irish communist activities under discussion. It is at best an oversimplification to argue that Murray, the CPI and other peripheral communist parties were only 'able to develop a more autonomous politics' in the wake of Stalin's death.[16] It fails to take into proper consideration a number of important factors: national specificities; internal deliberations; the Communist International (Comintern) bodies that sat outside Stalin's sphere of influence; the degree of latitude afforded by the Comintern on policy and tactics; and the decisions taken in direct contradiction to directives from Moscow.[17] It also detracts from a serious analysis of rapidly changing social, political and economic conditions in Ireland and the limited possibilities that these conditions afforded.

Isaac Deutscher has argued correctly that 'anybody who would try to comprehend the history of any communist party merely in the context of its own environment would fail'.[18] However, Milotte's book is perhaps best described as an Irish facsimile of traditional accounts of international communism, which place Stalin and the Communist Party of the Soviet Union (CPSU) above the remaining Comintern-affiliated parties as the fundamental source of ideological and tactical inspiration. For example, Borkenau asserts that

> The Comintern had been the primary expression of Russian revolutionism … It was unthinkable that the Comintern could have an ideology divergent from that imposed by the infallible leader of Russia. Here foreign policy did not even take place of honour. The Comintern from beginning to end remained a church where unity of the credo was the paramount consideration.[19]

Similarly, Duncan Hallas has written that 'it was one thing to "go to school" under the Russians but quite another to come to rely on the teachers to resolve the complex problems facing the German, Polish, British, United States or whatever parties'. The failure of the Comintern to spread the revolution westwards, according to Hallas, lay in the pupils' 'excessive dependence on the teacher'.[20] The release of the Comintern archives in the 1990s has enabled historians to shed greater light on the workings of its structures and centre-periphery relations, challenging grand narrative approaches to the history of international communism. The most important of these, written by Kevin McDermott and Jeremy Agnew, accepts the above charges in part while drawing attention to the relative autonomy enjoyed by communist and workers' parties on the question of tactics. These authors also make the important distinction between an early phase of 'Bolshevisation' and a later period of 'Stalinisation'.[21]

Debates between the contrasting schools of thought on the Comintern and 'Stalinism' are most pronounced in the case of the British party.[22] Emmet O'Connor has quite recently entered the fray with his work on Irish communism, which clearly owes a great deal to the more nuanced analytical framework endowed by McDermott and Agnew.[23] In line with recent trends in the historiography of communism, O'Connor uses the Comintern archives to correct the deficiencies of previous analyses of the CPI.[24] He argues that, 'The impact of the Comintern on Irish communist organisation and policy was fundamental, and largely positive.'[25] But he qualifies this by demonstrating that the Irish party endured a complex and difficult relationship with the international communist hierarchy and with the Communist Party of Great Britain (CPGB) in particular. He confirms Milotte's suspicions that the Comintern 'offered precise instructions on slogans, programmes, tactics, timing, and tone of statements' through its British intermediaries,[26] and argues convincingly that 'the British party invariably regarded Irish communists as subordinate to its own interests in Britain, or its agenda on Ireland'.[27] Interventions by the Comintern and CPGB in the affairs of the CPI 'made little allowance for the difficulties besetting its Irish section'.[28] For that reason, their instructions were not always welcome or taken on board, and were actively resisted in some instances.

Murray was at the reins of the nascent second CPI in 1932, 'the high tide of communism in Ireland'.[29] Yet, in O'Connor's estimation, the favourable conditions for building a party and a movement in cooperation with left republicans deteriorated quickly thereafter. The Comintern's adoption of 'class against class', a narrowly sectarian and self-defeating tactic, 'discourage[d] the strengthening of links with republicans when the IRA was most susceptible to communism'.[30]

Subsequently, the 'red scare' tactics of the Catholic Church and conservative media, combined with Unionist state repression, prevented the movement from recapturing the impetus and spirit of the late 1920s.[31] These points are compelling. However, O'Connor's focus on institutional relationships does not allow for a wider exploration of Murray's political career, of his response to events of international and domestic significance, of his own battles with the CPGB and Comintern, or why he continued to persevere in the face of extreme adversity. Building on O'Connor's work, this is an opportune time to examine Murray's political thought and determine the extent to which this was reflected in CPI policy and tactics.

Stephen Bowler's aptly-named essay, 'Seán Murray, 1898-1961, And the Pursuit of Stalinism in One Country', was the first attempt at a study devoted to Murray's life and politics. Like Milotte, Bowler did not have access to the Comintern archives. It is to his credit, therefore, that he recognises that CPI leaders such as Murray 'adapted to the particular pressures of the Irish context' and 'were neither pawns of Moscow, nor slaves to the rhythm of Irish nationalism'.[32] Yet the focus on Murray's communist apprenticeship at the expense of his early republican activities leads Bowler to neglect at least one formative influence on his subject. Consequently, he reaches the conclusion that it was Murray's

> misfortune to find himself at the Lenin School in Moscow during the period when Stalin was consolidating his grip. It would have been unthinkable for Murray to have emerged from his training with any serious doubts about the merits of defending 'socialism in one country'.[33]

Bowler characterises Murray as a 'Stalinist' representative in Ireland, under whose leadership it was 'the task of the Irish Communists to cohere such aspirations, in accord with many others who also went to make up the Comintern'.[34] This prompted the late Joe Deasy to contest the use of the term 'Stalinism' and its 'disparaging' connotations.[35] Ultimately, although Bowler is more sympathetic than Milotte in terms of the challenges of operating as a national section of a world communist party, his overall judgement is that compliance with instructions laid out by head office in Moscow led to successive CPI failures. This does not even begin to capture the complexities of Comintern organisation and procedures, or the important distinction between that body and the CPSU. Crucially, Bowler advances a one-dimensional interpretation of Murray's ideological make-up, which contrasts with the multi-faceted reality.

Aside from Bowler's overview and a short biographical essay by O'Connor in the *Dictionary of Labour Biography*,[36] the closest we have come to a full-length study of Murray's public life is a relatively unknown piece by Belfast-based historian, Denis Smyth. Smyth's work is more a romantic tribute to Murray's politics than a critical examination of them but, appositely, he acknowledges the limitations of his research and notes that 'there is still an enormous degree of research material, documentation and sources still to be tapped'.[37] Used in conjunction with material in the possession of Desmond Greaves' literary executor, Anthony Coughlan, this range of sources sheds great light on Murray's political career and allows one to get as close as possible to the 'full story'. The collection of four thousand documents retrieved from the Comintern archives in Moscow is but one example.[38] Another is the CPI Seán Nolan/Geoffrey Palmer Collection, recently deposited at the Dublin City Library and Archive. This collection includes draft policy documents, records of national leadership meetings and Dublin party branch minute books, all of which add great depth to the available contemporary sources on the Irish communist movement. The Irish Bureau of Military History contains valuable records of Murray's IRA career and the activities of his Antrim Brigade. As regards official sources, a detailed British intelligence file on Murray sits in the British National Archives in London. Records of the departments of Justice, Taoiseach and External Affairs in the National Archives of Ireland are a mine of information, as are Northern Ireland Ministry of Home Affairs files. For most of the period in question, the authorities paid close attention to the activities of the labour and republican movements. RUC and Garda Special Branch detectives were in regular attendance at meetings held by communists and allied groups, and the evidence suggests that both police forces had a few well-placed informants within the CPI. Finally, unlike Greaves, this generation of historians is in a position to benefit from the digitisation of newspapers and other manuscripts, which has provided, amongst other things, an insight into the conservative media's treatment of Murray.

Despite this, the process of writing this political biography was by no means straightforward. Seán Murray's private papers, held at the Public Record Office of Northern Ireland (PRONI), are a rich source of information, containing important details on party policy and Murray's political thought in the form of party circulars, manuscripts, surviving letters and notebooks. However, the collection has been physically damaged by years of wear and tear making it illegible in places, and documentary evidence has been lost as a result of removal, unauthorised or otherwise. This means that there are important facts and details about Murray's life and career forever lost to history. It is also the case that Murray was not inclined to record his private thoughts on paper. Peadar O'Donnell, his closest friend, said of this: 'He would write only on the current, concrete situation, and write brilliantly, but he had a strange reluctance to uncover his mind except in conversation.'[39] This has deprived scholars of a proper insight into his personal battles, with alcohol and in love for example, and a fuller understanding of his thought processes.

Fortunately, Murray was a prolific writer and propagandist, the editor and lead contributor of a series of short-lived radical newspapers. He published a number of pamphlets and left reams of political tracts unpublished. Where this book falls short in uncovering the stuff of personal biography, it succeeds in detailing Murray's considerable political activities and in delivering an intellectual history of Irish communism and socialist republicanism between 1916 and 1962. It documents Murray's considerable IRA activities during the Irish revolutionary period, his significant contribution to the 1932 outdoor relief strike and the short-lived Republican Congress initiative, and his crucial role in organising the Irish contingent of the International Brigades. It reveals how cross-pollination between the Irish socialist and left republican movements was maintained by virtue of Murray's relationships with a number of key individuals. The book also illuminates his connections in Britain and the US, his various trips to Moscow, and the difficult relationship he endured with the decision-making bodies of international communism as he attempted to reconcile their universal demands with conditions that were specific to Ireland, north and south. This is a story of how, in the face of adversity, Murray made a significant contribution to British and Irish leftist politics through his work as an activist and organiser, writer, propagandist and theorist.

NOTES

1 Seán Nolan (ed.), *Communist Party of Ireland Outline History* (Dublin, 1975), p.43.
2 Mike Milotte, *Communism in Modern Ireland: The Pursuit of the Workers' Republic since 1916* (Dublin, 1984).
3 Emmet O'Connor, *Reds and the Green: Ireland, Russia and the Communist Internationals, 1919-43* (Dublin, 2004).

4   Matt Treacy, *The Communist Party of Ireland 1921-2011: Vol. 1: 1921-1969* (Dublin, 2013).

5   Richard English, *Radicals and the Republic: Socialist Republicanism in the Irish Free State, 1925-1937* (Oxford, 1994); Adrian Grant, *Irish Socialist Republicanism, 1909-36* (Dublin, 2012); Brian Hanley, *The IRA, 1926-1936* (Dublin, 2002); Henry Patterson, *The Politics of Illusion: A Political History of the IRA* (London, 1997).

6   Fearghal McGarry, *Irish Politics and the Spanish Civil War* (Cork, 1999); Robert Stradling, *The Irish in the Spanish Civil War, 1936-39: Crusades in Conflict* (Manchester, 1999).

7   Emmet O'Connor and Conor McCabe, 'Ireland', in Joan Allen, Alan Campbell and John McIlroy (eds), *Histories of Labour: National and International Perspectives* (Pontypool, 2010), p.150.

8   E.H. Carr, *What is History?* (2nd ed., with new introduction by Richard J. Evans) (Basingstoke, 2001), p.18.

9   C. Desmond Greaves, *The Life and Times of James Connolly* (London, 1961).

10 C. Desmond Greaves, *Liam Mellows and the Irish Revolution* (London, 1971); *Seán O'Casey: Politics and Art* (London, 1971); *The Irish Transport and General Workers' Union: The Formative Years, 1909-1923* (Dublin, 1982).

11 Author's interview with Anthony Coughlan, 10 September 2010.

12 Seán Cronin, *Frank Ryan: The Search for the Republic* (Dublin, 1980); Adrian Hoar, *In Green and Red: The Lives of Frank Ryan* (Dingle, 2004); Fearghal McGarry, *Frank Ryan* (Dundalk, 2002).

13 *The Gates Flew Open* (London, 1932) is a record of his time in prison during the Irish Civil War; *Salud! An Irishman in Spain* (London, 1937) deals with the Spanish Civil War period; *There Will Be Another Day* (Dublin, 1963) is a recollection of the land annuities campaign; *Monkeys in the Superstructure: Reminiscences of Peadar O'Donnell* (Galway, 1986) is the last instalment of autobiographies, published shortly after his death at the behest of The Committee of Concerned University Staff.

14 Grattan Freyer, *Peadar O'Donnell* (Lewisburg, 1973); Peter Hegarty, *Peadar O'Donnell* (Cork, 1999); Michael McInerney, *Peadar O'Donnell: Irish Social Rebel* (Dublin, 1974); Donal Ó Drisceoil, *Peadar O'Donnell* (Cork, 2001).

15 Milotte, *Communism in Modern Ireland*, pp.4, 7-8.

16 Ibid., p.224.

17 Matt Treacy's *The Communist Party of Ireland* is beset with similar problems of a larger scale. See Seán Byers, 'The Communist Party of Ireland 1921-2011: Vol. 1: 1921-1969', *Irish Political Studies*, DOI: 10.1080/ 07907184.2014.900230.

18 Isaac Deutscher, *Stalin: A Political Biography* (London, 1964), p.394.

19 Franz Borkenau, *World Communism: A History of the Communist International* (Michigan, 1962), p.394.

20 Duncan Hallas, *The Comintern* (London, 1985), pp.70-1.

21 Kevin McDermott and Jeremy Agnew, *The Comintern: A History of International Communism from Lenin to Stalin* (Basingstoke, 1996).

22 John Newsinger, 'Recent Controversies in the History of British Communism (Review article)', *Journal of Contemporary History*, Vol. 41, No. 3 (2006), pp. 557-72; Kevin Morgan, 'The Trouble with Revisionism: or Communist History with the History Left in', *Labour/Le Travail*, Vol. 63 (Spring 2009), pp. 131-55; John McIlroy and Alan Campbell, 'A Peripheral Vision: Communist Historiography in Britain', *American Communist History*, Vol. 4, No. 2 (2005), pp. 125-57; Matthew Worley, 'The Communist International, The Communist Party of Great Britain, and the 'Third Period', 1928-1932', *European History Quarterly*, Vol. 30, No. 2 (2000), pp.185-208.

23 Emmet O'Connor, 'From Bolshevism to Stalinism: Communism and the Comintern in Ireland', in Norman LaPorte, Kevin Morgan and Matthew Worley (eds), *Bolshevism, Stalinism and the Comintern: Perspectives on Stalinization, 1917-1953* (Basingstoke, 2008).

24 O'Connor, *Reds and the Green: Ireland, Russia and the Communist Internationals, 1919-43*

25 Ibid., p.236.

26 Ibid., p.147.

27 Ibid., p.237.

28 Ibid., p.147.

29 Ibid., p.179.

30 Ibid., p.239.

31 Ibid., pp.166-88.

32 Stephen Bowler, 'Seán Murray, 1898-1961, And the Pursuit of Stalinism in One Country', *Saothar*, 18 (1993), p.44.

33 Ibid., p.50.

34 Ibid., p.51.

35 Joe Deasy, 'Seán Murray: Republican and Marxist' (correspondence), *Saothar*, 19 (1994), p.13.

36 Emmet O'Connor, 'John (Seán) Murray', in Keith Gildart, David Howell and Neville Kirk (eds), *Dictionary of Labour Biography, Vol. XI* (London, 2003).

37 Denis Smyth, *Sean Murray, A Pilgrim of Hope: The Life and Times of an Irish Communist, 1898-1961* (Belfast, 1998), pp.2-3.

38 Barry McLoughlin and Emmet O'Connor, 'Sources on Ireland and the Communist International, 1920-1943', *Saothar*, 21 (1995), pp.101-7.

39 McInerney, *Peadar O'Donnell*, p.98.

CHAPTER 1

The Making of an Irish Republican Bolshevik

Faced with the clearly expressed will of the people in a General Election, the Lloyd George Government answered with the Black and Tans. Finished fighting for "liberty" on the Continent, the knight-errants of imperialism launched their crusade against the declared will of the Irish people.

The struggle from January, 1919, till December, 1921, is the story of the continuation of the Easter rising fortified by the mass power of the people, on the one side, and the continuation on a corresponding scale of the Easter executions, proclamations, jailing and suppressions by the imperialist forces on the other. The Treaty of 1921 – a compromise fraught with disastrous consequences to Ireland – brought the unity of the anti-imperialist forces to an end, closed one chapter in the history of the Irish national struggle and opened another.[1]

Seán Murray was born on 15 June 1898 into a rural Catholic environment in Cushendall, the Glens of Antrim, to Patrick Murray and his wife, Mary Anne (née Gore). Christened John on 18 June at the local St. Mary's Church, family and friends would come to refer to him by his Gaelicised name.[2] What little we know about Murray's background is garnered from a short, hastily written autobiography dated 1932. He recalls that his father's brothers and their families were seamen and labourers, while some of his mother's siblings emigrated to England and the USA to find employment as railwaymen, carters and textile workers.[3] A rare surviving letter written on behalf of an aging and possibly illiterate Hugh Murray to his brother Pat in 1924 reveals that he has lived in Australia for twenty-five years and is working as a farmhand in the town of Wongan Hills.[4] It is unlikely that Murray had the opportunity to meet his uncle Hugh. The fortunes of his extended family form one small chapter of Irish emigrant and working life stories yet to be unearthed.

After inheriting the family farm at Ballybrack, a Cushendall townland, Pat remained in the locality and, with Mary Anne, settled into 'poor peasant' life.[5] It is difficult to ascertain the size of land holdings, but census records for 1901 and 1911 do reveal that the farm included one stable, a cow house, calf house and piggery. In the light of this evidence, it is perhaps most accurate to describe Murray as coming from small farming stock. Census records also indicate that he spent much of his childhood living on his maternal uncle James' farm at Laney, another Cushendall townland, along with his mother and three sisters, Mary, Kate and Margaret (Maggie). Whatever the reasons for these living arrangements – one can only assume they were born out of practical or financial necessity – we can be sure that Seán became immersed in agriculture at an early age. His claim to have 'started to work at 7 years of age on the land' is a stretch, though it would not have been uncommon at the time for a boy to lend assistance on the family farm throughout his school years.[6]

From the age of six, Murray attended Glenann National School, which operated under the management of the local clergy. Despite showing some promise under the tutelage of Master Joe MacNamee, he left school aged eleven. At this point he commenced full-time work on the family farm while availing himself of the scant opportunities there were for further education. This involved self-study and attendance for several years at evening classes run by MacNamee, a staunch Irish republican, in the winter months. Influenced strongly by his teacher, Murray took a keen interest in histories of 'Irish national struggle' and proceeded towards participation in that same struggle.[7]

Seán Murray the republican

Born in the year of the centenary of the 1798 United Irish rebellion, Murray came from a long line of republican activists. Indeed, his great-grandfather was a United Irishman and members of his family participated in the Young Ireland and Fenian uprisings of 1848 and 1867 respectively. It is fitting, then, that a chance encounter with Roger Casement reinforced his early interest in the struggle for national independence.[8] A proud Glens of Antrim native, Casement was instrumental in promoting Gaelic language and culture in the area and establishing the annual Feis na nGleann (Festival of the Glens), first held in Cushendall in 1904.[9] Casement is also said to have arranged a series of historical lectures across Antrim, which 'had sedition mixed up with them' and clearly had a profound effect on impressionable young activists' commitment to the republican cause.[10] Unsurprisingly, the Easter Rising was a formative event in Murray's political development. He described the execution of Connolly 'as among the blackest crimes of imperialism against the Irish nation and against the international Labour movement'. Crucially, in his estimation, Sinn Féin's landslide victory in the 1918 general election provided retrospective vindication for the Rising and presented republicans with a moral mandate for the armed insurrection that followed.[11]

Although Murray did not participate in the Rising, he became involved with the republican movement shortly afterwards, joining Sinn Féin in 1917. He became secretary of the local cumann and a 'leading member' of the district organisation.[12] Moreover, with the Irish language showing some resilience in the Glens of Antrim, one of the few surviving Gaeltacht areas of Ulster, he combined political activism with chairmanship of his local Gaelic League branch.[13] In the predominantly Protestant county of Antrim, the Catholic population was heavily concentrated in the Glens, leading to high levels of communal solidarity in the area – Sinn Féin, the Gaelic League and the GAA were all closely connected. IRA membership was perhaps not part of the inexorable progression of political activism, but in September 1918 Murray joined the organisation's 2nd (Antrim) Brigade, 3rd Northern Division and made rapid progress as a guerrilla leader in the early stages of the War of Independence. He also demonstrated some awareness of socialist republican thought and practice by participating in the 1918 general strike against conscription and by becoming 'acquainted with Marxian literature as a result of reading the works of Connolly'.[14] Meanwhile, his sister Kate, two years his junior, joined Cumann na mBan. She too would participate in the War of Independence, eventually receiving a service medal and military pension for her republican activities.

Throughout the revolutionary period, IRA violence in Ulster was disorganised and sporadic, though it grew in intensity after the 1921 truce. One reason for this was that the uncertainty around the negotiations taking place in London not only raised Unionist fears but hardened the resolve of northern republicans who increasingly began to look after their own areas following a GHQ moratorium on armed activity; another was the actions of the B Specials, the government's exclusively Protestant auxiliary police force, whose sectarian attacks on Catholics generated some sympathy for the IRA; the truce was further undermined by the sectarian dynamics in Belfast where the large-scale expulsion of Catholics from the shipyards and their homes contributed to an escalation of violence which spread across the province.[15] Due to the relative numerical weakness of republicans and the heavy presence of state forces, the IRA found Antrim one of the most difficult counties in which to organise and operate. In the course of a rare operation against a British Army patrol in mid-1920, Murray was arrested on his way to join an IRA flying column. Interned without charge or trial, he spent over one year in Crumlin Road Gaol, Belfast and the Curragh Camp, County Kildare.[16] Released following the Anglo-Irish truce, Murray returned home and resumed his IRA activities, having attained the dual rank of 3rd Battalion Intelligence Officer and First Lieutenant, B Company (Glenann).[17] Within weeks of the truce coming into effect, IRA training camps were established in the counties of Down and Antrim. The Antrim Brigade attended a camp in the mountains near Ballycastle, before making way for the Belfast Brigade. Thomas Fitzpatrick, who served as an officer with both brigades, claims that the threat of a B Specials attack loomed over volunteers for the duration of the training period.[18] The Anglo-Irish Treaty followed on 6 December. Signed by representatives of the British government and the de jure Irish Republic, the Treaty was then ratified by a vote of sixty-four to fifty-seven in the 'second Dáil'. Strongly opposed to the terms of compromise with Britain, Murray responded by helping to marshal the forces of republicanism in anticipation of a renewed campaign in the North.

In March 1922, senior anti-Treaty officers gathered at the Mansion House, Dublin with the intention of restoring the Army Executive as the main authority over the IRA. This convention went ahead in spite of a ban imposed by Richard Mulcahy, Minister of Defence, and his cabinet colleagues. In attendance were 211 delegates claiming to represent 95,000 men, or 80 percent of the IRA membership.[19] The newly elected IRA Executive issued a statement repudiating the authority of the Provisional Government and the Treatyite majority on GHQ staff. Of those representing the 3rd Northern Division, only Murray and Hugh Corvin of the Belfast Brigade spoke against GHQ; other officers were influenced by Eoin O'Duffy to adopt a pro-Treaty stance on the understanding that they would be supplied with arms and ammunition for a northern campaign.[20] This is the point at which anti-Treatyism became a fixed point on Murray's ideological compass. The convention also held great personal significance because of his introduction to the Donegal-born socialist republican, Peadar O'Donnell, who would become his closest confidant and most ardent supporter. O'Donnell's quixotic recollection of meeting Murray was simply: 'We found each other somehow.'[21]

Reflecting on the Treaty over a decade later, Murray described it as 'a compromise fraught with disastrous consequences to Ireland' and a clear demonstration that the Irish elite 'loved their country, but they loved their class more'.[22] Having made his position clear at the banned IRA convention, Murray returned to Antrim to participate in the widespread assault on Crown forces, police barracks and Unionist establishment figures north of the border. The original intention was for the five northern divisions to take part in this large-scale operation on 19 May, with auxiliary support provided by the 1st Midland Division in the form of raids from the South. In Belfast, the initial operation was an ambitious attack on Musgrave Street barracks on the night of 17 May, which, if successful, would have secured the use of armoured cars and a large cache of rifles as well as providing the impetus for the 19 May attacks across the North. Shortly after this operation commenced, a guard managed to fire a warning shot to alert those within the barracks. Machine gun fire rained down on the twenty-two strong IRA unit, which returned shots before retreating. This exchange left one Royal Irish Constabulary (RIC) officer dead and another wounded, the IRA disoriented and demoralised.[23]

The disastrous outcome of the Musgrave Street operation prompted the northern leadership to issue countermanding orders for the scheduled 19 May attacks. However, these orders failed to reach some areas and the Antrim Brigade proceeded with the original plan. Fate then conspired to make things even more difficult for the IRA's strengthened yet thinly-spread forces in the area. A lorry carrying a supply of rifles, revolvers, hand grenades, detonators and explosives from the South broke down outside the home of a British colonel in Carrickfergus, thus threatening to compound the failure to secure weapons in Belfast. Fortuitously, Colonel Steele was under the impression that the lorry – an oil tanker – contained petrol. He had the vehicle towed to the closest military barracks and repaired before seeing Charlie Connolly, the driver and Antrim Brigade Adjutant, on his way the next morning. The consignment arrived safely at Red Bay, Cushendall and was distributed among parties from each battalion.[24] Now in charge of operations, Murray directed the 3rd Battalion's attempt to capture Cushendun police barracks. This failed due to a lack of explosives, but was compensated for by the destruction of three bridges on the Larne-Cushendall coast. Men under his command were also responsible for one of the numerous 'big house' burnings in the Glens; Ronald McNeill, Unionist MP and Under-Secretary of State for Foreign Affairs, was the target.[25] Earning its reputation for brutality and haphazardness, Murray's battalion carried out twenty-six 'outrages' in the area over a six-day period, including an attack on Cushendall police station, the robbery and burning of a bank, and a series of arson attacks on the houses and property of notable figures.[26] That the countermanding orders failed to reach the area ensured that the Antrim Brigade worked in isolation and, due to the state forces concentrated in the area, always against the odds. The complaints emanating from the 3rd Northern Division leadership about the inaction of the 1st, 2nd and 4th Northern Divisions were made out of frustration and in the knowledge that the local population would suffer the consequences of their actions.[27]

A wave of repression swept the Glens in the aftermath of May's events. Feidhlim MacGuill, Antrim Brigade Intelligence Officer, painted a clear picture of what this entailed in his area:

> Since the Rising in the North had not been as general as first planned, it allowed the British to concentrate their forces on the areas where partial Risings took place. It soon became evident to us, after our Rising had failed, that to remain in Co. Antrim was almost an impossibility for those who had taken part in the Rising. Round ups and mass raids were the order of the day, not only for those who took an active part in the operations during the Rising but also for all those who were known to have Republican tendencies. Many active men were 'on the run' and trying to escape the drag-net which the British authorities were relentlessly using. Every day the possibility of evading arrest became more difficult.[28]

A raid by the notorious B Specials in Cushendall on 23 June, which left three men dead and two others wounded, is a chilling example of such measures in action. An inquiry into the incident found no evidence of the Specials receiving fire and concluded that James McAllister, John Gore and John Hill had been summarily executed. Two Special constables dragged McAllister into an alleyway between shops and, despite pleas for clemency from onlookers, shot him through the mouth. After taking refuge in a nearby shop with family and friends, Gore was shot dead as he emerged from behind a counter with his hands above his head. Another constable, meanwhile, interrogated Hill and Gore's brother, Pat. The latter secured a reprieve by referring to his service in the British Army, but Hill was taken into an alleyway and shot in the chest at close range.[29] The new-born Unionist government released a statement claiming that the killings were the unfortunate result of a botched ambush on a group of Specials.[30] T.F. Barrington-Ward, the barrister in charge of the inquiry, discredited these claims in his final report, which confirmed that the military incursions were a direct and coordinated response to the IRA's activities in May, that the victims were unarmed and 'innocently occupied', and that the B Special constables involved had attempted to present a fabricated version of events.[31] That McAllister, Hill and Gore were members of the local IRA indicates that they were persons of interest and were singled out for assassination by the B Specials. All signs pointed to a difficult existence for Murray had he decided to remain at home or in the vicinity.[32]

This round of reprisals prompted John (Jack) O'Loan to officially relinquish command of the 149-strong 3rd Battalion to Murray.[33] Along with Feidhlim MacGuill, whose name had found its way onto a B Specials list of targets, Murray and O'Loan travelled to Glasgow at the request of the brigade leadership. The purpose of the operation was twofold: to enable these three notable IRA figures to evade the clampdown in progress; and to track down an unnamed volunteer who had left Ireland in haste, accused of misappropriating around £400 from the bank raid in May. After questioning this individual and becoming sufficiently convinced of his innocence, they made their way directly to the Curragh to join up with other officers and volunteers from the 3rd Northern Division. The intention was that they would regroup, undergo intensive military training and return to their respective areas fully equipped to commit themselves afresh to the struggle. But in the context of a brutal civil war ripping through the South, the widespread feeling in anti-Treaty circles was that the Dublin leadership would not support another northern offensive.[34] This left a large number of Ulster volunteers, including those of the Antrim Brigade, residing in the South as refugees. There was no prospect of them returning north without facing imprisonment or retaliation at the hands of the B Specials, and emigration was the only option in lieu of specific guarantees from the northern government.

Captain Jack White, founder member of the ICA, a comrade of James Connolly, and a fellow Glens of Antrim native, had begun to petition Unionist ministers with a view to securing the guarantee of safe passage for the IRA volunteers in exile. Having assumed the role of spokesperson for the refugees, one of Murray's final acts as 3rd Batallion O/C was to make contact with White to see if anything could be done on their behalf. White wrote to Wilfrid B. Spender, secretary to the Northern Ireland Cabinet, who put him in touch with Dawson Bates, Minister for Home Affairs. The Unionist regime had already refused to entertain the notion of an amnesty in exchange for the pledge from republicans that they would not undertake unconstitutional actions on their return, and White found Bates just as unsympathetic to his overtures.[35] Murray's high profile, his association with the events of May 1922 and with the three assassinated volunteers of the Antrim Brigade, made him a likely target for arrest or reprisals. He therefore returned to Glasgow in December 1922, seeking work as a labourer on the Clyde.[36]

A British communist initiation

Murray arrived in Scotland during 'Red Clydeside', the celebrated period of industrial and political radicalism that began at the tail-end of wartime protests in Glasgow and its surrounding areas. Red Clydeside spawned such influential figures as John Maclean, Arthur MacManus, Harry McShane, Tom Bell and William Gallacher. The Irish connection with this Scottish labour tradition found its greatest expression in James Connolly and the Socialist Labour Party, established in 1903 as a breakaway from Hyndman's Social Democratic Federation.[37] Two notable graduates of 1916 – Connolly's son Roddy and Seán McLoughlin, the 'boy commandant' – plied their political trade in Glasgow between 1918 and 1920, establishing positive working relationships with Scottish socialists.[38] Their time on Clydeside did not overlap with Murray's, but these examples of interaction between British socialism and Irish socialist republicanism in the immediate aftermath of the October Revolution are important for their lines of continuity through Connolly and for arriving at an understanding of the origins of Irish Bolshevism.

In 1924, after gaining an introduction to militant trade unionism and communist politics, Murray left for London, where he found work as a labourer and became active as a member of the CPGB. He began organising the London Irish and was appointed district secretary of Jim Larkin's Irish Worker League (IWL) on the recommendation of Jack White who 'expressed a high opinion of Murray's abilities'.[39] Upon his return to Ireland in 1923, Larkin had set about launching the IWL as an alternative to Roddy Connolly's first CPI, which had fallen under Comintern control but quickly self-destructed amidst organisational and ideological disputes. In this context, the Comintern regarded Larkin as a more attractive option for organising in Ireland and winning the Irish working class in Britain to a communist programme. These overtures continued despite Connolly's ill-fated attempt to rally his supporters under the auspices of the Workers' Party of Ireland (WPI). As Emmet O'Connor has pointed out, 'The IWL never functioned as a communist party, and the "big noise" [Larkin] had an extraordinarily troubled relationship with the Comintern.'[40] Nevertheless, Murray continued to progress in English communist circles. By 1925 he was organiser for the CPGB's Islington branch and a member of the party's London district committee. This involved working closely with Joe Scott, a member of the national committee and leading Amalgamated Engineering Union (AEU) official, and one 'Comrade Robinson'. Murray was also a paid-up member of the Central London branch of the National Union of Distributive and Allied Workers (NUDAW). He participated in the 1926 general strike, which prompted the police to raid his lodgings, and earned NUDAW's nomination as a delegate to London Trades' Council.[41]

The All-Russian Co-operative Society (ARCOS) Ltd., a company formed by the Soviet government in 1921, seemed to offer the prospect of secure employment. However, in May 1927 the company closed its London offices amid accusations of espionage and communist propaganda. Compensated with a job in the London depot of Russian Oil Products (ROP), where he worked for a few months, his political work continued unabated.[42] Incidentally, a Dublin subsidiary of ROP was to become the centre of great controversy. Not only was the company investigated as a communist front operation for the duration of its existence,[43] but within two years of its formation the branch became part of an increasingly bitter dispute between Larkin and the Comintern. On this occasion, Larkin's grievance was that ROP had overlooked members of his Workers' Union of Ireland (WUI) in favour of non-union labour. After receiving what O'Connor describes as a 'weasel-worded letter' from Larkin seeking Stalin's arbitration in the dispute, the Comintern laid out instructions for the ROP to adopt a labour union only policy. At the same time, Stalin's Politburo made it clear that the company would not be allowed to grant the WUI a monopoly on employment or give Larkin access to oil deals.[44]

This affair marked the decisive rupture between Larkin and the Comintern, which had begun to make alternative arrangements for organising in Ireland. Between November 1927 and March 1928, the first Irish intake arrived at the International Lenin School in Moscow for preliminary training. The group included Pat Breslin, Bill Denn, Charlie Ashmore, Dan Buckley, Seán Shelly and Jim Larkin junior.[45] 'Young' Jim, as he was known, was a notable inclusion given his father's frosty relationship with Moscow. Regardless of what had gone before, he was keen to reassure the Executive Committee of the Comintern (ECCI) that the IWL had the capacity to function as a communist party if nudged in a particular direction. Big Jim, meanwhile, held residual hope that some IWL representation would help rescue his standing with Moscow. Jack Carney, his loyal lieutenant, encouraged this belief rather unnecessarily and it was only to Larkin's credit that he realised, albeit belatedly, that any lasting deal with the Comintern was out of reach.[46] In notifying Bukharin of his decision to withdraw from 'active work', he gave assurances that there would be 'no interference' in young Jim's activities and that his son was working 'in earnest.' He also requested that those placed in charge of the movement in Ireland 'receive undivided support' from the Comintern.[47] Though not exactly a ringing endorsement of decisions made in Moscow, Larkin's support for the new generation of leaders helped to create the space for the ECCI to press ahead with its new strategy in Ireland.

'Bolshevisation' and the International Lenin School

The fifth congress of the Comintern in 1924 marked out a policy of 'Bolshevisation' of affiliated parties. Devised by Comintern President, Grigory Zinoviev, with some help from an increasingly prominent Stalin, Bolshevisation reflected the absence of revolution in the West and the failure of united front tactics to win a majority of workers in advanced capitalist countries to communism. The individual experiences of Comintern-affiliated parties in the West fed into policy design but it was conceived with a universalising purpose and implemented with ideological zeal. Bolshevisation would therefore be characterised by greater deference to the Soviet Union as the only successful example of revolution and to Moscow as the bastion of global revolution. The intention was to create loyal (to the Comintern), disciplined, centralised parties based on Marxist-Leninist principles and in the image of the Soviet party. In practice, it would have the effect of 'Russifying the communist movement and, what is more, a Russification in an embryonic Stalinist form'.[48]

One important component of Bolshevisation was the establishment of party schools in Moscow for the benefit of foreign activists. In May 1926, the International Lenin School opened with the specific purpose of creating

> in every Party at least a small group of leaders capable of comprehending in a Leninist Bolshevik spirit the contradictions of the present historical epoch, analysing the concrete historical situation in their own country and of dialectically applying and distinguishing that part of the experience of the Russian Revolution which is applicable to all countries from that which is specifically Russian.[49]

According to the school curriculum, the first two terms were devoted mainly to the 'two fundamental subjects' of 'political economy and the history of the labour movement'. Naturally, the study of economics involved a specific focus on Marx's theories of capitalism and Lenin's contribution to the understanding of imperialism, while the (Vsesoyuznaya Kommunisticheskaya Partiya (Bolshevikov), VKP/b) formed a central part of the history course. These lectures were followed by seminars (groups of ten to fifteen people, sub-divided into groups of four or five for each particular topic) on Leninism, agriculture, agitation and propaganda, during which students were expected to grasp the organisational and tactical fundamentals expounded in key Leninist texts such as *What is to be Done?* and *Two Tactics of Social-Democracy in the Democratic Revolution*. The fourth and final term covered 'dialectical and historical materialism', the world economy and additional lessons on agitation and propaganda. In addition, the students were required to learn Russian for the duration of the course as well as to attend compulsory 'excursions' and participate in 'the practical work of the national sections of the Agitprop of the Comintern.'[50] The students lived together in a residential setting and studied in classrooms under the banner 'Without Revolutionary Theory, No Revolutionary Practice'.[51] In fact, theory (school lessons and private study) and practice (work-based activities) combined, amounted to some seventy-two hours per week.[52] The Lenin School was far from a holiday camp for even the most able scholars and activists in attendance.

Seán Murray joined the Irish students (under the pseudonym 'James Black') on 11 December 1927 after attending the CPGB national congress that October.[53] As with other members of the Irish group, Larkin junior to a lesser extent, Murray arrived untainted by the dramatic failure of successive Irish communist incarnations. Most significantly, although Murray travelled to Moscow with a view to eventually taking up a position in Ireland, he did so as one of ten CPGB delegates, not on the instructions of Dublin. The CPGB was in the midst of a transitory period, with internal and external pressures shifting the party hastily to the left and its relationship with the Comintern reaching a high point.[54] Most of the British party's delegates (86 percent) over the period 1929-34 had no more than an elementary schooling; less than one-third had theoretical training; and only six of these students had benefited from the intensive training provided by the Central Labour College (CLC). Consequently, the 'proletarian credentials' of its students have been described as 'second to none'.[55] Whether because or in spite of this lack of training and theoretical knowledge, the ECCI singled out the CPGB for its rigorous methods of selection for the Lenin School.[56] Either way, Murray was among the most experienced and educated of the first British and Irish cohorts.

Barry McLoughlin, a historian with an in-depth knowledge of the Comintern archives, is right to point out that the role reserved for Murray 'as Moscow's most important and trusted representative of Ireland was due to his long Party record and links with those British emissaries who supervised Comintern business in Ireland'.[57] At the behest of the Anglo-American secretariat, which generally dealt with Irish affairs, Tom Bell and Bob Stewart – two Scots – travelled to Ireland in September 1929 to oversee preparations for a new political formation under the slogan 'United Free Workers' and Peasants' Irish Republic'.[58] The Comintern deemed Bell and Stewart, two stalwarts of Irish communist efforts of the early 1920s, most capable of initiating the foundation of a new party. Their experience counted for much and it was anticipated that through the CPGB conduit they would develop effective lines of communication between Dublin and Moscow, which had been lacking in previous years. Larkin no longer commanded the respect or trust of key functionaries at international communism's head office. But nor did anyone else from the existing Irish communist leadership. Clearly Moscow intended on starting afresh. Bell and Stewart would prepare the ground with a rump of committed local activists, while Murray received the additional training necessary for organising and cultivating an Irish revolutionary party.

Murray at the Lenin School

Aged twenty-nine, and with ten years' political experience behind him, Murray was not a blank slate when he arrived at the Lenin School. Having enrolled on the longest and most demanding of the courses on offer, he made great strides to justify early admission to the VKP/b. By making his limited experience and political education pay, Murray quickly became one of the best performing English-speaking students. An early progress report stated: 'Worked well and has made progress. Good attitude to party and social work.' However, he still showed 'confusion on some questions, and should make a bigger effort to understand the fundamentals of Leninism'. A later report indicated that he had advanced sufficiently, describing Murray as 'very capable, very active' and praising his 'independence of thought'. More significantly, he had developed 'a good grasp of Marxist-Leninist methods': the primacy of democratic centralism; the role of the communist party as the vanguard party of the proletariat, led by a group of professional revolutionaries; and the importance of communist party agents penetrating and having a political influence at all levels of society. Murray's instructors would have viewed this as the most pleasing aspect of his development.[59]

By October 1929 the Comintern had rewarded Murray and Larkin junior with placements on a specialised agrarian group within the Anglo-American secretariat. They were required to attend meetings and conduct independent research, the culmination of which was the publication of a 100-page Marxist pamphlet on Irish conditions.[60] During their time at the Lenin School, each student would take up a special question on which they would eventually submit a short report to their instructors. But only the best of these research reports made it to publication.[61] It is clear that Murray and Larkin junior took their research very seriously. Spread over six chapters, *The Life and Struggle of the Working-Class and Peasantry in Ireland* addresses a wide range of questions – partition; the Irish Civil War; women's labour; land reform and the rural economy; trade unionism, living conditions; the role of labour and republican parties; and 'Anglo-American antagonism in Irish political life' – and looks forward to the establishment of a 'proletarian dictatorship' in Ireland. Translated into Russian and published with an initial print run of 7,000 copies, this pamphlet was a gauge of the two Irish students' progress and a positive indication of the Lenin School's faith in them as Marxist scholars.[62]

In the summer, the students had embarked on their second 'practical', which involved a short field trip to one of the Soviet regions. Accompanied by Harry Wicks and three others – Charlie Stead, a South Wales miner and organiser for the National Council of Labour Colleges, an Indian named 'Magharab' and a Canadian known only as 'Porter' – Murray and Larkin junior set off for Dagestan, one of the autonomous Soviet Republics in the North Caucasus region, bordering the Caspian Sea. Their first stop was Makhachkala, the region's capital, where they attended party meetings and had an opportunity to study the city's economy. Among the sights to which they were unaccustomed were the 'lavishness of hospitality' at meetings and the poor treatment of women. This certainly contrasted with their experience of Moscow. Making their way to Shamil, one of the remotest towns of the predominantly Muslim region, they witnessed further examples of primitive life. The people were uneducated, food was in short supply and again the treatment of women was slave-like. Wicks described the state of social relations as 'pre-feudal'. Returning to Moscow with a greater understanding of realities on the periphery and the challenges of building socialism in rural areas, they all agreed that the trip challenged their 'desire to be loyal party concepts'.[63]

Because their time at the Lenin School coincided with a momentous shift to the left in Soviet politics and international communism, the Irish students did not have to wait long for their faith in the 'party' to be tested. Initiated and developed by Nikolai Bukharin, a leading Bolshevik, revolutionary theorist and key Comintern functionary, the term 'Third Period' referred to an era of global capitalist rationalisation and stabilisation which was characterised by a crisis of profitability, rising unemployment and a decline in working-class standards of living. These conditions, the theory ran, would lead to an intensification of class conflict, undermine working-class support for social democracy and instigate a new round of imperialist wars, thus creating a revolutionary situation. Internationally, communist parties were expected to accelerate this process and promote their independent identity, in the political and industrial spheres, with tactics that opposed social democracy as a pillar of capitalism. The derogatory theory of 'social fascism' was resurrected to depict social democracy as a variant of fascism because it shared the economic corporatist model and stood in the way of the imminent revolution, while the slogan 'class against class' came to define the renewed revolutionary struggle in absolutist terms. This left turn had far-reaching implications for the internal power struggle for control of the

Russian party. Having followed an essentially Bukharinist line until the end of 1927, Stalin began, in 1928, to appropriate Third Period theory and employ its terminology against 'right-wing deviationists' who dared to question the imminent collapse of capitalism or the wisdom of breakneck collectivisation and industrialisation en route to socialist reconstruction. Conveniently, this offered a pretext for the discrediting and removal of all those who put up any resistance to the Stalinist faction's rise to power.[64]

Although Bukharin had not departed radically from his 1926-27 position, he had expressed reservations about the use of extreme coercion and advocated more nuanced tactics to the blatant sectarianism on offer. This in itself was enough to warrant expulsion from the ECCI in July 1929, one of several enforced personnel changes within the Comintern hierarchy. Bukharin would be removed as Director of the Lenin School in February 1930, but it was the real evaporation of his influence in 1929 that enabled the replication of purification measures across the board. Consequently, the school instructors initiated a *chistka* or 'cleansing', which lasted a few weeks and caused the suspension of all other activity. In the case of the Irish students, the most intense scrutiny fell on those suspected of 'right-wing' Larkinite sympathies. Thus, the first significant act of the *chistka* was to replace Larkin junior with Harry Wicks as *partorg* (party organiser) or *starosta* (head/elder) of the Anglo-Irish group. Losing such an important position, which entailed responsibility for 'all political aspects of student life', was a significant blow to the Irish contingent.[65] Yet there is no evidence to suggest that the episode had a destructive impact on Wicks' relationship with his Irish comrades. Wicks remembered the Irish students as 'good militants' and knew Larkin junior in particular 'very well'. He had also travelled with Larkin and Murray because 'we fitted each other's interests and temperaments'. Besides, all students had experienced the same humiliating process to some extent. Even though Wicks' classmates failed to speak in his favour during a particularly brutal grilling, his memoirs do not reveal any deep feelings of resentment about the incident or towards the Irish group in general.[66]

For the Irish students, the most frustrating aspect of the *chistka* was that the Comintern and caretaker leadership in Dublin elected to bypass them during policy negotiations. Undoubtedly, this was a precaution against Larkin senior catching wind of the Comintern's plans for the foundation of a new Irish party. A letter from 'Arthur'[67] to Tom Bell on 17 November noted 'strained and difficult' relations within the school. At a special commission set up to deal with the Irish students' grievances, the group (with Murray's 'objective support') presented a number of accusations. The main concern was that 'there had taken place a progressive and intentional exclusion of the Irish students from the discussion of Irish questions'. Harry Haywood, an influential American communist and pan-African theorist, was appointed chair of the commission.[68] An imposing figure, Haywood shared a room with Murray at the Lenin School and counted him as a close friend. He was 'excited' by his encounters with the 'Irish revolutionaries' as he described them, with whom he shared a lot in common as 'members of oppressed nations'.[69] After a long drawn out investigation, Haywood adopted a minority position on the commission, coming down strongly on the side of the Irish students and sustaining their objections. He argued for an outright condemnation of the methods used by Bell and Buckley (the latter had made an early return to Ireland to assist Bell and Stewart) and of 'the complete ignoring of the Irish students who must form a basis for the carrying out of the CI line'. This contrasted with the majority report, which rejected charges of 'fractionalism' and 'intrigue' and attacked young Jim for holding his ground in the face of criticism.[70]

The impression given by 'Arthur' was that the Irish group's most serious grievances centred on young Jim's enforced demotion and the complicity of Bell and Buckley in the Lenin School's move against Larkinites. The climate that prevailed within the VKP/b, combined with the fact that Bell was acting on his authority as chair of Sector 'E' (the Anglo-Irish sector) and part of the Comintern officialdom (a member of its presidium and political secretariat), rendered it highly imprudent for Larkin junior and his supporters to challenge these methods more forcefully.[71] That an internal commission was established to investigate their claims underlines the gravity of the situation and the full extent of the Irish students' concerns with the form and content of Third Period sectarianism. Indeed, Larkin junior warned that the replication of these methods in Ireland would be 'harmful' in terms of opening up divisions. But there was never any question that the dispute would be resolved to the complete satisfaction of the Irish students. The imminent arrival of an Irish trade union delegation for the twelfth anniversary of the Bolshevik Revolution prompted an intervention by Harry Wicks, who helped to broker a meeting between the Irish group and members of the commission. The final resolution acknowledged the mistake of the Lenin School management in failing to give the Irish students more attention, while placing on record Larkin junior's apparent commitment to the Comintern line. Ultimately, it was agreed to sweep the whole affair under the carpet and proceed in attempting to win over the Irish group, 'without of course disregarding or glossing over any political differences that may arise'.[72]

In an interesting footnote, 'Arthur' suggested that 'it was a tactical mistake to have excluded' Murray from discussions relating to Irish affairs.[73] One possible reason for this is that as a CPGB delegate with experience of political activism in Britain and Ireland, Murray was held in higher regard than were fellow members of the Irish group. A related explanation is that he demonstrated a certain level of aptitude to justify a positive assessment and therefore establish himself, in Arthur's eyes, as someone who could have contributed to policy formulation and implementation. It is also significant that he had not incurred any major blemishes on his record since arriving in Moscow. By contrast, Larkin junior and Charlie Ashmore were censured when they failed to keep in step with the notion of 'socialist competition' and meet the expected contribution of two to three months' rather than month's allowance to the national loan scheme, created to fund the industrialisation programme of the Five Year Plan.[74] The former was also compelled to undertake self-criticism and repudiate his father's politics, which was a particularly degrading aspect of the purge.[75] And even this paled in comparison to the fate suffered by Pat Breslin, whose 'unusual' political ideas drew criticism from his fellow students and eventually precipitated his expulsion from the school.[76] In light of this, one can begin to understand why Murray was singled out and why he enjoyed a comparatively smooth passage through the Lenin School.

In the same year, Breslin married a Russian woman named Katya and successfully applied for Soviet citizenship. Murray also married a local woman, a fellow member of the VKP/b, and signalled his intention to bring her to Ireland upon completion of the 'long' course. Assuring the party that he and his wife would take steps to address the language barrier in preparation for moving to Ireland, Murray continued to learn Russian – his notebooks reveal that he used the síneadh fada (Gaelic acute accent) to help with pronunciation – and presumably began to teach his wife English. Crucially, the Murrays deferred to the party for approval or otherwise of their relationship:

Their advice is that it would not be correct for her to register as my wife etc without first having the permission of the party leading organs. That this will be allright there is no suggestion [sic] my wife, quite correctly, refuses to do anything without the full consent of the party. I agree with this.[77]

In the event, Murray neither managed to secure his wife a passport for a return to Ireland nor was prepared to take up Soviet citizenship in order to remain in Moscow. This contrasted with Breslin's decision to surrender Irish citizenship, which effectively sealed his fate. Breslin later fell foul of the Soviet authorities, who refused him permission to return home to be with his second wife, 'Daisy' McMackin from Belfast. He eventually died of ill-health in a prison camp in Kazan in 1942. This is significant because not only was Murray one of Breslin's classmates, but he became friendly with McMackin and kept in contact with her throughout the 1930s. He provided her with a reference to gain employment in Moscow and commissioned her to write an Irish translation of the *Communist Manifesto*.[78] Murray and Breslin's radically different trajectories highlight not only the former's good fortune but also his proximity to political repression in the Soviet Union. This raises questions about his knowledge of the full extent of Stalin's purges and of how Breslin met his end.

Despite calls from Tom Bell for their early repatriation, the remaining Irish students from the first deputation completed the long course in the summer of 1930.[79] For Murray, his time at the Lenin School was a mixed bag of problems and useful experiences. The trip to Dagestan was an education, though it exposed the limitations of Socialism in One Country in primitive areas. The *chistka* could not have had any other effect than to leave him with unpleasant memories of isolation and infighting as well as feelings of disillusionment about Third Period methods. Notwithstanding Murray's ultimate demonstration of faith in the party regarding his Russian wife, mystery continues to shroud the precise role of the VKP/b and Soviet authorities in preventing the couple from making their marriage official. Whether due to cravenness, heartlessness or, most likely, the weeding out of his private papers, Murray reveals nothing in his writings about this important event in his life, other than to restate his unmarried status to the Comintern in 1932.[80] More positively, he escaped from the Lenin School relatively unscathed in comparison to a number of fellow students. He gained vital knowledge of international socialist history and Marxist theory, and an equally consequential introduction to Leninist methods of party organisation and discipline, which had been lacking in previous Irish communist leaderships. Finally, he added to his arsenal a number of contacts from which he and the Irish communist movement could draw inspiration and assistance in subsequent years. Not quite a deviationist, nor a fully-fledged apparatchik, Murray left Moscow a Bolshevik with some comprehension of the demands of Third Periodism.

Taking the reins

Upon completion of the long course, all but one of the successful Irish students made their way to Dublin to commence party work. Murray was first required to report to CPGB headquarters at King Street, London, for debriefing where he was accompanied by Charlie Stead and Harry Wicks.[81] Incidentally, in the midst of his studies, Murray had attended the CPGB's eleventh national congress, November 1929, as a 'delegate from the Lenin School nucleus'.[82] Wicks' memoirs reveal that one of Murray's key duties was to convey the ECCI's basic policy message to the CPGB rank and file: 'These two [Murray and Bob McIlhone, a Scottish steel worker of Irish descent] were expected to plug the Comintern's "left" line as against the "right" one represented by the British Central Committee.'[83] Although Wicks' expulsion from the CPGB in 1932 for involvement with an early British Trotskyist group obfuscates definitions of 'left' and 'right', his recollections give the impression that the Comintern viewed Murray, rightly or wrongly, as a reliable and effective transmitter of Third Period policy and tactics.

Prior to Murray and Larkin junior's return to Ireland, the ECCI had been prepared to work closely with left-wing republicans in areas of mutual interest. IRA members were involved with united front groups of the 1920s, for example the Irish section of International Class War Prisoners' Aid (ICWPA), the INUM and the ILDL, and prominent republicans such as David Fitzgerald, Mick Fitzpatrick and Peadar O'Donnell liaised directly with Moscow throughout the decade.[84] O'Donnell played a leading role in the formation of an Irish Working Farmers' Committee (IWFC) and in March 1930 led a delegation to the European Peasants' Congress in Berlin. In the same year, he joined twenty-nine fellow IRA members on a Preparatory Committee for the Formation of a Workers' Revolutionary Party. However, Murray and Larkin junior would be parachuted into an environment shaped by the ECCI's decision to extend 'class against class' to republicans, not to mention Tom Bell's polemics against those who operated outside the narrow confines of Third Period doctrine. Although this shift was designed to bring a new sense of urgency to the formation of an Irish communist party, Moscow failed to understand the wider implications of applying the tactic universally to erstwhile allies:

It was a rash move against a constituency on which the Irish secretariat was heavily dependent. In addition to supplying the core of the Dublin

communist group, republicans dominated all of the communist fronts, and had proved useful in INUM demonstrations, the bus strike [May 1930], and providing sympathetic coverage in *An Phoblacht*, which claimed to sell 8,000 copies per week.[85]

This would act as the first litmus test of Murray's Bolshevik credentials, his capacity to put republican sympathies to one side, and his commitment to a policy of rejecting united frontism in practice.

Upon his arrival in Dublin in July (without his Russian wife) Murray became a paid organiser on the Comintern's books[86] and was immediately confronted with the difficulties arising out of the escalation of 'class against class'. Not content with launching a ruthless assault on trade union leaders, including the WUI, Bell proceeded in encouraging an ill-tempered exchange with left republicans in the pages of *An Phoblacht* and the *Workers' Voice*, organ of what was now known as the Revolutionary Workers' Party (RWP). The IRA drew condemnation for its neglect of American imperialism and of problems facing the Irish working class, while one communist contributor described the boycott of British goods as 'nonsense' and another directed personal insults at *An Phoblacht* editor, Frank Ryan. O'Donnell described the articles as the work of 'imbeciles' and attributed their publication to the 'unfathomable stupidity' of lax editorial oversight.[87] This betrayed his blissful ignorance of Bell's deeply negative view of republicans and the likelihood that the Scot commissioned the most vitriolic criticisms of the republican movement.[88]

In a measured contribution entitled 'What next?' Murray suggested that much work remained in clarifying the position of 'all comrades', not just those attached to the IRA. Drawing on the Bolsheviks' participation in the bourgeois-democratic revolutions of 1905 and February/March 1917, he supported Connolly's decision to take part in the Easter Rising. At the same time, he argued that Ireland had entered into a new era of class struggle:

I think it will generally be agreed that we are now in a different stage. The Irish bourgeoisie are no longer 'oppressed' by British imperialism, but are ruling Ireland, North and South, in alliance with British capitalism … They have abandoned the struggle for the Republic … Not a single move can now be made for independence without a struggle to overthrow the Irish capitalist class … This means that old slogans (correct in their time) of

'Ireland against England', 'Independence', 'Republic', must now be replaced by the slogan of class against class.[89]

Written with one eye on Moscow, Murray's intervention was perceptive in its assessment of limited political independence and the role of a native comprador class in upholding the British economic system in Ireland. Crucially, while downplaying the significance of British imperialism, he did not explicitly rule out anti-imperialist alliances. Nor did he descend into indiscriminate attacks on the republican movement. Rather, he identified a radical strain within the IRA, exemplified by an *An Phoblacht* statement criticising Fianna Fáil's 'reformist tinkering', and reserved a role for this type of thinking in the 'revolutionary party of the workers and poor peasants'.[90] However, this was not enough to dissuade Bell from publishing further attacks on left republicans or to prevent O'Donnell's departure from the RWP's embryonic central committee.[91]

To compensate for the loss of O'Donnell, the ECCI revised its attitude towards the WUI and decided to explore the possibility of accessing and utilising the union. On Moscow's instruction, Murray and Larkin junior made contact with the latter's father in August 1930. Their report on this conversation and various meetings with prominent officials and rank-and-file members outlined the delicate and complex nature of WUI organisation and internal dynamics. Membership figures had reached approximately 15,000, including recently recruited busmen and rail workers, which made the WUI one of the numerically strongest unions in Ireland. Yet, because no previous attempt had been made to approach the union, Murray and Larkin junior encountered what they described as an 'extremely difficult and very embittered' atmosphere, not just with Big Jim but across the membership more generally. Prevalent among WUI officials and grassroots was the view that the Comintern had prosecuted a 'struggle against their section of the movement'. Struggling to hide their frustration that the WUI had suffered such neglect, Murray and young Jim explained that any 'tendencies towards reformism' had grown out of a detachment from the RWP and 'the international revolutionary movement' i.e. the Comintern. Although there existed a widespread 'desire for political activity and education', such was Larkin senior's influence on, and standing with, the workers of Dublin that only through cooperation with him would it be possible to transform the WUI into a revolutionary vehicle. They advised the Comintern to entrust a 'responsible party comrade' with the task of dealing with Larkin's misgivings about the ROP affair, in the hope that this would pave the way to further rapprochement.[92]

At one level, Murray and Larkin junior's report reveals the degree of acrimony between the WUI and Comintern. At another, it strongly indicates that a dividing line had formed between the RWP caretaker leadership and the Larkinites, which represented a hangover from the *chistka*. Quoting from specific issues of the *Workers' Voice*, the two Lenin School graduates levied criticisms at the tone of Bell's editorials, which had adopted 'an anti-Larkinite policy' and tarred the WUI with the same brush as the 'reformist' National Union of Railwaymen (NUR) and ITGWU. They requested assurances that Bell's virulent anti-Larkinism sat 'in complete contradiction to the actual instructions' handed down by the ECCI. Finally, in a thinly veiled jibe at Bell, Murray and young Jim called for a period of self-reflection and a change in tack: 'Only by proving our group to be worthy of serious consideration and not of ridicule can we expect to be seriously accepted by the WUI section of the workers in Dublin and by the workers in general.'[93] This was their way of informing the Comintern that they saw a bleak future for the communist movement so long as it continued along the self-defeating path of left sectarianism.

At a RWP meeting in Belfast on 24 August, chaired by Arthur Griffin, Murray used his newly acquired knowledge of Marxist economics and history to deliver a long-winded analysis of the Wall Street crash and its local implications. Naturally, he prescribed the solution embraced by the Russian workers and peasants and brought the meeting to a close for the 100 people in attendance with the exhortation 'to come into the ranks and fight in the terrific struggle for the overthrow of capitalism'.[94] On a practical level, the communist groupings had begun to reap in small amounts the rewards of their efforts through the INUM and trade unions. In the Dublin municipal council elections that September, Larkin junior won a seat for the RWP with 967 votes. Representation in local government gave the party the necessary platform to press ahead with a recruitment drive. Significant also was Larkin senior's election on an IWL ticket, which, despite reports that he planned to retire from politics and concentrate on industrial agitation, reinforced the view that he remained a formidable political force.[95] Astonishingly, however, Bell continued to use the *Workers' Voice* as a blunt instrument against Big Jim, even though he had defended the RWP from Catholic pressure groups and arranged for his Camac Press to produce the paper in lieu of another publisher willing to associate with communist activities.[96] Bell, it seems, was bent on damaging relations between Larkin and the RWP beyond repair.

A letter from the ECCI in September announced that, due to his 'sectarian attitude', Bell would be removed from his position with immediate effect and replaced by Murray, Larkin junior and Bill Denn, three of the strongest Lenin School graduates. The diligent Bob Stewart would remain in place for the meantime and continue to assist preparations for the formation of a new party. Paradoxically, the letter also stated that the line pursued by Bell and articulated in the *Workers' Voice* was fundamentally correct, but had failed in its application to differentiate between the WUI and 'social fascist' unions and pay sufficient attention to Ireland's relationship with Britain. The former concession arguably came too late to bring Larkin back into the fold. The latter came with the considerable caveat that, in the face of stark realities, the Irish cadres would be required to separate the 'semi-proletarian and proletarian elements' of the IRA from its 'petty bourgeois leadership' and bring them under communist control. Whereas the Comintern was more than willing to enforce personnel changes where it felt it was being failed, there was little movement regarding tactics.[97] Bell appears to have been implementing 'class against class' with a fundamentalism that did not sit well with Murray and Larkin junior, but the new leadership would be expected to pursue the Comintern line in a less erratic fashion.

Bell's dismissal and return to Moscow preceded the removal of Christy Ferguson, another troublesome figure. Having returned from the Lenin School in disgrace after just a few days, Ferguson took up work with the INUM. Shortly after gaining influence within what was now known as the Revolutionary Workers' Groups (RWG), he formed an oppositional section and announced his intention to establish a 'Workers' International Party'. In contravention of a Dublin secretariat resolution, he began to organise and pursue militant tactics in Cork and other southern parts of the island, before travelling to Belfast to deliver his message to the local branch.[98] This had the desired effect of disrupting the activities of the Belfast group, which had not yet affiliated to the Comintern and was therefore largely unacquainted with Bolshevik methods of organisation, but it also prompted the Dublin leadership to censure him for 'unprincipled' conduct. Given his behaviour at the Lenin School, his hostility to republicans and alleged poor leadership of the INUM, this subversion of the secretariat's authority constituted the final straw. Ferguson's expulsion was negotiated between Dublin and Moscow, and eventually confirmed in early 1931. This marked the continuation of an incongruous process of centralisation within the RWG leadership.[99]

The direction of travel set out by the Lenin School graduates from their Dublin base gave the Belfast comrades cause for concern. At a meeting with Murray, Larkin junior and Bob Stewart, who had begun overseeing RWG activities in the city, William Boyd and M. McLarnon raised a number of taxing questions on behalf of the Belfast group. What is the state of the RWG's relationship with Larkin and the WUI? In response, Murray repeated his criticisms of Bell's left sectarianism and joined Larkin junior and William Boyd from Belfast in affirming support for Big Jim. These fundamental differences, Stewart added, made it necessary to remove Bell and proceed without him. What is the connection between the RWG, Peadar O'Donnell and the IRA? Stewart explained with misguided optimism that the Comintern line allowed for cooperation with O'Donnell and the establishment of a united front of the working class and peasantry under the umbrella of anti-imperialism. Murray further argued 'there was no part of the country where the fight against Imperialism was more necessary than in Belfast'. At the same time, Stewart attempted to assuage concerns about a republican takeover, noting that fewer than half of RWG national committee members were republicans and emphasising that all but one came from working-class backgrounds. Although the secretariat rejected or deftly avoided a number of questions, the Belfast cadres 'expressed themselves as generally satisfied' and admitted to forejudging the RWG's relationship with the republican movement.[100]

Despite these assurances, McLarnon proceeded in complaining to the Anglo-American secretariat that the national committee had not yet been restored and that control of the RWG now resided 'in the hands of three persons who have constituted themselves a dictatorship'. An accompanying statement to the ECCI criticised the neglect of the industrial North and the decision to base Murray and Denn in Dublin, from where they 'dole out their training in the form of resolutions from which there can be no appeal'. The removal of Bell and Ferguson remained sore points, while Murray's recent visit to Coleraine had taken place under the 'pretext of assisting us' and with the aim of 'bring[ing] another newly-formed contact (Ballymoney) under the direct control of Dublin'. And to the extreme displeasure of their comrades, James Kater and Loftus Johnston, two leading Belfast cadres, had begun to assist the Dublin secretariat through their close association with Murray and Stewart. Expressing a reluctance to work under the direction of the latter, who was guilty of 'pandering to a clerically-dominated, fascist-in-embryo Republican Party through its leader Peadar O'Donnell and the Peasants' Movement', the Belfast group informed the ECCI of its decision, with four dissensions, to split with the Dublin secretariat. They remained committed to the goal of establishing an Irish communist party, but insisted that the ECCI take steps to change or at least clarify Belfast's role vis-à-vis the movement's increasingly Dublin-centric organisational structures.[101]

The prevailing disunity within the RWG resulted in a brief souring of relations between the dissident Belfast group and Harry Pollitt, CPGB general secretary and member of the Anglo-American secretariat, who consequently abandoned plans to travel across for an unemployed meeting.[102] Meanwhile, the Belfast cadres met with Murray again on 8 March and were sufficiently assuaged to fall in behind the Dublin leadership, pending further instructions from the ECCI.[103] When these instructions finally came in May, they brought the dispute to a swift end, stating in no uncertain terms that the Belfast group had taken 'a wrong attitude' towards Dublin and that centralised structures were among the 'pre-requisites' for developing the RWG and establishing a communist party. Although the ECCI insisted that a Belfast representative be appointed to the central secretariat, the implication was clear: the Irish communist party would be founded on bureaucratic, rather than democratic, centralism; and the central trinity of Murray, Denn and Larkin junior would be sacrosanct as long as they continued to prosecute the Comintern line to Moscow's satisfaction.[104]

Bolshevisation, left republicanism and the united front

Throughout this tumultuous period, 1930-31, Murray continued to play a prominent role in united front organisations such as the Irish Friends of Soviet Russia and the Irish section of the League Against Imperialism (LAI), which drew its delegates from colonial countries and had become almost inoperative, as a global organisation, due to the escalation of 'class against class'.[105] He shared public platforms with Peadar O'Donnell, Roddy Connolly, Seán MacBride, the socialist-feminists, Charlotte Despard and Hanna Sheehy Skeffington, Fianna Fáil leader, Éamon de Valera, and Frank Ryan, who had assumed editorial control of *An Phoblacht* and who concluded LAI meetings with 'three cheers for India and then three more for the Workers' Revolutionary Party'.[106] Murray qualified his support for broad anti-imperialist resolutions with a warning against the likely 'betrayal' of the masses by bourgeois nationalism in India and Ireland,[107] and his attendance at an Armistice Day protest with a reminder that he stood opposed to British, French, Italian, American and Irish imperialism.[108] However, the Irish section was predominantly republican in content and personnel, and its anti-imperialism was directed primarily at the British state, the imperial power with the greatest influence on Irish affairs. Indeed, a rather opportunistic 'anti-imperialist' IRA campaign ran concurrently with these events and targeted mainly symbolic figures of local resentment such as moneylenders, ex-servicemen and British monuments. Only the least militaristic of the IRA's activities – Poppy Day protests, which did involve clashes with poppy sellers, the British Legion and black-shirted members of the British Fascists – had 'an appeal beyond their ranks'.[109] In fact, these were 'the primary LAI activity in Ireland' between 1930 and 1932.[110]

According to Roddy Connolly's biographer, Murray's open association with republicanism and involvement with the LAI was indicative of possibilities on the ground, almost two thousand miles away from head office in Moscow.[111] Moreover, although the Dublin secretariat generally avoided engaging with the IRA in the *Workers' Voice*, Murray was as late as October 1930 distinguishing class-based republicanism from the 'petty-bourgeois elements under clerical and other anti-revolutionary pressure'. O'Donnell and David Fitzgerald were examples of the former variant of republicanism, which deserved a sympathetic hearing: 'The fight to give clarity to the gallant working class fighters within the ranks of revolutionary republicanism is one which will have the support of every class-conscious worker.'[112] The primary difficulty of translating this analysis into tangible cooperation between the RWG and the 'revolutionary' IRA would lie in reconciling pragmatism with adherence to the Comintern line.

As outlined above, Murray and Larkin junior in particular had genuine reservations about the potential implications of creating a movement in isolation from Larkinism and left republicanism. Ultimately, however, they subordinated these concerns to the retention of access to the international communist apparatus. The process of Bolshevisation gathered pace in late 1930 with the establishment of factory cells and the division of the Dublin RWG into four groups: Inchicore and the railwaymen; the docks and factories; Guinness and Jacob's; and Broadstone. More significantly, in lieu of further clarification from Moscow on tactical flexibility, the RWG's inaugural congress, January 1931, formally endorsed 'class against class'. Irish capitalism and British imperialism remained the dual enemies of the working class, whose unity with the 'peasantry and discontented bourgeoisie' in a mass movement was the objective of the RWG. At the same time, the 'conference emphasised the necessity of tirelessly exposing the character of petty-bourgeois nationalism in the leadership of the Irish Republican Army'. Cooperation with republicans would therefore take place from below and only in the interests of bolstering the ranks of the RWG.[113]

In a similar vein, the RWG now stressed the importance of delivering 'the clearest revolutionary criticism of the "centrist" policy of the [WUI] leadership, which threatened to transform this organisation of revolutionary workers into a "left" screen for the Labor [sic] Party'.[114] It is clear that despite Murray and young Jim's efforts, the Comintern's inability or unwillingness to reach out to Larkin left the Dublin secretariat with little option but to take the path that excluded the WUI. Incidentally, one can find scant evidence of the term 'social fascist' in usage, whether in RWG publications or statements. However, Murray was comfortable with using the *Workers' Voice* to denounce as 'traitors' the NUR and Building Trades Council leaders in Belfast, which included RWG cadres, for agreeing pay cuts with employers. Likewise, the party's relationship with the Northern Ireland Labour Party (NILP) deteriorated during this period. Specifically, the RWG dismissed the NILP's proposals for greater regulation of industry as a cynical attempt to 'prevent the collapse of their [capitalist] system'.[115] Whatever his concerns about alienating potential allies, Murray gradually succumbed to left sectarianism in policy and practice.

While the RWG leadership moved to jettison what little prospect there was of reaching out to left republicans on a meaningful scale, the IRA had identified, in the context of the global economic downturn and continued growth of Fianna Fáil, an opportunity to consider a more radical social programme. Not surprisingly, O'Donnell and George Gilmore, a socialist republican of northern origins, were among the main protagonists. At the same time, the importance of pitching the message to a wider republican audience drew the contribution of Moss Twomey, the IRA Chief of Staff. Under the pen name 'Manus O'Ruairc', Twomey published in *An Phoblacht* a draft document entitled 'The Sovereignty of the People'. Murray clearly had this initiative in mind when referring to the 'revolutionary' potential within republicanism. The failure to go beyond this and offer concrete proposals of his own reflected, in large part, a lack of clarity regarding the position to adopt towards radicals within the IRA.[116]

Adopting the language of 'Pearsean communalism', Twomey's tract provoked intense debates around the issue of private ownership and accentuated tensions within the IRA on the role of Catholic social teaching.[117] Yet, while ideology and resistance to radical change played a role in fomenting internal divisions, Brian Hanley and Adrian Grant have argued convincingly that strategic considerations were of equal, if not greater, importance. Indeed, that the IRA leadership was open to left-wing ideas and the formation of a political wing is evident from the fact that the ensuing debate was open-ended and sanctioned at an Army convention. In Grant's estimation, Twomey's critical failure was twofold: that he underestimated the extent of Catholic reaction against socialistic ideas; and that in his desire to keep the republican movement together as a broad church, he refused to cut loose a minority of right-wing enthusiasts within the IRA and reach a compromise with O'Donnell.[118] For the RWG's part, token references to Connolly and attendance at the Easter commemoration alongside O'Donnell failed to disguise the most consequential development within its ranks.[119] The decision to launch a communist party, *the vanguard party*, marked the conclusion to the process of Bolshevisation that had begun around 1927.[120]

Two developments effectively condemned united front politics to failure. Firstly, the RWG leadership's conscious decision to embrace Third Period doctrines had, and would continue to have, far-reaching implications for the communists' relationships with rival labour formations across the island. Secondly, the decision to form Saor Éire saw a band of progressive republicans make what O'Donnell described as 'a great lurch to the left on definite terms'.[121] It is indicative of the direction in which republican figures such as O'Donnell, Gilmore and even Seán MacBride were heading that they had begun to speak in terms of the abolition of capitalism and private property. They had also dismissed Michael Price, one of their distributivist critics, as a 'Treatyite of the third phase' – in other words, someone who was prepared to reach a compromise with capitalism in the most crucial stage of revolutionary struggle.[122] Although Saor Éire initially carried the Army's stamp of approval, its radicalism quickly went beyond a reticent IRA leadership, which had begun to flounder in the effort of self-preservation and direct its energy towards retaining the loyalty of rank-and-file members. At the same time, just as preparations for the launch of Saor Éire had commenced, the RWG shifted the goalposts hastily to the left and closed out cooperation between the two groups. Grant puts it very succinctly: 'Irish communists and leftist republicans were now on parallel tracks on route to similar destinations. Comintern strategy acted as the sleeper between the tracks preventing any official crossover.'[123]

In different circumstances, Murray might have been in a stronger position to pursue alliances with the WUI and left republicans. One does not have to dig deep to find evidence of his affinity with Larkinism and anti-Treaty socialist republicanism, both of which had a formative influence on his political outlook. The sectarian hangover of Bell's brief tenure and the conditionality of Comintern support during the Third Period trumped these tendencies without quite eradicating them. Murray was tied to and constrained by shifts in Comintern thinking, and the small Irish communist movement relied on Moscow for 'the myth, the model of organisation, the cadres, and, to a degree, the finance which made the struggle possible'.[124] There was little or no scope within these parameters for improvisation of the Comintern line or the development of a distinct Irish path to Bolshevisation. In short, Murray's early political career epitomised the central contradiction of Comintern-periphery relations: the tension between 'Bolshevik universalism and national specificity'.[125]

NOTES

1   Seán Murray, *The Irish Revolt: 1916 and After* (London, 1936), p.10.
2   Emmet O'Connor, 'John (Seán) Murray', in Keith Gildart, David Howell and Neville Kirk (eds), *Dictionary of Labour Biography, Vol. XI* (London, 2003), p.200.
3   Russian State Archive for Social and Political History (Rossiiskii Gosudartsvennyi Arkhiv Sotsial'no-Politischeskoi Istorii, RGASPI), 495/218/1/57-63, Seán Murray autobiography, 11 August 1932.
4   Public Record Office of Northern Ireland (PRONI), Seán Murray Papers, D2162/M/1, Letter from Wongan Hills, Western Australia to Pat Murray, 14 November 1924.
5   RGASPI, 495/218/1/57-63, Seán Murray autobiography, 11 August 1932.
6   Ibid.
7   Ibid. I am obliged to Fionntán McElheran for additional information relating to Murray's background.
8   Author's interview with Eoin Ó Murchú, 17 May 2010; PRONI, Seán Murray Papers, D2162/I/43, Irish Section of the British-Hungarian Friendship Society, 'In Memoriam and Dedicated to Seán Murray: A Courageous Irishman and Valiant Fighter for International Peace' (1961).

9 Stephanie Millar, 'Roger Casement and North Antrim', in Eamon Phoenix, Padraic O Cleireachain, Eileen McAuley and Nuala McSparran (eds), *Feis na nGleann: A Century of Gaelic Culture in the Antrim Glens* (Belfast, 2005), pp.53-64.

10 Bureau of Military History (BMH), Witness Statements, WS. 762, Liam McMullen, p.3.

11 Murray, *The Irish Revolt*, pp.5, 8.

12 RGASPI, 495/218/1/57-63, Seán Murray autobiography, 11 August 1932.

13 *Irish Review*, April 1945.

14 RGASPI, 495/218/1/57-63, Seán Murray autobiography, 11 August 1932.

15 Robert Lynch, *The IRA and the Early Years of Partition* (Dublin, 2006), pp.66-128.

16 Emmet O'Connor, 'John (Seán) Murray', in Keith Gildart, David Howell and Neville Kirk (eds), *Dictionary of Labour Biography, Vol. XI* (London, 2003), p.200.

17 BMH, Military Service Pensions Collection, MA/MSPC/RO/410, 3rd Northern Division, 2nd Brigade, 3rd Battalion.

18 BMH, WS. 395, Thomas Fitzpatrick (Bob McDonnell), p.7.

19 Conor Kostick, *Revolution in Ireland: Popular Militancy 1917 to 1923* (London & Chicago, 1996), p.170.

20 BMH, WS. 389, Roger E. McCorley, 33-37; WS. 762, Liam McMullen, p.24.

21 Michael McInerney, *Peadar O'Donnell: Irish Social Rebel* (Dublin, 1974), p.97.

22 Murray, *The Irish Revolt*, pp.10-11.

23 BMH, WS. 389, Roger E. McCorley, p. 32; WS. 412, Joseph Murray, p.26.

24 BMH, WS. 395, Thomas Fitzpatrick (Bob McDonnell), pp.8-9; WS. 609, Feidhlim S. MacGuill, p.9.

25 BMH, WS. 395, Thomas Fitzpatrick (Bob McDonnell), p.10.

26 National Archives UK (NAUK), CAB/24/138, T.F. Barrington-Ward, K.C., 'The Cushendall Enquiry', 9 September 1922.

27 Michael Hopkinson, *Green Against Green: The Irish Civil War* (2nd ed.) (Dublin, 2004), p.84.

28 BMH, WS. 609, Feidhlim S. MacGuill, p.13.

29 NAUK, CAB/24/138, 'The Cushendall Enquiry'.

30 *Irish Times*, 9 September 1922.

31 NAUK, CAB/24/138, 'The Cushendall Enquiry'.

32 BMH, Military Service Pensions Collection, MA/MSPC/RO/410, 3rd Northern Division, 2nd Brigade, 3rd Battalion.

33 Ibid.

34 BMH, WS. 609, Feidhlim S. MacGuill, pp.13-15.

35 Leo Keohane, *Captain Jack White: Imperialism, Anarchism and the Irish Citizen Army* (Sallins, 2014), pp.217-18.

36 RGASPI, 495/218/1/57-63, Seán Murray autobiography, 11 August 1932.

37   David Howell, *A Lost Left: Three Studies in Socialism and Nationalism* (Manchester, 1986).

38   Charlie McGuire, *Seán McLoughlin: Ireland's Forgotten Revolutionary* (Pontypool, 2011), pp.50-8.

39   University College Dublin Archives (UCDA), Seán MacEntee Papers, P67/528(1), Department of Justice 'Notes on Communism in Saorstát Éireann' (1937).

40   Emmet O'Connor, *Reds and the Green: Ireland, Russia and the Communist Internationals, 1919-43* (Dublin, 2004), p.3. See Ch. 5 for the collapse of the IWL and the deterioration of Larkin's relationship with Moscow.

41   O'Connor, 'John (Seán) Murray', p.201; RGASPI, 495/218/1/57-63, Seán Murray autobiography, 11 August 1932.

42   UCDA, P67/528(1), Department of Justice 'Notes on Communism in Saorstát Éireann' (1937).

43   National Archives of Ireland (NAI), Department of Justice (DJ), 2007/56/120, 'Russian Oil Products Company' (1928-1931).

44   Emmet O'Connor, 'Bolshevising Irish Communism, 1927-31', *Irish Historical Studies*, 33: 132 (2003), p.455.

45   Barry McLoughlin, 'Proletarian Academics or Party Functionaries? Irish Communists at the International Lenin School, Moscow, 1927-37', *Saothar*, 22 (1997), p.64.

46   O'Connor, *Reds and the Green*, pp.127-39.

47   RGASPI, 495/89/49/18-19, Letter from Larkin to Bukharin (1929).

48   Kevin McDermott and Jeremy Agnew, *The Comintern: A History of International Communism from Lenin to Stalin* (Basingstoke, 1996), p.45.

49   RGASPI, 495/164/500/50-72, Sixth ECCI Plenum, 8 March 1926.

50   Ibid.

51   James K. Hopkins, *Into the Heart of the Fire: The British in the Spanish Civil War* (Stanford, 1998), p.100.

52   Barry McLoughlin, *Left to the Wolves: Irish Victims of Stalinist Terror* (Dublin, 2007), p.25.

53   RGASPI, 495/218/1/57-63, Seán Murray autobiography, 11 August 1932.

54   Andrew Thorpe, *The British Communist Party and Moscow, 1920-43* (Manchester, 2000), pp.117-55.

55   Gidon Cohen and Kevin Morgan, 'Stalin's Sausage Machine. British Students at the Lenin School, 1926-37', *Twentieth Century British History*, Vol. 13, No. 4 (2002), pp.334-7.

56   RGASPI, 495/164/500/50-72, Sixth ECCI Plenum, 8 March 1926.

57   McLoughlin, *Left to the Wolves*, p.25.

58 O'Connor, 'Bolshevising Irish Communism', p.458.

59 O'Connor, 'John (Seán) Murray', p.201.

60 James Larkin junior and Seán Murray, *The Life and Struggle of the Working-Class and Peasantry in Ireland* (Translated from English by N. Kaminskaya) (Moscow, 1930).

61 RGASPI, 495/164/500/50-72, Sixth ECCI Plenum, 8 March 1926.

62 I am obliged to Stephen White for this information.

63 The account of this trip is solely that of Harry Wicks, *Keeping My Head: Memoirs of a British Bolshevik* (London, 1992), pp.109-13.

64 McDermott and Agnew, *The Comintern*, pp.68-90.

65 McLoughlin, 'Proletarian Academics or Party Functionaries?', p.68.

66 Wicks, *Keeping My Head*, pp.90-2, 109.

67 'Arthur' is likely to have been Arthur Horner, the Welsh miner, trade union official and one-time member of the Anglo-American secretariat. During the First World War, Horner's decision to avoid conscription had led him to Ireland and into the ranks of the ICA. He was in Moscow during the *chistka* and appears to have had an input into how 'rightists' were treated at the Lenin School and within the CPGB. See Arthur Horner, *Incorrigible Rebel* (London, 1960), pp.107-13; Thorpe, *The British Communist Party*, pp.142-70.

68 RGASPI, 495/89/54/53-61, Letter from 'Arthur' to 'Frank', 17 November 1929.

69 Harry Haywood, *Black Bolshevik: Autobiography of an Afro-American Communist* (Chicago, 1978), p.205.

70 RGASPI, 495/89/54/53-61, Letter from 'Arthur' to 'Frank', 17 November 1929.

71 McLoughlin, 'Proletarian Academics or Party Functionaries?', p.70.

72 RGASPI, 495/89/54/53-61, Letter from 'Arthur' to 'Frank', 17 November 1929.

73 Ibid.

74 McLoughlin, 'Proletarian Academics or Party Functionaries?', p.70.

75 O'Connor, *Reds and the Green*, p.145.

76 McLoughlin, *Left to the Wolves*, pp.34-8.

77 RGASPI, 495/14/335/21-23, Letter from Murray to I. Mingulin, Lenin School instructor and member of the Anglo-American secretariat (c. 1929).

78 McLoughlin, *Left to the Wolves*, Part 1.

79 O'Connor, *Reds and the Green*, pp.149-50.

80 RGASPI, 495/218/1/57-63, Seán Murray autobiography, 11 August 1932.

81 Wicks, *Keeping My Head*, p.126.

82 RGASPI, 495/218/1/57-63, Seán Murray autobiography, 11 August 1932.

83 Wicks, *Keeping My Head*, p.93.

84 Adrian Grant, *Irish Socialist Republicanism, 1909-36* (Dublin, 2012), Ch. 5.

85 O'Connor, *Reds and the Green*, p.153.

86 RGASPI, 495/218/1/57-63, Seán Murray autobiography, 11 August 1932; UCDA, Seán MacEntee Papers, P67/528(1), Department of Justice 'Notes on Communism in Saorstát Éireann' (1937).
87 *Workers' Voice*, 28 June 1930; *An Phoblacht*, 5 July 1930.
88 O'Connor, *Reds and the Green*, pp.152, 155.
89 *Workers' Voice*, 19 July 1930.
90 Ibid.
91 Ibid., 30 August 1930; *An Phoblacht*, 6 September 1930.
92 RGASPI, 495/89/63/20-27, Seán Murray and Jim Larkin junior, Joint report on the WUI, 2 August 1930.
93 Ibid.
94 PRONI, Ministry of Home Affairs, HA/32/1/545, RUC Special Branch report, 27 August 1930.
95 Mike Milotte, *Communism in Modern Ireland: The Pursuit of the Workers' Republic Since 1916* (Dublin, 1984), p.103.
96 O'Connor, *Reds and the Green*, p.157.
97 RGASPI, 495/89/61/19-22, Draft resolution on Ireland, 1 September 1930.
98 PRONI, HA/32/1/546, RUC Special Branch report, 28 January 1931.
99 RGASPI, 495/89/65/7-8, Case of F. (1930); O'Connor, *Reds and the Green*, pp.158-9.
100 RGASPI, 495/89/65/9-11, Minutes of RWG meeting, 12 January 1931.
101 RGASPI, 495/89/66/16-21, Letter from M. McLarnon to Anglo-American secretariat; Statement to the ECCI, 28 February 1931.
102 RGASPI, 495/89/66/21-23, Letters between M. McLarnon and Harry Pollitt, 19 February - 6 March 1931.
103 RGASPI, 495/89/66/24, Letter from M. McLarnon to RWG secretariat, 9 March 1931.
104 RGASPI 495/4/102/35-39, Instructions on Ireland, 16 May 1931.
105 Kate O'Malley, 'The League Against Imperialism: British, Irish and Indian connections', *Communist History Network Newsletter*, 14 (Spring, 2003).
106 Grant, *Irish Socialist Republicanism*, p.170.
107 *An Phoblacht*, 4 October 1930.
108 Ibid., 15 November 1930.
109 Brian Hanley, *The IRA, 1926-1936* (Dublin, 2002), pp.71-6.
110 Donal Ó Drisceoil, *Peadar O'Donnell* (Cork, 2001), p.63.
111 Charlie McGuire, *Roddy Connolly and the Struggle for Socialism in Ireland* (Cork, 2008), pp.132-5.
112 *Workers' Voice*, 25 October 1930.

113   O'Connor, *Reds and the Green*, pp.158-9.

114   Ibid., p.160.

115   *Workers' Voice*, 11 April, 9, 16 May 1931.

116   Ibid., 25 October 1930.

117   Richard English, *Radicals and the Republic: Socialist Republicanism in the Irish Free State, 1925-37* (Oxford, 1994), pp.124-6.

118   Brian Hanley, 'Moss Twomey, Radicalism and the IRA, 1931-1933: A Reassessment', *Saothar*, 26 (2001), pp.53-60; Grant, *Irish Socialist Republicanism*, pp.171-7.

119   *Workers' Voice*, 4, 11 April 1931.

120   O'Connor, *Reds and the Green*, p.159.

121   Henry Patterson, *The Politics of Illusion: A Political History of the IRA* (London, 1997), p.52.

122   Jonathan Hamill, 'Saor Éire and the IRA: An Exercise in Deception?', *Saothar*, 20 (1995), p.60.

123   Grant, *Irish Socialist Republicanism*, p.170.

124   O'Connor, *Reds and the Green*, p.160.

125   McDermott and Agnew, *The Comintern*, p.65.

CHAPTER 2

Reviving the United Front

I am a servant of two masters ... The imperial British state ... and the holy Roman Catholic and apostolic Church.[1]

At a meeting with the Anglo-American secretariat in June 1932, Murray attempted to clarify the RWG's attitude towards Saor Éire. He explained that while he had opposed the formation of a rival political party, he was also keen to avoid alienating 'the revolutionary elements' mobilised by O'Donnell. That Murray had encouraged attempts to develop class-based republicanism in 1930 and the early part of 1931 is supportive of this description of events. Less convincing is his retrospective claim to tactical clarity:

> We did not call it names, say it was a petty bourgeois party and did not tell them we were the only people that would lead the revolution because we were not at that time in a position to come forward with our own party and give it as an alternative ... The rank and file of the IRA were undoubtedly moving forward and Saor Eire represented an attempt of the proletarian and revolutionary peasant elements within Republican Ireland to escape from bankrupt policies of the old nationalist movement, to seek a revolutionary way out. At the same time it ... represented an attempt on the part of a section of the leadership, such as the MacBrides and those people who are really representatives of De Valera within the IRA, to hold back the development of the revolutionary movement and keep it within the petty bourgeois nationalist orbit, and the fact is we were not long in seeing the futility of endeavouring to form a revolutionary Party on the basis on which Saor Eire was formed.[2]

At the time, Murray had occupied a much more ambiguous position in practice. Not only was he a delegate to Saor Éire's founding congress in September 1931, but he had assisted David Fitzgerald, an old War of Independence comrade, in drafting its programme. Following this, he shared a platform with O'Donnell and Shapurji Saklatvala of the CPGB at public meetings to form local branches.[3] This cooperation stands in contrast to Tom Bell's view of Saor Éire as 'an attempt on the part of petit bourgeois leaders [in the IRA] to … prevent the formation of a Communist Party'.[4] If Bell's was the interpretation shared by the Comintern and IRA leadership, it did not reflect the stance adopted by Murray and the architects of Saor Éire.

The inaugural Saor Éire congress convened on the last weekend of September, with 120 delegates and around twenty observers in attendance. Seán Hayes of the IRA and IWFC chaired, while Nixie Boran, the Kilkenny miner, gave the RWG representation on the executive. The new left-wing organisation counted among its main objectives the overthrow of British imperialism and Irish capitalism, and 'the possession and administration by the workers and working farmers, of the land, the instruments of production, distribution and exchange'.[5] From the outset, however, the Saor Éire project drew the opprobrium of the authorities and Catholic Church. In the first instance, the arrest of Seán MacBride in the possession of Saor Éire documents in July confirmed the state's suspicions of an IRA flirtation with communism.[6] This corresponded with a revival of Catholic social teaching and activism, fortified by the 1929 centenary of Catholic emancipation and the circulation of Pope Pius XI's *Quadragesimo Anno* (1931). On 17 September, the Department of Justice sent a detailed intelligence report to Cardinal Joseph MacRory and bishops across the island, drawing attention to the emergence of Saor Éire and alleging an IRA-communist conspiracy.[7] Thus the Church and state agencies stirred one another into an anti-communist frenzy and set in motion an orchestrated assault on leftist groups. The 'red scare' would condemn Saor Éire to failure and create the conditions whereby the RWG would encounter great difficulty in organising and advancing its programme.

It was the murders of Pat Carroll, an IRA informer, and Garda Superintendent Seán Curtin that provided the Cumann na nGaedheal government with a pretext for the introduction of coercive legislation. Dáil debates on the subject paid some attention to the murders and other IRA activities, but the formation of Saor Éire dominated exchanges in the chamber.[8] On 18 October, after further contact between the bishops and government, priests in every parish read out a pastoral letter condemning Saor Éire for attempting to 'impose upon the Catholic soil of Ireland the same materialistic regime, with its fanatical hatred of God, as now dominates Russia and threatens to dominate Spain'.[9] The letter concluded with a stern reminder that 'you cannot be a Catholic and a Communist. One stands for Christ, the other for anti-Christ'. This was followed closely by the passage of William T. Cosgrave's Constitution (Amendment No. 17) Bill, which inserted Article 2A (a Public Safety Act) into the constitution. The bill would enable censorship, the proscription of anti-state organisations and their literature, the establishment of military tribunals, and an extension of Garda powers. As the legislation came into effect, Garda Commissioner Eoin O'Duffy began identifying 'communist agitators' by name and successfully requested an additional 200 Special Branch officers to put in place his favoured measures of repression.[10] Serious problems lay ahead for O'Duffy's political opponents in the anti-Treaty left republican and communist milieu.

These mechanisms succeeded in their primary objective of putting Saor Éire out of commission. Leaving nothing to chance, the authorities proscribed a number of groups including the IRA, Fianna Éireann, Cumann na mBan, the ILDL, the Irish Friends of Soviet Russia, the IWFC and the Workers' Defence Corps. The RWG only escaped proscription because it had replaced the RWP.[11] Where government measures failed to handicap the RWG, the Catholic public relations machine succeeded as the *Workers' Voice* lost the support of three different publishers over a period of around twelve months. When the paper resumed publication, it attempted an uncomfortable compromise, balancing criticisms of clericalism at home with praise for religious freedom in the Soviet Union.[12] Murray assured the radical feminist, Hanna Sheehy Skeffington that the RWG would 'take up a correct position on this dirty business [religious interference] which is becoming very prevalent down here'.[13] He subsequently went to great lengths to make religion a non-issue within the Irish communist movement. One sign of this was the adoption of a less pronounced stance on religious belief in the *Workers' Voice* from early 1932, which indicates that Murray grasped the significance of clerical reaction at an early stage in the RWG's development.

Catholic anti-communism also had a hand in shaping the political landscape of the North. According to William McMullen, a Protestant disciple of Connolly, Catholic denunciations of socialism had the effect of preventing the spread of radical politics in nationalist areas. In support of McMullen's claim, the Nationalist

Party leader, Joe Devlin, described the Church as 'the greatest obstacle facing the Labour movement if it hoped to appeal to the Catholic working-class'.[14] Of course, Devlin's close association with a distinctly Catholic-nationalist political current obscures his position vis-à-vis the labour movement. Graham Walker explains that

> McMullen and others were to find that Catholic anti-socialist propaganda from the pulpit and in the pages of the *Irish News*, the mouthpiece of the Nationalist Party led by Joe Devlin, was an obstacle just as daunting as the unionist-Orange machine on the other side of the sectarian divide.[15]

Nor was there anything particularly new about this problem. Connolly had written extensively on the negative role of 'the national movement' and his experience of Belfast politics provoked a few choice words about 'wee' Joe, the Ancient Order of Hibernians (AOH) and the 'poisonous suggestion' used by *Irish News* editors to undermine the efforts of labour activists.[16] The Church did lack institutional power in the North. As a defender of minority rights, supporter of Irish nationalism, educational authority and social services provider, it endured an antagonistic relationship with the Unionist regime. But for much the same reason, it remained a big factor in determining the social and political attitudes of working-class Catholics during Murray's era.[17]

Extreme Protestant fundamentalism posed a relatively minor threat to the Belfast communist movement in its own right; it was when these ideas emerged from, or drew the support of, the ruling Unionist Party that the left had greater cause for concern.[18] In terms of the state and power relations, the northern ruling elite of industrialists, merchants and landed gentry had a material interest in maintaining their dominant political position. The Special Powers Act (1922), uglier sister of the Public Safety Act, provided the authorities with the necessary cover to harass, imprison and exclude 'subversive' elements. Right up until the onset of the Second World War, the government devoted considerable resources to monitoring the activities of communists and other labour activists. Plain clothes RUC Special Branch detectives were ubiquitous observers (and meticulous note-takers) at leftist meetings throughout the 1930s, reporting to the Ministry of Home Affairs almost on a weekly basis. Dawson Bates, the long-serving minister, took the lead in employing Special Powers with little restraint and to the detriment of labour activists. In September 1930, Loftus Johnston became the first of many communists jailed for sedition under this legislation.[19] For his part in organising workers and the unemployed on both sides of the border, Murray would eventually feel the full weight of legal measures available to Bates and the RUC.

In a perverse sense, the precarious economic climate presented an opening for labour groups by threatening a dispersal of working-class loyalties away from the Unionist Party and conservative northern nationalism. The Great Depression hit the industrialised north-east hard, with unemployment rising from 35,000 in 1929 to 72,000 in 1930 and 76,000 in 1932.[20] These figures worked out at an annual rate of 27 percent, compared with 22 percent in Britain.[21] In response, the militant Ulster Protestant League (UPL) emerged in 1931 to launch a 'jobs for Protestants' appeal, while the Orange Order experienced some success in expanding its membership.[22] Prime Minister James Craig did not yield to this reaction directly, though he and his dominant 'populist' wing certainly played to the gallery. Against the advice of the 'anti-populist' Minister of Finance, Hugh Pollock, Craig extended specific aspects of British social legislation to the North. This he did with the support of Bates and John Andrews, Minister of Labour and head of the Ulster Unionist Labour Association (UULA), which had fallen under the direction of the Unionist Party in 1918.[23] As Walker notes, this step by step approach 'could be touted by the unionists as proof that they in Northern Ireland were no less British when it came to material benefits'.[24] Complicating labour politics further was the emergence of the anti-partitionist Northern Ireland Socialist Party (NISP) from the ashes of the Belfast-based Independent Labour Party (ILP), and the continued strength of the pinkish NILP, which moved in a Unionist direction under Harry Midgley's leadership. Politically, the labour movement in the North was deeply fragmented, but the severity of the recession created windows of opportunity for the communists to make an impact on social and economic issues.

Due to the absence of heavy industries and a reliance on agricultural and cattle exports, the impact of the global downturn was more gradual in the South. However, emigration figures between 1921 and 1931, averaging at 33,000 per annum, were disconcerting. Higher than the rate for the previous two decades, these numbers underlined a failure to create new employment in the form of native industries and a strong export base.[25] These emigration levels and the corresponding rate of unemployment were an indictment of Cumann na nGaedheal's economic liberalism and fiscal and monetary prudence. Consequently, they heightened the popular appeal of Fianna Fáil's programme, which appropriated Peadar O'Donnell's land annuities campaign, promised radical agricultural reforms in favour of labour-intensive production, and committed to economic-nationalist industrialisation behind protective barriers.[26] In the 1932 election, the anti-Treaty party increased its share of the vote from 35.2 percent to 44.5 percent. Labour lost six deputies, but its transfers and support for de Valera as Taoiseach were determining factors in the consolidation of Fianna Fáil's strong position.[27] As one historian of Fianna Fáil's adolescent years has noted, the Labour Party 'effectively fought in 1932 on a platform that accepted Fianna Fáil leadership of the country'.[28] Cooperation with Labour continued into and beyond the 1933 snap election, in which de Valera's party increased its share of the vote to a commanding 49.7 percent and secured an overall majority.[29] Labour transfers continued to head in Fianna Fáil's direction, while the IRA leadership lent support to de Valera in both elections in return for the suspension of Cosgrave's Public Safety Act. This Faustian Pact allowed the release of republican prisoners and enabled the IRA to regroup. It also precipitated the formation of the anti-republican and anti-socialist Army Comrades' Association (ACA), thus introducing a new but all too familiar dimension to Civil War politics.[30] A high concentration of working-class support thus formed the basis of Fianna Fáil's success. Nevertheless, since Saor Éire had vacated the scene, there existed a degree of political space for a radical movement to step into the breach and act as a small thorn in the government's left side.

Building a local base

Murray rose to prominence as the leading RWG representative in late 1931. As such, he assumed responsibility for communicating the theory underpinning RWG activities. With Bob Stewart organising in Belfast and William Denn occupied with trade union work, Jim Hale and Joseph Troy joined the Dublin secretariat in their place, though Hale left for the Lenin School in December. The RWG in the South proved effective in organising on the shop floor. It played a leading role in the Dublin building strike at the beginning of 1932 and made some progress recruiting within the WUI. However, this support dissipated just as quickly in the atmosphere of Catholic reaction, leaving the group back at square one. Polling figures for Larkin junior and Troy in the 1932 election – 917 and 170 votes respectively – were an accurate reflection of the party's progress, even accounting for the fact that Troy was forced to run against Larkin senior in North

Dublin. A recruitment drive in the North looked to capitalise on the British Labour government's collapse, deploying Tom Mann, a veteran of the Industrial Workers of the World (IWW) or 'Wobblies', as its trump card. This faltered dramatically in a hostile environment fostered by a reactionary Unionist state on the defensive. By May 1932, the RWG had an estimated Belfast membership of just fifty.[31] Murray reported a lack of 'effective political leadership' in the North. Membership figures for the Dublin group – seventy-eight members, fifty-eight of whom were active – were only marginally better.[32] The RWG leadership's critical task was to consolidate support in the South and identify opportunities for a breakthrough in the North.

Assessing the 1932 election, the Comintern stated that Fianna Fáil had raised false hopes with 'extravagant election promises'. The RWG campaign, on the other hand, had favoured 'the phraseology of nationalism' and failed to focus enough critical attention on the capitalist parties. This analysis obscured the potent legacy of the Irish Civil War and blurred the distinction between the two parties' programmes. In the same communication, Moscow criticised the Irish communists for failing to apply the united front to the 'militant workers' of the WUI and IRA members 'who are breaking away from their petty-bourgeois leadership'. Herein lay a spectacular failure to understand the appeal that Fianna Fáil held for urban and agrarian workers, which included republican grassroots. Combining its socio-economic programme with a promise to continue the national struggle, Fianna Fáil won over the very constituency the Comintern believed it could reach with 'revolutionary' sloganeering.[33] De Valera's party promised to dismantle Cumann na nGaedheal's comprador capitalism, abolish the Oath of Allegiance and achieve full political independence. In this limited sense, Murray and RWG could view Fianna Fáil as an anti-imperialist ally.

As early as mid-1932, there were clear signs that Murray had expended all patience with the obsolescent 'class against class' policy. Upon its reappearance on 9 April, the *Workers' Voice* warned de Valera against pursuing Cumann na nGaedheal's programme 'under other forms and phrases'.[34] Yet the nostalgic republican focus of subsequent issues expressed Murray's proclivity for a nationally specific strategy and hinted at the RWG lending critical support to Fianna Fáil. Firstly, against the backdrop of impending land reforms, an image of Charles Stewart Parnell occupied the front page of one issue. Inside, Murray contributed a piece relating the Irish national struggle to anti-colonial movements in India and China, accompanied by an instalment from Liam Mellows' *Notes from*

Mountjoy (1922) on the same subject.[35] In the absence of chastisement from London or Moscow, the editorial line continued in much the same vein, with the writings of John Mitchel and James Fintan Lalor featuring in quick succession.[36] Most interestingly, Murray reproduced extracts from Lenin's positive contribution on the principle of national self-determination, which represented a rare example of socialist republican literature going beyond Marx and Engels.[37] On 4 June, he finally circumvented all ambiguity, switching critical attention from de Valera to Cosgrave and tying the concept of a successful 'national struggle against Britain' to the fortunes of the working class.[38] With this, he responded to qualitative changes in the political environment and signalled an end to the short Third Period in Ireland.

Having indicated a shift in the RWG's orientation, Murray and Joe Troy travelled to Moscow to present their case to the Anglo-American secretariat. Troy concentrated on trade union matters, while Murray proceeded in addressing the more politically precarious issues of policy and tactics. He bemoaned the absence of an anti-imperialist aspect to RWG activities, argued that the communists had regrettably been 'too sharp' with de Valera and concluded that the Comintern line had simply proved unworkable in Ireland. The clear alternative, he asserted, was for the *Workers' Voice* to persevere with its republican language and for party policy to reflect the fact that Ireland was 'engaged in a struggle with British imperialism' and its native agents.[39] This position could be justified with reference to the classical 'stageist' conception of the revolution, first articulated by Lenin in 1920: in underdeveloped and colonial countries, communists must assist radical bourgeois-national movements in the achievement of democracy and liberation, in anticipation of the struggle for socialism.

Murray found support for his position in the work of the influential German communist, Gerhart Eisler, who, in May 1932, published an article on Ireland in the *Communist International* journal. Eisler noted the significance of the land annuities campaign and the recent draft legislation introduced by de Valera providing for the removal of the Oath of Allegiance. This converged neatly with Murray's analysis and therefore boosted the RWG's chances of gaining policy concessions from the Comintern. In a further effort to bolster the Irish cadres' case, Eisler helped Murray draft a letter correcting the CPGB's 'vulgar distortion' and 'deep-rooted misunderstanding' of the Irish national struggle. The latter's main transgression was a *Daily Worker* article that downplayed the significance of the conflict between Ireland and Britain.[40] Although it would take the pol-commission (Comintern political sub-committee) over two months to deal with Murray's concerns directly, it was prepared to request in the interim that the CPGB support Irish national independence and reach out to the Irish diaspora in working-class areas of Britain.[41] The Comintern also issued letters in Britain and America to raise funds for the RWG, while granting Murray a subvention of $1,088 to cover wages, printing debts and costs incurred during the election.[42]

Murray ratcheted up the pressure at the end of August, delivering what the attending Special Branch detective described as 'a vehement, eloquent and lengthy … Irish rebel's speech' at an LAI meeting in Liverpool. He concluded with a call for the revival of dormant anti-imperialist alliances under the LAI umbrella, involving all republican and workers' organisations.[43] Another Special Branch report claims that Murray had, in fact, rejoined the IRA in 1932 with the CPGB's support and secured a position on the GHQ_staff.[44] Eoin MacNamee, a prominent northern IRA volunteer, recalls meeting with Murray along with Jimmy Joe Reynolds, a traditionalist republican from Leitrim. They discussed general political questions but, contrary to rumours that were later to surface, the 'typical Glensman' was not provided with reports of Army conventions.[45] In lieu of more convincing archival evidence, one must assume that the British authorities had Murray confused with the London-based volunteer of the same name.

On 9 September, Murray did inform the Comintern by letter of his intention to work with David Fitzgerald, an old War of Independence comrade and founding member of Saor Éire. The purpose was the establishment of a joint training and education centre with left republicans, which he sold as a last resort and a means of reducing the RWG's outgoings. This was necessary, he claimed, because the Anglo-American secretariat had reneged on its promise of financial assistance. In addition, he delivered a strongly worded reminder that Moscow had not yet allayed his policy-related concerns. Seeking to 'popularise the way out' of the capitalist crisis, Murray argued that the time was ripe to pressurise Fianna Fáil on its left flank and force the government's hand. That the RWG had not yet attempted to do this was an opportunity missed. The letter in question lays bare Murray's frustration with Moscow. He blamed the Comintern hierarchy for the RWG's 'puny' national progress and requested support for a change in tack.[46]

This policy tug of war continued with four communications from Moscow over a short period, which conveyed mixed messages on Murray's leadership.

On the one hand, the Comintern acknowledged that, regardless of its directives, he had already implemented significant changes on the ground. Most notably, it accepted the necessity of the RWG connecting with workers and small farmers among the ranks of the IRA, Fianna Fáil and even the Labour Party. Against these concessions, it looked to reassert its authority on a number of issues. Firstly, it addressed the content of the *Workers' Voice* in detail, noting 'the deliberate avoidance of even the word Communist' and an editorial policy 'diametrically opposed to the line laid down for the guidance of the comrades in Ireland'. No leeway given on this subject, this letter duly emphasised the importance of the paper in preparing the ground for the formation of a new Irish communist party. Secondly, it reiterated the importance of applying 'class against class' to 'bourgeois and petty bourgeois' political leaderships. Thirdly, that pooling resources with republicans was not an acceptable substitute for a communist training centre in its own right. Fourthly, that the RWG should avoid succumbing to clerical pressure and instead educate supporters tainted with 'religious prejudices'. Finally, taking aim at Murray's cavalier approach to Dublin-Moscow communications, the Comintern requested 'more elaborate and concrete' reports on the Irish party in future.[47]

Murray took these few concessions and applied them liberally. On 8 October, in order to maximise its appeal in republican circles, the *Workers' Voice* became the *Irish Workers' Voice*. Murray continued to develop links with left republicans, taking up a position on the executive of the Boycott British [Goods] League. On 3 November, the RWG and its allies launched a Workers' College in the home of Charlotte Despard, a quintessential fellow traveller of the Irish labour movement. Mrs Despard acted as president; the governing committee consisted of Murray, Peadar O'Donnell, David Fitzgerald, Jim Larkin junior, Betty Sinclair and Bob Stewart.[48] Almost without exception, the joint initiatives of the communist and left republican movements had in common Murray and O'Donnell's close involvement. The latter was even prepared to relinquish his position as head of the IWFC in order for Murray to resuscitate the movement and lead a new campaign: 'He, too, is of small farming stock and upbringing. His being a communist would be no barrier, for my being no communist is no asset!' In the end, this plan gave way to a more roundly supported system of collective leadership.[49] However, O'Donnell's gesture was typical of his and Murray's willingness to exchange places as subordinate allies in the interest of political progress.

Economic conditions ensured that the united front on offer in the North was an easy sell in the short term. As noted above, the recession brought about a sharp increase in unemployment, pushing levels in excess of the British average. When Ramsay MacDonald's national government cut unemployment benefit by 10 percent, the number of cases recorded by the Poor Law Guardians increased dramatically, from 884 cases in early January, involving 4,008 people, to 2,612 in September, involving 11,983 people.[50] Drawing on the support of labour activists of different hues, the communists formed an outdoor relief workers' committee with the intention of bringing relief rates into line with Britain and winning reform of the Board of Guardians' administration of relief payments. On 11 September, Murray travelled to Belfast to deliver a typically long-winded speech to a crowd of around 800 at Custom House steps. After describing the paltry donations offered by the crowd as 'scandalous', for the lack of financial commitment to the party was a particular vexation of his, he proceeded in attacking the widespread introduction of the means test. He praised the efforts of the Belfast communists, who had launched what he termed 'united front committees' in solidarity with the relief workers, and predicted gains for the Belfast working class before concluding with a verse from Connolly's 'The Watchword of Labour'.[51]

On 3 October, the outdoor relief workers' committee called a strike and mass demonstration, which escalated into an unprecedented campaign for improved wages and working conditions. Headed by the Duke of York Accordion Band and carrying the banner 'Abolish all task work', a crowd numbering 30,000 marched from the Labour Exchange on Frederick Street to Custom House Square, where Murray shared the main platform with Betty Sinclair and Jack Beattie. He assured those involved that they would receive the full support of the Dublin RWG; Tommy Geehan, a popular trade unionist and secretary of the outdoor relief committee, mooted the reorganisation of the ILDL to protect the dependents of those imprisoned.[52] For its part, the Belfast RWG had some success in connecting the relief workers' grievances to the plight of the city's unemployed, who received no benefits from the Labour Exchange. The outdoor relief committee also drew inspiration and encouragement from ongoing struggles of a similar nature in Birkenhead and Liverpool. The Belfast protests reached a climax on 11 October, when the striking workers defied the ban imposed on another demonstration. This led to intense rioting in working-class areas of the city, with Catholics and Protestants uniting in clashes with heavily armed RUC officers.[53] With two workers dead, fifteen wounded by gunshot and nineteen others injured, RWG delegates to Belfast Trades Council called for an extension of the fight to the factories and for a widespread cessation of work. Ultimately, the resolution fell due to NILP opposition and because the 1927 Trade Disputes and Trade Unions Act deemed general strikes illegal and subject to swift punishment.[54]

The outdoor relief riots are etched into the collective consciousness of the northern labour movement.[55] Based in Dublin, Murray played a less prominent role than did Belfast activists such as Geehan, Sinclair and Tommy Watters. Generally, though, the communists were justified in claiming the concessions granted by the government and Board of Guardians as the fruit of their efforts. The events of October 1932 ignited a renewed wave of agitation by the INUM, which formed new groups in Belfast, Carrick on Suir, Clonmel, Dublin, Longford and Waterford. Moreover, the brief transcendence of religious antagonisms in the north-east coincided with a rapprochement between Belfast and Dublin communism and an upturn in support for the RWG. From about 200 in June, RWG membership increased to 339 in November. Over the same period, weekly circulation figures for the (Irish) Workers' Voice doubled to 3,000.[56] An aura of 'class against class' superiority pervaded the attitudes of individual RWG representatives during and in the immediate aftermath of the strikes.[57] Murray was critical of the NILP and trade union leadership for preventing an escalation in strike activity, but praised the efforts of Jack Beattie in the same breath. While these instances of left sectarianism were self-defeating in the long run, they do not detract from Murray's view of the strike as a welcome coalescence of labour forces in the North. He described the campaign as a 'model' for the working class in the six counties and informed Moscow that the Irish party had taken a step forward: 'All we can say at the moment is that we have got a place in the mass movement.'[58]

Unlike Betty Sinclair and Tommy Geehan, Murray had an existing relationship with the IRA that extended back to the War of Independence. During the strikes, he made contact with the Belfast IRA in an effort to secure protection for outdoor relief committee meetings – 'not to indulge in warfare, but to be there', in Sinclair's words.[59] That the local IRA leadership rejected these overtures and dismissed the prospect of successful agitation on the eve of the strike was, according to O'Donnell, a major dereliction of duty. Davy Matthews, Jack Brady, Liam Mulholland and a young man named Joe Cahill were among those who participated in the strikes and the subsequent riots on an individual basis. Cumann na mBan held a flag protest in support of the workers and encouraged its members to join trade unions.[60] As an organisation, the IRA missed a golden opportunity to involve itself in cross-community agitation and end its separation from the Protestant working class. Brian Hanley notes that over the following year the republican leadership would reflect upon this inaction with regret, which in turn encouraged participation in various industrial disputes over the course of the 1930s.[61] Despite the IRA's poor showing on this occasion, Murray's faith in left republicanism remained intact. At a CPGB congress in November, he reaffirmed the RWG's commitment to an anti-imperialist programme and to the achievement of full independence en route to socialism:

> The Communist Party must be the party of national independence ... This national issue is not something in the road of the CP keeping back the struggle, but is the most powerful weapon in the hands of the working class in Ireland.[62]

Murray continued to work within the progressive republican milieu for support, leaving the Belfast group to pursue tactics that suited local conditions. The RWG remained united in structural and ideological terms. However, anti-imperialism did stretch the capacity of the party to mobilise its two strands in unison, particularly as the IRA remained aloof from the labour movement in the North.

The second Communist Party of Ireland

Increased circulation of the *Irish Workers' Voice* coincided with the commencement of weekly education sessions at the Workers' College. A syllabus in the possession of Garda Special Branch outlines an intensive education programme involving lectures on feudalism, Marxist political economy, theories of money, rent, surplus value and *Imperialism: The Highest Stage of Capitalism*.[63] RWG intellectuals such as Murray, Joss and Brian O'Neill also spoke on the more popular subjects of the French Revolution, Young Ireland, the Fenians and Connolly's political thought, while O'Donnell dealt with the implications of the Anglo-Irish Treaty. He was the cause of a full-blown row at one of Joss' lectures in late 1932, when he held aloft a copy of the Catholic *Standard* and accused one J. McMullen of passing confidential documents to the paper. Seán McCool, a committed, acutely political

IRA man from Donegal, now on the Workers' College governing committee, warned that the damaging work of 'undesirables' would not be tolerated. This says something of the clandestine environment in which the left operated and the levels of suspicion that prevailed across that political milieu. Even if McMullen was innocent, the threat of infiltration by Catholic organs and Garda informants always loomed large.[64]

Fitzgerald, O'Donnell and McCool were not the only left-wing IRA members associated with the Workers' College. In April 1933, Frank Ryan delivered a lecture entitled 'The Motives of Irish Revolutions from the year 1798 to 1932'. Quite controversially, he argued that Connolly was not a communist but a socialist in a much looser sense. Ryan also informed his RWG comrades that he would not join a communist party or countenance any direct association with the international communist movement. Instead, he encouraged continued cooperation between the IRA and RWG, promoting the formation of a National Workers' Revolutionary Party as a compromise between left republicanism and communism. Murray and O'Donnell greeted Ryan's proposal warmly during the ensuing discussion, despite their knowledge that plans for the launch of a communist party were already well underway.[65] It is likely that they wished to ensure that Ryan stayed on board in the event that the new party took on an anti-imperialist form at the outset.

In January 1933, the RWG's Sphinx Publications distributed *The Irish Case for Communism*, Murray's first attempt at a draft programme for the CPI. Although one historian of inter-war socialist republicanism has reduced the pamphlet to 'misguidedness and crudity' in one fell swoop,[66] Murray, in fact, based his analysis of Irish capitalism and global economic recession on meticulous primary research. If one cross-references *The Irish Case for Communism* with more recent studies of Irish political economy, it emerges that Murray was quite accurate on a number of questions: the Cosgrave administration's eradication of social services and attack on living standards; the Irish banking system and its subservience to British finance capital; the debilitating effects of the parity link between the Free State currency and the pound; and the class nature of the Treaty split.[67] In terms of solutions, the pamphlet is excessively ambitious. It aspires to the creation of a 'Workers' and Farmers' Republic', entailing the nationalisation of key industries; confiscation of 'the property of all traitors, and imperialist British interests'; the establishment of workers' and farmers' committees to replace the parliamentary system; free and nondenominational education; and the guarantee of religious liberty across the island.[68] Beyond this immediately unattainable programme, there is no indication of how the communists were to unite industrial and rural workers and instil them with the necessary class-consciousness to advance towards the proposed republic. If the draft manifesto was strong in diagnosis, it was also light in prescription.

In conjunction with this abstract thinking, Murray crossed swords with the British party over the Irish group's working relationship with republicans and the RWG's 1933 election manifesto. Although the Anglo-American secretariat had identified an opportunity to recruit from the IRA 'the best revolutionary elements among the workers and farmers', this did not extend to leaders such as O'Donnell, whose commitment to anti-capitalism was apparently 'wavering'.[69] The upper limit of Comintern flexibility on tactics was therefore the united front from below, which the CPGB feared Murray had bypassed in favour of cooperation with O'Donnell and support for republican election candidates.[70] And to all intents and purposes, he had. To rectify this, the British party called Murray to its colonial committee and instructed him to distinguish the RWG from the IRA by removing from its literature all flattering references to Fianna Fáil.[71]

This interference foreshadowed an embittered dispute between Murray and the CPGB on the issue of forming a new Irish political party with 'communist' in its name. In discussion with RWG grassroots, Murray attempted to assuage concerns about the potential ramifications of forming a Moscow-led party in Ireland. Privately, he opposed the launch of a communist party without adequate preparation and informed the CPGB that the strength of religious opposition to communism in Ireland was such that it would be imprudent to attack the Catholic Church. Given that this was at the height of the 'red scare', it is easy to see why Murray became 'indignant' at being instructed by the CPGB executive committee not 'to run away from the enemy'. Consequently, he wrote to William Gallacher seeking arbitration. Before Gallacher could reply, Harry Pollitt intervened on behalf of the Anglo-American secretariat and directed Murray to proceed with the formation of a communist party along the lines laid down by the Comintern. In truly duplicitous fashion, he also assured Murray of the international communist hierarchy's faith in him as head of the Irish communist movement, while in fact the CPGB leadership had debated removing him for insubordination.[72] This adds weight to the view that the Comintern delegated to the British party responsibility for reining in the Irish party where there was a danger of the latter becoming too autonomous.

Whereas Murray had articulated what Gramsci would later describe as the 'war of position', the slow-burning cultural and ideological battle to undermine the state and win influence,[73] the CPGB clearly underestimated the challenges facing the Irish movement. In the year that Ireland played host to the Eucharistic Congress, Murray's legitimate fears about entering into a collision course with the Catholic hierarchy were quickly realised. One example of hostilities fomented by the clergy is the vilification of Jim Gralton, a leading RWG figure in Leitrim and subject of Ken Loach's eponymous film *Jimmy's Hall* (2014). Murray corresponded with Gralton and was instrumental in the formation of defence committees in Dublin, Leitrim and elsewhere, but ultimately could not compete with the government's determination to deport his comrade to the US.[74] At the same time, the National Guard – formerly the ACA, soon to be known colloquially as the Blueshirts – began to escalate its campaign against Fianna Fáil's redistributive land reforms while taking aim at the communist movement and the IRA.[75] De Valera's crackdown on the Blueshirts invoked the language of the Public Safety Act, which also served to legitimise attacks on the RWG and affiliated individuals. Organisations such as St. Patrick's Anti-Communist League recruited large numbers of impressionable and anti-social youths into its ranks and, as anti-communism became more organised, attacks on meetings became more frequent and malicious. At one public meeting on Cathal Brugha Street, Murray survived an attempted stabbing, with the blade just piercing his precious agitator's overcoat. As Manus O'Riordan remarks, this was 'a relatively mild foretaste of what was yet to come'.[76]

In preparation for the launch of a new party, the RWG opened a head office at Connolly House, 64 Great Strand Street, on 11 March. Two weeks later, on 27 March, a mob of around six thousand, inflamed by a pastoral letter read during the Lenten mission at the Dublin Pro-Cathedral, marched to Connolly House and laid siege to it for three days and nights. Leading RWG figures such as Murray, Joe Troy, Seán Nolan, Jim Prendergast and Donie O'Neill were among the fourteen that 'mounted a stern defence' of the building by throwing slates, bricks and a range of other objects from a top-floor window. On the last day of the siege, around midnight, the crowd stormed the building and set it alight. When the house filled with smoke, Murray gave the order to retire and escape across the glass rooftops. Despite injuring his ankle, Murray managed to evade his attackers and seek refuge nearby. On the orders of George Gilmore, a number of sympathetic IRA men – Charlie Gilmore, Jack Nalty, Donie O'Reilly and Bill

Gannon, brother of Murray's partner, Margaret – came to the RWG's aid. Charlie Gilmore fired shots to hold off the advancing crowd and O'Reilly received a beating from the police for his efforts. Gardaí arrested Gilmore as he attempted to flee, though he was later acquitted of all charges.[77]

The social historian, Donal Fallon, has challenged retrospective claims that the much maligned and misunderstood Animal Gang was responsible for the siege of Connolly House.[78] Along with George McLay and Jack Carney, Murray had recruited a number of the newsboys into a section of the WUI. The *Workers' Voice* supported a boycott of the pro-government *Irish Press,* during which vans carrying the paper to shops were attacked, and congratulated the newsboys for 'living up to their great tradition they held when they beat the D.M.P. to a frazzle' in 1913.[79] This makes it unlikely that they were involved in the Connolly House attack or in harassing Murray more generally. The main antagonists were Catholic action groups and the violent elements that latched onto their protests. Murray's attempt to speak at a later public meeting was met with boos and shouts of 'Go back to Russia!' Communist literature and newspapers were torn up, before a band of young men rushed the platform. While fighting broke out, Gardaí were forced to form a cordon around Murray and then escort him, followed by the crowd, to Pearse Street station and to safety.[80] On another occasion, he had to run from attackers from Upper Abbey Street to O'Connell Street, where he escaped by getting on a bus.[81] Murray would continue to endure harassment throughout the year and into 1934. This and the visit of several strangers to his lodgings prompted him to begin carrying a gun and to keep on the move.[82]

Murray continued to test left republican waters prior to the launch of the CPI in June. This involved the formation of a committee whose purpose was to bring together kindred spirits in the discussion and dissemination of Connolly's works. Prominent among those involved were Murray, Larkin junior, the ubiquitous O'Donnell, the Gilmore brothers, Jack Carney and the radical journalist Rosamond Jacob. The committee's main aim was to give the communist movement a 'national flavour' by presenting its programme in the language of Connollyism.[83] However, this proved a pyrrhic victory for Murray in the context of an IRA shift away from communism. The leadership's refusal to sanction the protection of Connolly House in March reflected the increasing hostility of junior officers to left-wing politics and to the RWG in particular. So too did the participation of IRA members in the hounding of Jim Gralton. The new atmosphere of virulent anti-communism in the Free State forced these sentiments to the surface, exacerbating divisions within the organisation and rendering tactical alliances with the RWG a much less attractive proposition for the leadership.

The tensions between left-wing politicos and traditionalist elements were evident at the Army convention that year, which took place one week before the Connolly House attack. A number of units put forward motions against the adoption of social policy and others called for the organisation to disassociate itself from communism, a motion that was marginally defeated by twenty-nine votes to twenty-six. The Dublin Brigade was split down the middle, with four battalions voting for and four voting against. Bill Gannon argued that politics were essential to the movement's survival and that it would be 'very undemocratic to deprive a man of his political education'. He was forthright in proclaiming to be a communist and therefore opposed to the anti-communist motion. O'Donnell described it as 'shameful' and urged delegates not to 'throw men like Seán Murray to the wolves'.[84] The straw that broke the camel's back for a number of left republicans was the introduction of a rule that prohibited membership of political organisations. At least two RWG members made it clear that they would instead resign from the IRA. Frank Ryan relinquished his position as editor of *An Phoblacht* in protest and refused to put his name forward for the executive. Hanna Sheehy Skeffington resigned as deputy editor, while Peadar O'Donnell also withdrew from the executive.[85] O'Donnell's parting shot implied that, by preventing members from participating in left-wing politics, the leadership had abandoned the IRA's raison d'être:

> My first allegiance has always been to the Irish Working Class movement. The I.R.A. was the most intense form of this. This is why I joined the I.R.A. It is men outside the I.R.A. like Seán Murray who was at one time an Officer in the I.R.A. who are collecting this unrest ... If you carry this resolution through in the spirit in which it is offered it is the end of the I.R.A. as a revolutionary body. You will find that men who were heart and soul in this organisation will be elsewhere.[86]

One historian of the IRA has since arrived at a similar conclusion: 'The aftermath of the 1933 convention marked the IRA's abandonment of openly socialist policies. Those within the IRA with an *ideological* commitment to these policies would either re-evaluate them or leave the organisation.'[87]

On 4-5 June 1933, in entirely inauspicious circumstances, the RWG convened under the auspices of the Dublin Total Abstinence Society to launch a new party, the Communist Party of Ireland. In the preceding weeks and months, the *Standard* had kept a watchful eye on the RWG's preparations and had now procured a number of internal documents relating to the CPI's inaugural congress, which it described as an 'impudent challenge to the Irish people'.[88] Larkin junior chaired the gathering of forty-five delegates, with Charlotte Despard, Nora Connolly and Bob McIlhone, Murray's Lenin School classmate, in attendance as observers. Members of the first central committee included Nixie Boran, Tommy Geehan, Loftus Johnston, Betty Sinclair and Seán Nolan. Murray used his first speech as general secretary to outline the CPI manifesto, *Ireland's Path to Freedom,* and to describe the party as 'the United Irishmen of the 20th Century'. He drew on Connolly's *Socialism Made Easy* (1909) and at the same time paraphrased Engels and Lenin to underline Ireland's role in hastening the demise of the British Empire: 'The Communists who talk about Internationalism are [sic] so because they are the greatest exponents of the National Independence struggles.' The first major task of the CPI, then, was to help 'change the class leadership of the national struggle', or the bourgeois revolution in Marxist terms. To compensate for this, he conceded that support for the CPI in Belfast would depend in part on successful engagement with 'the mass economic struggles'. But he was unmoved by Larkin's contention that *Ireland's Path to Freedom* paid disproportionate attention to the national question 'to the exclusion of the class issue'. Crucially, the party membership adopted Murray's manifesto without amendment, confirming the popularity of an approach to communism that was Connollyist and anti-imperialist whilst honouring the Marxist-Leninist conception of the revolution.[89]

Scholars of the period have insisted on equating *Ireland's Path to Freedom* with *The Irish Case for Communism*, despite significant changes and the possibility that the former was, according to one note in the CPI's archives, 'drafted by Moscow'.[90] One of the most radical amendments was the substitution of references to Cosgrave with sharp criticisms of de Valera, now likened to Daniel O'Connell and Arthur Griffith and referred to as the 'custodian of the interests of Irish capitalism'.[91] This was due in no small part to Murray's dressing down in London. Importantly, it also reflected a growing perception on the republican left that, despite its considerable social reforms, Fianna Fáil had failed to demonstrate a commitment to full political and economic independence.[92] Where Murray diverged slightly from O'Donnell was in his acutely dismissive view of the Irish peasantry, including the agricultural labourers whom O'Donnell remained keen to mobilise. *Ireland's Path to Freedom* argued that rural workers would 'become a powerful and decisive force only under the leadership of another revolutionary class which is in such conditions that it can organise its forces' i.e. the industrial working class.[93] Without a spontaneous epoch-defining event to stir these potential support bases into action, Murray's attitude did nothing to convince the Irish rural majority of his project's viability.

Moscow and London's imprint on *Ireland's Path to Freedom* is evident from its references to the 'triumphant' USSR and the removal of a clause guaranteeing religious freedom. Rayner Lysaght argues quite unfairly that the document was significant only in its 'blunting of potential', but is right to point out that 'there was no programme whether Transitional, Maximum or Minimum'.[94] In lieu of a concrete programme, the modest and ambiguous pledge to work for 'the destruction of national and social oppression' was a more accurate reflection of possibilities in the Free State at the time. Another pragmatic amendment was the removal of a passage that lent conditional support to the Nationalist Party. Murray now claimed that Joe Devlin and Cahir Healy were as guilty as the Unionist Party of making 'demagogic appeals to religious prejudice' in order to win working class support.[95] This represented a significant admission that the CPI would have to confront and overcome sectarian divisions if it wished to make progress in Belfast. Indeed a report to the ECCI in July confirmed that the party intended to concentrate its efforts on winning over 'the non-nationalist section'.[96] However, this jarred against Murray's revised analysis of the outdoor relief strikes as one stage in the 'conflict with British imperialism' and his belief that 'the national liberation of Ireland is an inevitable task which it [the CPI] will carry out on the way to Socialism'.[97] In *Ireland's Path to Freedom* he balanced rather than synthesised Soviet Marxism and 'stageist' revolutionary thinking with anti-imperialist Connollyism.

The CPI had a strong representation at the annual Wolfe Tone commemoration at Bodenstown on 18 June. However, in the fallout from the IRA Army convention, tensions flared and the IRA clashed with the CPI delegation, seizing communist literature. Moss Twomey also used the occasion to continue his revisionist campaign of refuting all links, past or present, between republicanism and communism. He emphasised the supposed 'atheism and irreligion' of the latter and, despite retaining a commitment to challenging 'existing social and economic conditions', ruled out future alliances with the communist movement. In response, the CPI released an oddly sympathetic statement acknowledging that the IRA leadership had 'felt called upon to declare where they officially stand' due to the 'pressure of the reaction'. But whatever his reasons, the statement continued, Twomey had signalled an abandonment of his organisation's working-class membership in favour 'joining the chorus' of anti-communism.[98] In an appeal to IRA leftists who had left or were considering their future in the organisation, Murray harked back to the defunct Saor Éire, which at least 'had something to say about capitalists, their wealth, private property and so on', and assured republicans that it was 'not inconsistent for a Catholic to be a communist'.[99] At this stage, the IRA leadership was 'generally more radical than their junior officers and certainly more so than their rank and file'.[100] Murray understood this. If O'Donnell, Ryan, Gilmore and other prominent socialist republicans were highly unlikely to join the CPI, the best he could hope for was tactical support on questions of common concern.

A subsequent report to Moscow gave the impression that the CPI in Dublin had made adequate progress.[101] However, two factors suggest that the party's secretariat was merely putting on a brave front. Firstly, the performance of the two CPI candidates in June's municipal elections – Murray received an embarrassing seventy-five votes and Larkin junior lost his seat – paints a clearer picture of the Sisyphean task facing the party.[102] Secondly, although Murray understood the risks of going down the route of illegality, the party decided that meetings would be organised through factory and street cells until further notice.[103] The CPI leadership did not entirely accept its role as a clandestine organisation. For example, despite their fears of being attacked, comrades were instructed to attend a Connolly commemoration on 4 June at the Mansion House, where Murray spoke alongside Nora and Roddy Connolly, Hanna Sheehy Skeffington and Rosamond Jacob. Prior to the event, O'Donnell and Gilmore organised a march of fifty IRA men to act as stewards. IRA volunteers were also on hand to 'squash' disruption at the launch of the CPI's 1933 municipal election campaign.[104] In spite of this, with the Connolly House attack fresh in their minds, the CPI cadres recognised that circumstances had taken a turn against the party and that Leninist methods offered some means of organising under the radar of its most dangerous opponents.

In the year following the outdoor relief strikes, relations within the labour movement had deteriorated considerably. The *Irish Workers' Voice* reported as early as January 1933 that the gains of the outdoor relief workers were 'being systematically smashed' in the absence of labour unity.[105] The RWG played only a marginal role in an abortive NUR strike in January, with the British railway vigilance representative, William Cowe, delivering a sobering assessment of work levels and the calibre of leadership in Belfast.[106] On 6 October, a group of party members connected to the INUM left Dublin with the intention of marching to Belfast and securing a propaganda coup for the movement. The occasion was the first anniversary of the outdoor relief strikes. Most of the group were prevented from entering the six counties by the RUC, while twenty others succeeded in making it across the border before being rounded up in Newry and escorted back to the South. Two members, Paul Murphy and Christopher Norton, passed the same RUC officers on bicycles and reached Belfast, where they remained for almost two weeks.[107] The questionable actions of the police were covered under Special Powers legislation. And if the Stormont government was not already acting in a repressive manner, the shooting of an RUC man by the IRA gave the authorities the perfect excuse to ban all demonstrations.[108]

Part of the government's response was to deport prominent individuals such as Harry Pollitt and Tom Mann as soon as they set foot on Irish soil. According to Loftus Johnston, the detective tasked with preventing Murray from entering the North 'was seen on Saturday dashing from bus to bus in Lisburn', but failed to track his target.[109] Murray made it onto the platform at the ILP Hall in Belfast on 15 October and began to address the banned outdoor relief strike meeting. He was hauled from the platform by two detectives brandishing revolvers, taken to the border and immediately served with an exclusion order that prohibited him from entering the territory of Northern Ireland with the exception of Clogher, a rural village in County Tyrone. In violation of this order, he returned to Belfast to see out his commitments for the week, including another unemployed workers' demonstration on 22 October. Arrested the next day at comrade James Kater's house, he received a sentence of one month's hard labour and returned to Crumlin Road Gaol, more than ten years after his previous visit; Kater would later receive the more severe punishment of five months' hard labour for harbouring the CPI general secretary.[110]

During his stay at His Majesty's pleasure, Murray received a number of letters and postcards. One, from Kater, pledges to 'carry on the good work' in his absence, to send books and to request that his sister Kate get in contact.[111] A postcard from his sister followed:

I was most surprised to hear of your new address. I hope you enjoy Halloween in your new surroundings. We are all OK here. Mother doesn't know you are there yet but father does. He doesn't worry. Quite a lot of fuss around here. The young lad is talking now, he is very amusing. I hope this card finds you in good health.[112]

With the support of the usual left republican suspects, the CPI launched a campaign for the immediate release of its leader.[113] After serving his full sentence, Murray returned to Dublin on 6 December and was greeted by 300 people at the Foresters' Hall, Parnell Square. There was a sizeable IRA contingent present, including Frank Ryan and George Gilmore. Although both were listed to address the meeting, strict orders from the IRA leadership prevented them from doing so.[114] A few days later, on 11 December, the CPI held a dance at the Teachers' Club to celebrate Murray's release. The function was attended by another 300 people, including all prominent members of the CPI, plus Ryan, Gilmore and Mick Fitzpatrick. A collection in aid of 'political and class war prisoners' was held at the event, raising the modest sum of £3.[115]

Among the leading Belfast members to experience the full effects of the Ministry of Home Affairs clampdown on 'subversives' were Arthur Griffin and Val Morahan, who were imprisoned in quick succession in the same year. In response to this outright denial of political expression, the CPI began campaigning not only for the release of its members but for all political prisoners, republicans included, and for the full repeal of both the Special Powers Act and Public Safety Act.[116] One of the first coherent political declarations on civil and political liberties in Northern Ireland, the CPI's campaign anticipated a National Council for Civil Liberties (NCCL) investigation into the extension and application of Special Powers legislation. When the NCCL reported in 1936, it used Murray's imprisonment and exclusion as a case study demonstration of the state's arbitrary use of Special Powers. The NCCL described the legislation as 'contrary to the fundamental principles of democratic government, in that it imperils the rights and freedoms of law-abiding citizens',[117] and confirmed that labour activists were being targeted by the Ministry of Home Affairs and RUC for harassment:

It is striking that the Northern Irish Government has freely employed Special Powers in dealing with incidents arising from the natural revulsion of the working-class against their depressed conditions. Not only have important incidents such as the October 1932 strike seen the use of Special Powers in their full force and measure, but there is abundant evidence of the daily use of such powers against individuals active in the working-class movement, particularly on its left wing. Domiciliary visits, searches, interrogations, detentions and Exclusion Orders appear, in this way, to have been freely employed.[118]

The report concluded:

It is sad that in the guise of temporary and emergency legislation there should have been created under the shadow of the British Constitution a permanent machine of dictatorship – a standing temptation to whatever intolerant or bigoted section may attain power to abuse its authority at the expense of the people it rules.[119]

Whereas sections of Catholic community suffered discrimination in housing and employment at the hands of a sectarian administration, the labour movement was in conflict with the bourgeois state – the landed gentry, industrialists and merchant class of the Unionist Party. The CPI's analysis of and practical response to the use of repressive legislation demonstrated an early understanding of the significance of civil and political liberties being denied in Northern Ireland, far beyond what the NILP was prepared to countenance. These efforts deserve recognition in any examination of the inter-generational struggle for civil rights.

The second CPI could not have conceived of a more difficult teething period, so to have survived the difficulties of 1933 was a major achievement, even if the party existed in a debilitated state. End of year membership figures fell short of the lofty expectations of 1932, which had predicted an active membership of between five and six hundred.[120] Printer boycotts ensured that only nine issues of the *Irish Workers' Voice* were published between April and mid-October, and the paper struggled to attract contributors from outside the CPI milieu. Naturally, sympathisers within the IRA were reluctant to contribute for fear of harassment or expulsion from the organisation.[121] Murray claimed that weekly circulation of the paper had fallen dramatically from a high of 2,000 to just twenty-one.[122] Furthermore, a number of pamphlets drafted by party intellectuals, including a biography of James Connolly by Brian O'Neill and a treatise on 'The Ulster Question' by Murray, stood little chance of reaching publication.[123] These problems were compounded by the revelation that one party member, Frank Breen, had been working as an informant for the Garda, Eoin O'Duffy, the *Daily Express* and the *Standard* newspaper. During an internal inquiry, Breen admitted that he had received payment for gathering information on the inner workings of the CPI, but insisted that he had fabricated many of the stories relayed to his employers. However, Breen's exposure as an informant explains how the *Standard* came into possession of several confidential CPI documents and why the paper was able to report on the party's activities with great accuracy in the early part of 1933. For this unforgivable transgression, he was expelled from the CPI and ordered 'to leave Ireland within ten hours'.[124]

Emmet O'Connor writes that by 1934 the CPI was 'teetering on the brink of extinction outside Dublin and Belfast', particularly in areas where the IRA had traditionally provided fertile ground for recruitment. Close links with republicans were maintained in the party's two main urban centres of activity. For instance, in the lead up to the November 1933 Stormont elections, the party endorsed the IRA candidate over Joe Devlin. The *Irish Workers' Voice* praised the formation of a 'united front' in Tralee, where trade unionists and Fianna Fáil activists protested against the arrest of twelve republicans for attacking a Blueshirt demonstration.[125] Despite these strained efforts to avoid painting itself into an ideological corner, the CPI remained mired in policy confusion and organisational malaise. A few days after the funeral of David Fitzgerald, who passed away tragically early after battling a debilitating illness, all Dublin groups assembled at Connolly House to discuss the party's future in the city. A heated debate ensued and vented frustrations led quickly to insults. Donie O'Reilly, Brian O'Neill, Larkin and Murray, all Lenin School graduates, came under the most sustained criticism for neglecting their duties and for their routine failure to attend meetings. All with the exception of O'Reilly conceded that they had been inactive and Larkin and Murray were charged with neglecting their duties and routinely failing to attend meetings. Before long, O'Reilly would eventually be excluded from all decision making bodies, including the central committee, for his attitude towards party work and rejection of self-criticism. The others agreed to devote more time to the practical aspects of organisation, including measures to improve collective leadership and an escalation of industrial and IRA 'cell' activity.[126]

The criticisms forthcoming from the CPGB were no less severe. Bob McIlhone bemoaned the 'lack of cadres, of leading local, district and national comrades who have some knowledge of Leninist strategy and tactics, who are able to give political direction to the party work'.[127] During a meeting with the Irish secretariat, Harry Pollitt charged Murray with neglect of duty and with failing to develop organised programmes of propaganda. Murray explained in response that local conditions were not conducive to this type of work. The hostility of IRA officers and the Dublin population to communism made it difficult to hold public meetings and distribute literature, while the party's activities within the republican movement had suffered a blow with the expulsion of its members from the IRA. For these pleas, he gained the concession of a reconstituted ILDL to defend 'all class war and political prisoners', which provided the party with a platform for winning the support of IRA members and 'all persons interested in the defence of the IRA prisoners'.[128]

In accordance with Third Period doctrines, Moscow insisted, in a progress report delivered towards the end of 1933, that the Irish party row back from its left republican position and maintain its independent identity:

> Since the party Congress very little has been done to popularise the manifesto adopted by the Congress. Besides some speeches delivered at the Congress (in which the erroneous conception is put forward that the CPI is a '20th century Society of the United Irishmen') the Workers' Voice has printed only one article on the manifesto ... and in its contents appears more as a Left republican journal rather than the organ of the CPI.

The report also reprimanded the CPI for displaying united front tendencies and using the language of the united front in its publications.[129] On more than one occasion, the *Irish Workers' Voice* had called for alliances with republican 'anti-imperialists' in opposition to the Blueshirts and the Public Safety Act, and with the NILP in opposition to the Special Powers Act. Continued efforts to secure the release of all political prisoners in both jurisdictions enabled the party to present these parallel campaigns as a coherent whole.[130] Editorials running into 1934 continued along this vein, expressing a clear preference for united front action. There was indeed a vast gulf between Comintern policy, which ruled out cooperation with social democrats and other reformists, and CPI practice.

It would be a mistake to think that Murray was on the verge of breaking with the Comintern's analysis or painting himself as some sort of oppositionist. He always kept within touching distance of Comintern directives, and criticism from London and Moscow ensured that he did not stray too far from the official position on fascism. At an important meeting of the CPI central committee in March 1934, Murray praised the bravery of those who had taken to the streets in Austria, France and Spain, including in Paris where socialists and communists had combined to prevent a fascist uprising. At the same time, he asserted that social democracy was to blame for the rise of fascism in those countries, in Germany and across Europe. He argued that the crisis of capitalism was deepening and spoke of the growing militancy of the working class. The conditions for revolution were favourable, he contended, but social democracy continued to act as 'the main social prop of the bourgeoisie; this is the absolutely correct estimation of the role of the Irish Labour Party and the Trade Union leadership'. Only Loftus Johnston refused to share in this enthusiasm about the likelihood of the economic crisis being transformed into a revolutionary crisis. Consequently, the central committee passed a resolution endorsing the decisions of the ECCI at its thirteenth plenum, which associated the party with the deeply flawed and naïve characterisation of fascism as capitalism in its death throes.[131]

Towards the end of January, with the descent from illegality into what Murray termed 'passivity' nearing, he and a number of other CPI delegates attended the relaunch of the ILDL. A glance at the list of personalities involved leaves one in no doubt that it was conceived as a united front initiative. Mae Murray took up a position on the preparatory committee in her capacity as a Sinn Féin representative; Roddy Connolly, now a member of the Labour Party, assumed the role of chairman; and Hanna Sheehy Skeffington committed to the new anti-fascist movement as a disaffected representative of the Irish republican left.[132] An *Irish Workers' Voice* editorial asked rhetorically:

> Is there any way of defeating the Fascists and opening the path to Independence, except by the joint action of the entire working masses, regardless of present political differences? Is there any other path other than that put forward by the Communist Party, the organisation of the anti-Fascist United Front? There isn't.[133]

External pressure and events on the ground ensured that the CPI retained a rhetorical commitment to the left sectarian policies of the Third Period. When the Labour-dominated executive committee of Dublin Trades Council refused to endorse a call by delegates to make 1 May a day of anti-fascist action involving a general strike and mass demonstrations across the city, the communist paper held nothing back in denouncing the 'treachery' of P.T. Daly and other 'miscalled leaders' of the labour movement. In the event, these May Day demonstrations saw many of the usual suspects grace the platform and the march itself lead to scuffles with police after a section the crowd surged towards the Blueshirts' offices near Parnell Square.[134] The CPI's position was therefore conflicted and complex, but implicitly favourable to united front tactics in practice.

The Republican Congress

Murray travelled to Moscow at the beginning of April 1934 and, like Connolly and George Gilmore before him, proceeded to the US to embark on a prearranged speaking tour. Bob Stewart returned to Dublin in a supervisory capacity, while Brian O'Neill temporarily assumed the role of the CPI's main theoretician. Murray's first stop was Cleveland, Ohio, where he addressed the eighth national congress of the Communist Party of the USA (CPUSA) and was reacquainted with Harry Haywood, his comrade from the Lenin School.[135] He then visited Irish Workers' Clubs in New York and a number of big cities in the east and mid-west, increasing the number of branches from two to sixteen and securing financial support for the CPI. The Workers' Clubs, led by Jim Gralton, also published Murray's latest pamphlet, *Ireland's Fight for Freedom and the Irish in the USA*, which lionised the role of the Irish diaspora in the national struggle and expressed great disappointment with the Ireland that emerged out of the revolutionary period.[136]

During Murray's brief absence, the republican movement was hit by an historic development within its ranks. When on 17-18 March an IRA Army convention rejected proposals for an anti-imperialist republican congress, the preeminent representatives of left republicanism – Peadar O'Donnell, Frank Ryan and George Gilmore – made a prompt exit from the IRA. Michael Price, a more complex figure with inclinations towards Catholic social teaching, left at an earlier stage when the convention defeated his specific resolution for a workers' republic. Other socialist republicans, for example Seán McCool, retained a commitment to Army discipline and so chose to remain with the organisation. On 7-8 April, over 200 IRA officers, prominent socialists and trade unionists convened at Athlone and issued a radical manifesto that urged all progressives to rally around Connolly's slogan 'We cannot conceive of a free Ireland with a subject working class; we cannot conceive of a subject Ireland with a free working class'. It aimed to capitalise on disillusionment among the industrial working class, rural workers, small farmers, shop workers and domestic servants, and replace Fianna Fáil at the head of the national movement whilst advancing a socialistic programme.[137]

In lieu of direction from the Comintern or from Murray, the CPI welcomed the Republican Congress as a 'united front movement' but warned against any attempt to form a new political party of the working class.[138] Brian O'Neill, for one, was not as comfortable as Murray would have been with advocating a deliberate deviation from the Comintern line. Events in France during February-July, which led to a united front agreement between the communist and socialist parties and helped to accelerate the gradual transition out of the Third Period,[139] created enough space for the CPI to offer the left republicans its qualified support. Throughout the summer months, as Congress activity gathered pace, the *Irish Workers' Voice* added calls for a greater focus on fascism, the operation of coercive legislation across the island, INUM activities and the working conditions of the agricultural labourer.[140] Within the framework of the united front, the CPI extended comradeship to Labour Party and trade union branches as well as Fianna Fáil cumainn. The respective leaderships of these organisations and the NILP would be excluded from any proposed alliance. In response, the organising committee of the Republican Congress noted that the communists had suggested work 'that the Bureau has been carrying through' and that the CPI letter 'does not seem to have raised anything new'.[141]

On the surface, then, there was little separating the two groups. However, the circumstances surrounding the violent clashes at Bodenstown that year suggest that the CPI's attitude towards the Republican Congress and the IRA remained ambiguous. After disregarding a ban on unauthorised banners, the Congress contingent, including Protestant socialists from Ballymacarrett and the Shankill Road areas of Belfast, were attacked on the orders of the IRA leadership and their banners confiscated. Whether the attacks were sectarian is a matter of debate. Significantly, the CPI obeyed the IRA order and was not drawn into the fracas, indicating that the party was not fully committed to the Republican Congress ideal.[142] Official Comintern policy of the united front from below prevented the communists from displaying open enthusiasm for a much broader socialist republican united front. Indeed, Moscow insisted that any tactical alliance would be 'conditional on the party playing the leading role'.[143] The architects of the

Congress would therefore have to wait for Murray's return before they could be certain of CPI support for their initiative.

With Murray back at the helm, the CPI belatedly lent its support to the anti-imperialist Congress and set about mobilising its members towards that end. The inaugural meeting of the Congress took place at Rathmines Town Hall on 29-30 September. It was attended by 186 delegates and around 250 non-delegates, including representatives from the ITGWU, WUI, Bray Trades Council, the Labour League Against Fascism, ICA Veterans, the Tenants' League and the NISP. Murray put his weight behind O'Donnell's minority resolution, which initially called for a 'united front of the working class and small farmers' to smash 'Imperialist and native exploiters' and progress towards an 'Irish Republic', before O'Donnell amended the wording to entail a commitment to the 'Republic'. In opposition, Michael Price presented his 'Workers' Republic' resolution, which differed in substance only in the precedence it assigned to the struggle with Irish capitalism.[144] Addressing the one major interpretative problem facing the two groups, Murray took issue with Price's underlying contention that the British and Irish variants of capitalism worked in isolation:

> We must be definitely clear on this point: we cannot rid ourselves of capitalist oppression until we destroy the power of British imperialism. And the majority resolution advocates the opposite – that we must have capitalism abolished before we can destroy English imperialist power … This Congress … will fulfil its task by the creation of a united front as the way forward to the unity and independence of Ireland and the realisation of the ultimate goal of Connolly, the Workers' Republic.[145]

Thus while he envisaged precisely the same end goal as the faction led by Price, Roddy Connolly and Nora Connolly O'Brien, Murray's commitment to anti-imperialism led to the adoption of divergent tactics. He claimed, without foundation, that unity under the 'Republic' banner would enable the industrial working class and rural workers to 'get acquainted in the fight with the common enemy, imperialism' en route to socialism, whereas Price insisted that the 'Workers' Republic' slogan held greater appeal for Belfast Protestants. In retrospect, George Gilmore, both a supporter of the minority resolution and a northern Protestant, conceded that Price had a point.[146] After all, one contemporary estimate of the East Belfast Republican Congress marchers at Bodenstown was just thirty-six.[147]

Ultimately, Murray had attempted to remain loyal to Connolly whilst committing the CPI to a 'stageist' conception of the revolution.

If the disputes around interpretation and tactics were not intractable, it quickly became apparent that there existed an unbridgeable gap in thinking around organisation. Whereas Price called for the formation of a political party, the minority resolution backed by O'Donnell, Gilmore, Murray and Ryan insisted that it was more appropriate to embed and fortify the united front. Invoking Connolly's participation in the united front of Easter 1916, Murray claimed that, this time around, a united front Congress would enable the working class to assume leadership of the struggles for national and social liberation.[148] George Gilmore would later claim that the Congress was Murray and O'Donnell's joint idea, which would help to explain why they were singing off the same hymn sheet.[149] Murray's enthusiasm for the united front is also significant because one of his tasks as CPI general secretary was to ensure that the Congress did not threaten the independent work of the party. The Comintern had always feared the emergence of a rival socialist republican formation and so devoted much of its energy to ensuring that the Irish comrades not only cooperated with but, more importantly, recruited from the IRA. After being advised by Willie Gallacher to do what he thought best, Murray advanced an analysis that closely reflected the one constant in the Comintern's shifting strategic position.

Most of the main resolutions debated at Rathmines – on agriculture, industrial activity, unemployment, fascism, the Gaeltacht and political prisoners – were passed with little opposition. Murray's contribution ensured that, when it came to the two main resolutions, the CPI delegates voted in favour of O'Donnell's proposals for the 'Republic' and the united front by a margin of ninety-nine votes to eighty-four. Consequently, Price and Connolly O'Brien declined to put their names forward for the executive and resigned from the Congress with immediate effect, though Roddy Connolly would remain a member until at least 1935. A reformed ICA took Price's side and followed him out of the Congress. These departures left the prospect of success substantially weakened.[150]

The Comintern archives contain damning evidence that CPGB interference prevented Murray from receiving detailed instructions from Moscow regarding the line to be adopted at Rathmines. The ECCI memo in question, dated 16 September, presented the bones of a proposal that straddled the 'Republic' and 'Workers' Republic' 'resolution'. This committed the party to a 'united front of workers, farmers and agricultural labourers against hunger, fascism and war', giving formal expression to the CPI's pronouncements and activities in the lead up to the Congress gathering at Athlone. The memo included a fifteen-point programme that had much in common with the CPI's manifesto and contained nothing radically different from that adopted by the Congress at Rathmines. Also, and even more crucially, it endorsed the slogan of a 'Workers' and Farmers' Republic', which had been coined by Murray and included in *The Irish Case for Communism*.[151] Harry Pollitt stands accused of failing to pass on instructions that reflected the clarity of the ECCI document and, in light of his clear antipathy to Murray, it is conceivable that he did so out of malevolence. The case against the CPGB general secretary is compelling and raises the question of whether he was interested in damaging his Irish counterpart's standing in Moscow.[152]

In the most thorough academic discussion of the Republican Congress, Adrian Grant argues that had Murray been in a position to present and convince O'Donnell of the merits of the 'Workers' and Farmers' Republic' compromise, 'perhaps they could have carried a larger majority and minimized the devastation of the split'.[153] The strength of Grant's analysis lies in his contention that the Rathmines split was not primarily ideological, but tactical. There are, however, a number of flaws with this interpretation as he presents it. Firstly, there is the problem of counterfactual history and the questionable value of mapping out unprovable imagined alternatives. It could be argued that Grant over-speculates on what might have been, which detracts from his otherwise excellent analysis of the events in question. Secondly, Grant does not do enough to address the issue of political space. Specifically, the dominance of Fianna Fáil and the Unionist Party in their respective jurisdictions casts into doubt his optimistic assessment of the Republican Congress and its prospects at the early stages of its development. A related problem is his neglect of the Protestant working class, whose limited support for the Congress was significant but not enough to warrant the belief expressed in the *Republican Congress* newspaper that there was an appetite among Protestant workers generally for a break with Britain.[154] Finally, Grant's focus on the wording of the republican resolution involves an attempt to downplay the role of ideology in informing CPI support for the united front. The concept of the vanguard party of the working class, fundamental to Marxist-Leninist thinking, meant that the communists could never have contemplated the emergence of a new political party. In this sense, then, ideology and tactics were inseparable.

Although the Republican Congress remained in existence until 1938, the Rathmines split condemned the initiative to failure. It represented the end of another serious left republican engagement with communism and the wider labour movement. In terms of revolutionary strategy, Murray's decision to fall in behind O'Donnell reflected the reality that he and his supporters within republicanism had proved the most consistent of the CPI's allies and that the left sectarianism of the Third Period had damaged the chances of fruitful cooperation with social democrats. However, the circumstances surrounding the collapse of the Congress and Murray's role in bringing about that collapse would make it difficult for him to take the party forward with the same purpose and authority that had hitherto characterised his leadership.

NOTES

1 Stephen Dedalus, in James Joyce's *Ulysses* (U 1.638-44).
2 RGASPI, 495/72/188/164-165, Seán Murray report to meeting of the Anglo-American secretariat, 10 June 1932.
3 Seán Nolan (ed.), *Communist Party of Ireland Outline History* (Dublin, 1975), p. 48;Donal Ó Drisceoil, *Peadar O'Donnell* (Cork, 2001), p.67.
4 RGASPI, Material for Anglo-American secretariat meeting, 6 November 1931.
5 Ó Drisceoil, *Peadar O'Donnell*, p.67.
6 Adrian Grant, *Irish Socialist Republicanism, 1909-36* (Dublin, 2012), p.178.
7 Patrick Murray, *Oracles of God: The Roman Catholic Church and Irish Politics, 1922-37* (Dublin, 2000), pp.320-1.
8 *Dáil Debates*, Vol. 40, No. 1-3, 14-16 October 1931.
9 Dermot Keogh, *Ireland and the Vatican: The Politics and Diplomacy of Church-State Relations, 1922-1960* (Cork, 1995), p.83.
10 *Acts of the Oireachtas*, Constitution (Amendment No. 17) Act, 1931; Mike Milotte, *Communism in Modern Ireland: The Pursuit of the Workers' Republic since 1916* (Dublin, 1984), p.110.
11 Grant, *Irish Socialist Republicanism*, p.179.
12 Emmet O'Connor, *Reds and the Green: Ireland, Russia and the Communist Internationals, 1919-43* (Dublin, 2004), pp.166-7.
13 National Library of Ireland (NLI), Hanna Sheehy Skeffington Papers, MS 41178, Letter from Murray to Hanna (1931).
14 Diarmaid Ferriter, *The Transformation of Ireland: 1900-2000* (London, 2004), p.439.
15 Graham Walker, 'The Northern Ireland Labour Party, 1924-45', in Fintan Lane and Donal Ó Drisceoil (eds), *Politics and the Irish Working Class, 1830-1945* (Basingstoke, 2005), pp.234-5.

16   James Connolly, 'Press Poisoners in Ireland,' in *Ireland Upon the Dissecting Table: James Connolly on Ulster and Partition* (Cork, 1975), pp.48-52.

17   Mary Harris, 'Catholicism, Nationalism and the Labour Question in Belfast, 1935-1938', *Bullán*, No. 1 (1997), pp.15-32.

18   Graham Walker, '"Protestantism Before Party!": The Ulster Protestant League in the 1930s', *The Historical Journal*, Vol. 28, No. 4 (1985), pp.961-7.

19   Milotte, *Communism in Modern Ireland*, p.126-7.

20   Michael Farrell, *Northern Ireland: The Orange State* (2nd ed.) (London, 1980), p.117.

21   Thomas Hennessey, *A History of Northern Ireland, 1920-1996* (Dublin, 1997), p.59.

22   Emmet O'Connor, *A Labour History of Ireland, 1824-2000* (Dublin, 2011), p.200.

23   Paul Bew, Peter Gibbon and Henry Patterson, *Northern Ireland, 1921-2001: Political Forces and Social Classes* (London, 2002), pp.52-5, 60-1.

24   Walker, 'The Northern Ireland Labour Party', p.235.

25   Kieran A. Kennedy, Thomas Giblin and Deirdre McHugh, *The Economic Development of Ireland in the Twentieth Century* (London, 1988), p.39.

26   Paul Bew, Ellen Hazelkorn and Henry Patterson, *The Dynamics of Irish Politics* (London, 1989), pp.37-42.

27   J.J. Lee, *Ireland, 1912-1985: Politics and Society* (Cambridge, 1989), pp.170-1.

28   Richard Dunphy, 'Fianna Fáil and the Irish Working Class, 1926-38', in Lane and Ó Drisceoil (eds), *Politics and the Irish Working Class*, p.258.

29   Lee, *Ireland*, p.179.

30   Henry Patterson, *The Politics of Illusion: A Political History of the IRA* (London, 1997), pp.61-2; Brian Hanley, *The IRA, 1926-1936* (Dublin, 2002), pp.14-16.

31   O'Connor, *Reds and the Green*, pp.162-5, 175.

32   RGASPI, 495/89/78/30-37, Murray report on Ireland, Group Organisation, 8 June 1932.

33   RGASPI, 495/72/197/14-16, Results of the Irish Free State Elections (1932).

34   *Workers' Voice*, 9 April 1932.

35   Ibid., 16 April 1932.

36   Ibid., 23, 30 April 1932.

37   Ibid., 7 May 1932.

38   Ibid., 4 June 1932.

39   O'Connor, *Reds and the Green*, pp.176-7.

40   Barry McLoughlin, *Left to the Wolves: Irish Victims of Stalinist Terror* (Dublin, 2007), p.59.

41   RGASPI, 495/4/207/168-171, Letter to the CPGB on the Irish Question, 13 August 1932.

42   McLoughlin, *Left to the Wolves*, p.60.

43 NAUK, KV2/1185, Serial 18c, Extract from Metropolitan Police Special Branch report, 3 October 1933.

44 NAUK, KV2/1185, Serial 17a, Extract from Metropolitan Police Special Branch report, 22 October 1932.

45 NLI, Sean O'Mahony Papers, MS 44,113/4, Typescript copy of Eoin MacNamee's memoirs (n.d.).

46 RGASPI, 495/89/83/42-44, Murray to Moscow, 9 September 1932.

47 RGASPI, 495/89/75/22-25, Letter to Ireland, 17 September 1932; 495/20/251/89-98, Letter to Ireland, 23 September 1932; 495/89/75/26-28, Letter to Ireland, 1 October 1932; 495/89/75/29-30, Letter to Ireland, 20 October 1932.

48 NAI, Department of Taoiseach (DT), 97/9/73, General O'Duffy's memo on communism and other kindred organisations, 24 November 1932.

49 Ó Drisceoil, *Peadar O'Donnell*, pp.78-9.

50 Hennessey, *A History of Northern Ireland*, p.60.

51 PRONI, HA/32/1/547, RUC Special Branch report, 12 September 1932.

52 PRONI, HA/8/276, RUC Special Branch report, 3 October 1932.

53 Tom Bell, *The Struggle of the Unemployed in Belfast, Oct. 1932* (Cork, 1976).

54 *Irish Press*, 15 October 1932; *Irish Workers' Voice*, 29 October 1932.

55 Paddy Devlin, *Yes We Have No Bananas: Outdoor Relief in Belfast, 1920-39* (Belfast, 1981), pp.116-36.

56 O'Connor, *Reds and the Green*, pp.179-80

57 Bell, *The Struggle of the Unemployed in Belfast*; Milotte, *Communism in Modern Ireland*, pp.132-6.

58 *Irish Workers' Voice*, 29 October 1932; RGASPI, 495/89/83/42-44, Murray to Moscow, 9 September 1932.

59 Ronnie Munck and Bill Rolston (with Gerry Moore), *Belfast in the 1930s: An Oral History* (Belfast, 1987), p.154.

60 Hanley, *The IRA*, pp.102, 150-1; Munck and Rolston, *Belfast in the 1930s*, pp.169-78.

61 Brian Hanley, 'The IRA and Trade Unionism, 1922-72', in Francis Devine, Fintan Lane and Niamh Puirséil (eds), *Essays in Irish Labour History: A Festschrift for Elizabeth and John W. Boyle* (Sallins, 2008), pp.162-7.

62 Milotte, *Communism in Modern Ireland*, p.114.

63 NAI, DJ, 2008/117/38, Copy of Irish Workers' College syllabus; Garda Special Branch report, 2 March 1933.

64 Ibid.

65 NAI, DJ, 2008/117/38, Garda Special Branch report, 4 May 1933; RGASPI, 495/89/82/14-18, Report re national meeting of RWG, 5-6 November 1932.

66 Richard English, *Radicals and the Republic: Socialist Republicanism and the Irish Free State, 1925-1937* (Oxford,1994), p.181.

67 Bew, Hazelkorn and Patterson, *The Dynamics of Irish Politics*, pp.26-33; Brian Girvin, *Between Two Worlds: Politics and Economy in Independent Ireland* (Dublin, 1989), pp.55-7; Lee, *Ireland*, pp.121-4; Conor McCabe, *Sins of the Father: Tracing the Decisions that Shaped the Irish Economy* (Dublin, 2011), pp.125-32.

68 Seán Murray, *The Irish Case for Communism* (Dublin, 1933).

69 RGASPI, 495.89/84/15-21, Tactics of the RWG towards the IRA, 1 January 1933.

70 RGASPI, 495/89/90/23-30, The General Election in Ireland, January 1933.

71 O'Connor, *Reds and the Green*, p.182.

72 NAUK, KV2/1185, Serial 21f, Cross-reference to Metropolitan Police Special Branch report, 6 April 1933; KV2/1185, Serial 22, Metropolitan Police Special Branch report on communism, 12 April 1933; KV2/1185, Serial 23a, Cross-reference to Metropolitan Police Special Branch report, 1 May 1933.

73 Quintin Hoare and Geoffrey Nowell Smith (eds), *Antonio Gramsci: Selections from the Prison Note books* (London, 1971).

74 RGASPI, 495/89/83/8-9, Letter from Jim Gralton to Murray, 19 April 1932; Pat Feeley, *The Gralton Affair: The Story of the Deportation of Jim Gralton, a Leitrim Socialist* (Dublin, 1986); 'Labour and local history: The Case of Jim Gralton', *Saothar*, 14 (1989), pp.85-94; Nolan (ed.), *CPI Outline History*, pp.48-50.

75 Mike Cronin, *The Blueshirts and Irish Politics* (Dublin, 1997), Ch. 6; Fearghal McGarry, *Eoin O'Duffy: A Self-Made Hero* (Oxford, 2005), pp.211-33.

76 Manus O'Riordan, 'Communism in Dublin in the 1930s: The Struggle against Fascism', in H. Gustav Klaus (ed.), *Strong Words, Brave Deeds: The Poetry, Life and Times of Thomas O'Brien, Volunteer in the Spanish Civil War* (Dublin, 1994), p.220.

77 Patrick Byrne, *The Republican Congress Revisited* (London, 1994), p.26; Brian Hanley, 'The Storming of Connolly House', *History Ireland*, Vol. 7, No. 2 (Summer 1999), pp.5-7; *Irish Times*, 2 May 1933; NAI, DJ, JUS8/711, 'Garda Special Branch reports, 26, 30 March, 5 April 1933; O'Riordan, 'Communism in Dublin', p.221.

78 Donal Fallon, 'Newsboys and the "Animal Gang" in 1930s Dublin', in David Convery (ed.), *Locked Out: A Century of Working-Class Life* (Sallins, 2013).

79 NAI, DT, 97/9/73, General O'Duffy's memo on communism and other kindred organisations, 24 November 1932; *Workers' Voice*, 29 October 1932.

80 *Standard*, 22 July 1933.

81 Nolan (ed.), *CPI Outline History*, p.21.

82 NAUK, KV2/1185, Serial 21f, Cross-reference to Metropolitan Police Special Branch report, 6 April 1933.

83 NAI, DJ, 2007/56/176, Garda Special Branch report, 18 May 1933.

84 UCDA, Moss Twomey Papers, P69/187 (104-108), IRA General Army Convention, 17-19 March 1933.

85 Grant, *Irish Socialist Republicanism*, pp.187-98; *Irish Workers' Voice*, 24 June 1933; Hanley, *The IRA*, pp.105, 180-1.

86 UCDA, Moss Twomey Papers, P69/187 (104), IRA General Army Convention, 17-19 March 1933.

87 Hanley, *The IRA*, p.180.

88 *Standard*, 10 June 1933.

89 RGASPI, 495/89/90/39-40, Report on CPI founding congress, 3-4 June 1933; 495/89/88/14-30, Speeches from CPI founding congress, 4-5 June 1933.

90 Matt Treacy, *The Communist Party of Ireland 1921-2011: Vol. 1: 1921-1969* (Dublin, 2013), p.55.

91 Seán Murray, *Ireland's Path to Freedom* (Dublin, 1933), p.12.

92 Richard Dunphy, *The Making of Fianna Fáil Power in Ireland, 1923-1948* (Oxford, 1995), pp.187-8.

93 Murray, *Ireland's Path to Freedom*, p.9.

94 D.R. O'Connor Lysaght, 'The Communist Party of Ireland: A Critical History', Part 2 (1976), http://www.workersrepublic.org/Pages/Ireland/Communism/cpihistory2.html (accessed 20 July 2014).

95 Murray, *Ireland's Path to Freedom*, pp.13-14.

96 RGASPI, 495/89/91/23, Report from Ireland to the ECCI, July 1933.

97 Murray, *Ireland's Path to Freedom*, pp.2, 9.

98 *An Phoblacht*, 17 June 1933; NAI, DJ, 2007/56/176, Garda Special Branch report, 26 June 1933.

99 *Irish Workers' Voice*, 24 June 1933; *Irish Independent*, 7 June 1933.

100 Hanley, *The IRA*, p.181.

101 RGASPI, 495/89/90/13-18, Report from Ireland, July 1933.

102 Milotte, *Communism in Modern Ireland*, p.143; RGASPI, 495/89/88/14-30, Speeches from CPI founding congress, 4-5 June 1933.

103 NAI, DJ, 2007/56/176, Garda Special Branch report, 24 July 1933.

104 O'Connor, *Reds and the Green*, p.190.

105 *Irish Workers' Voice*, 10 January 1933.

106 O'Connor, *Reds and the Green*, pp.183-4.

107 NAI, DJ, 2008/117/38, Garda Special branch report, 23 October 1933.

108 O'Connor, *Reds and the Green*, p.194.

109 PRONI, HA/32/1/549, RUC Special Branch report, 23 October 1933.

110 PRONI, Seán Murray Papers, D2162/M/2, Letter from RUC District Inspector to Murray, 4 November 1933; CAB/9/B/215/1, Cabinet record of exclusion order, 5 December 1933; *Irish Workers' Voice*, 9, 16 December 1933; Milotte, *Communism in Modern Ireland*, pp.146-7.

111 PRONI, Seán Murray Papers, D2162/M/3, Postcard from James Kater (1933).

112 PRONI, Seán Murray Papers, D2162/5/1, Postcard from Kate, 30 October 1933.

113 RGASPI, 495/89/89/27, 'Demand Seán Murray's release', November 1933.

114 NAI, DJ, 2008/117/38, Garda Special Branch report, 11 December 1933.

115 NAI, DJ, 2008/117/38, Garda Special Branch report, 9 January 1934.

116 RGASPI, 495/89/89/24, 'To the working people of Ireland!', November 1933. *Irish Workers' Voice*, 28 October, 4, 18, 25 November, 16, 23 December 1933, 13 January 1934.

117 National Council for Civil Liberties (NCCL), *The Special Powers Acts of Northern Ireland: Report of a Commission of Inquiry appointed to examine the purpose and effect of Civil Authorities (Special Powers) Acts (Northern Ireland) 1922 & 1933* (London, 1936), p.22.

118 Ibid., p.32.

119 Ibid., p.40.

120 RGASPI, 495/89/73/75-95, Tasks of the Revolutionary Workers' Groups in Ireland, 1 August 1932; 495/89/99/2-3, CPI politburo report, 10 March 1934.

121 Milotte, *Communism in Modern Ireland*, p.142.

122 NAI, DJ, 2008/117/38, Garda Special Branch report, 9 January 1934.

123 RGASPI, 495/89/99/2-3, Position re printing of Irish Workers' Voice, etc., 8 February 1934.

124 RGASPI, 495/89/89/1-2, 'General O'Duffy Hoaxed!: We Expose Source of Anti-Communist Propaganda' (1933); NAI, DJ, 2007/56/176, Garda Special Branch report, 24 July 1933; 2008/117/38, Garda Special Branch report, 23 October 1933.

125 O'Connor, *Reds and the Green*, p.194.

126 NAI, DJ, 2008/117/38, Garda Special Branch report, 11 September 1933; RGASPI, 495/89/99/13-16, Meeting of the CPI politburo and central committee, 10-11 March 1934.

127 Milotte, *Communism in Modern Ireland*, p.144.

128 NAI, DJ, 2008/117/38, Garda Special Branch report, 20 January 1934.

129 O'Connor, *Reds and the Green*, p.195.

130 RGASPI, 495/89/89/10, 'The Fascist Danger, And the Workers' Struggle against it!'; *Irish Workers' Voice*, 19 August, 3 September, 4 November 1933.

131 RGASPI, 495/89/99/16, Meeting of the CPI central committee, 10-11 March 1934.

132 NAI, DJ, JUS8/739, Garda Special Branch report, 22 January 1934.

133 *Irish Workers' Voice*, 20 January 1934.

134 Ibid., 24 March, 5 May 1934; *Irish Times*, 2 May 1934.

135 Harry Haywood, *Black Bolshevik: Autobiography of an Afro-American Communist* (Chicago, Illinois, 1978), p.418.

136 Seán Murray, *Ireland's Fight for Freedom and the Irish in the USA* (New York, 1934).

137 Byrne, *The Republican Congress Revisited*, pp.13-14; English, *Radicals and the Republic*, p.188; Grant, *Irish Socialist Republicanism*, pp.199-202; *Irish Workers' Voice*, 14 April 1934.

138 Ibid.

139 Stephen Hopkins, 'French Communism, The Comintern and Class Against Class: Interpretations and Rationales', in Matthew Worley (ed.), *In Search of Revolution: International Communist Parties in the Third Period* (London, 2004), pp.120-8.

140 *Irish Workers' Voice*, 21 April, 5 May, 5, 23 June 1934.

141 Ibid., 9, 16 June 1934.

142 Byrne, *The Republican Congress Revisited*, p.23; Hanley, *The IRA*, p.107.

143 Grant, *Irish Socialist Republicanism*, p.210.

144 George Gilmore, *The Irish Republican Congress* (Cork, 1979), pp.47-51; *Republican Congress*, 13 October 1934.

145 *Irish Workers' Voice*, 6 October 1934.

146 Gilmore, *The Irish Republican Congress*, p.57.

147 Hanley, *The IRA*, p.107.

148 *Irish Workers' Voice*, 6 October 1934; *Republican Congress*, 6, 13 October 1934.

149 Ó Drisceoil, *Peadar O'Donnell*, p.88.

150 Grant, *Irish Socialist Republicanism*, p.215.

151 RGASPI, 495/89/96/46-47, ECCI memo on the Republican Congress, 16 September 1934.

152 O'Connor, *Reds and the Green*, p.201.

153 Grant, *Irish Socialist Republicanism*, p.212.

154 Patterson, *The Politics of Illusion*, p.72.

CHAPTER **3**

The Improvised Popular Front

'But look, Roberto,' Agustín said. 'They say the government moves further to the right each day. That in the Republic they no longer say Comrade but Señor and Señora ... Are we to win this war and lose the revolution?'

'Nay,' Robert Jordan said. 'But if we do not win this war there will be no revolution nor any Republic nor any thou nor any me nor anything but the most grand carajo.'[1]

By the close of 1934, Murray had been striving to bridge the gap between the communist movement and its erstwhile allies for well over a year. Despite being on the opposing side during the Rathmines debate, Roddy Connolly had become convinced of the utility of an alliance with the CPI against 'capitalism, fascism, international war and imperialism'.[2] Although his motion to this effect fell at the annual Labour Party conference in October, the Labour leadership's conservatism did not get in the way of grassroots united front action on the streets. In November, the CPI and its front organisations, the INUM and the Labour League Against Fascism, campaigned alongside Labour Party branches, the Republican Congress, trade unions and the IRA in opposition to the Unemployment Assistance Act (1933), securing a 25 percent increase in benefits from the government.[3] Pre-1934 united front traditions also helped to encourage cooperation, with the Congress leading a 2,000-strong joint counter-demonstration on Armistice Day involving British ex-servicemen opposed to war. Another important unifying factor was the commitment to build and protect democracy in Ireland, to which the Blueshirts posed a threat. Murray is credited, along with O'Donnell, Ryan, Gilmore, Tom Barry (IRA) and Kit Conway (CPI), with leading 'a fighting united front' involving violent clashes with O'Duffy's men.[4] Socialist republican opposition to the Blueshirts disrupted efforts at fascist organisation whilst boosting the morale of the labour movement and republican left in difficult circumstances.[5]

However, the demoralising Rathmines split left the CPI no nearer to establishing the concrete socialist republican alliance coveted by Murray. In fact, as Frank Ryan noted in a letter to Gerald O'Reilly, a member of Clan na Gael in New York, O'Donnell had 'drifted away out of touch' with his friend, the CPI general secretary.[6] Not only did Murray's personal relationships suffer but once again his position as leading Irish cadre came under intense scrutiny. Unaware of, or unwilling to admit to, Pollitt's role in contributing to the confusion at Rathmines, the Anglo-American secretariat placed the onus of blame on Murray for 'supporting a policy of REVOLUTIONARY NATIONAL REPUBLICANISM as AGAINST a so-called PROLETARIAN REPUBLICANISM' and failing to argue for 'Workers' and Farmers' Republic' compromise. He had also continued to oversee, in the secretariat's view, a dilution of the party's 'Communist identity'. It therefore demanded that the CPI make overtures to advocates of the 'Workers' Republic' resolution and that it cease operating like the 'tailend of the O'Donnellite Left Republicans'. The directive also carried 'suggestions' regarding an escalation of work with unemployed groups; trade union organisation and party recruitment; and an overhaul of the Irish Workers' Voice to include the establishment of an editorial board tasked with giving 'a Communist policy to every problem and task confronting the workers and farmers'.[7]

Whilst addressing the specifics of the Congress fallout, this amounted to a critique of Murray's leadership. On 16 November, the Comintern reinforced its analysis and instructions with a more concise and, it must be said, temperate letter. The message remained the same: the CPI had, under Murray's direction, failed to 'stand out independently in the Congress'.[8] A party circular admitted to mistakes at Rathmines but gave little indication that this would lead to full implementation of Moscow's recommendations.[9] This fits the pattern of Murray's response to directives with which he was at odds and indicates that he carried the support of the CPI central committee. What is particularly surprising is that he did not fight his corner more vigorously and outline the circumstances that led him to fall in behind O'Donnell. Consequently, the Comintern seconded

Pat Devine of the CPGB to work as a full-time instructor in Dublin. O'Connor remarks that Murray 'probably held his post as general secretary by default', given the absence of local cadres with the appetite or ability to step into his invidious position.[10] His much-vaunted affability and popularity with grassroots members must have also been a factor. However, the signs of dissatisfaction emanating from London and Moscow, culminating in the direct imposition of a trusted representative to supervise CPI activities, seriously dented his authority.

The thankless task of negotiating the CPI through rough terrain, therefore, carried the risk of receiving all of the blame for its many failures and none of the credit for its relative successes. Murray's growing prominence over the course of 1933 and 1934 also drew the unwelcome attention – opprobrium is too strong a description – of *United Ireland*, weekly organ of the pro-Treaty party Fine Gael. *United Ireland* treated Murray with a combination of patronising contempt and grudging respect: patronising contempt because of his political views; grudging respect because he was 'evidently a man with the courage of his convictions'.[11] This was the view held by Blueshirt intellectual, James Hogan, Professor of History at University College Cork, author of *Could Ireland Become Communist?*[12] and close confidant of O'Duffy, who expressed his preference for Murray's 'disciplined' communism over the 'Communism without discipline' promoted by O'Donnell. Furthermore, in typically condescending fashion, he identified texts that would enable them to see the error of their ways.[13] Had readers and contributors been more acutely aware of Murray's IRA past and his anti-Treaty credentials in particular – one article described him as belonging to 'that large class of patriots who in times of war are men of peace, and, accordingly, is talking from theory rather than experience'[14] – they may have reserved more vitriol for him.

Either way, Catholic anti-communism would continue to work against Murray, the CPI and the republican left in the South. Towards the end of 1934, in a re-run of the Gralton affair, Bishop Kinane of Waterford and Lismore removed the Belfast-born teacher Frank Edwards from his post at Mount Sion Christian Brothers' School after learning of his involvement with the Republican Congress and leading role in campaigns against slum landlords. Frank Ryan and Peadar O'Donnell lent Edwards their support by writing to various newspapers to dispute the reasons for the bishop's decision and by establishing Frank Edwards defence committees. Even the IRA leadership released a statement deploring the bishop's behaviour.[15] Murray spoke at a number of protest meetings for Edwards, and used the *Irish Workers' Voice* to encourage participation in the campaign for his reinstatement. At one meeting in Dublin, he argued that Dr. Kinane only opposed the type of republicanism that questioned the legitimacy of private property and, after reading from a list of people worth £80,000 or more, asked why there were scant pastorals dealing with inequality across the island.[16] Despite the national attention given to Edwards' plight and the popular support he enjoyed locally, the Church held firm and retained the loyalty of Waterford City Corporation on the issue, securing yet another victory for conservative Ireland.[17]

In the North, ethno-religious divisions bubbled to the surface to the detriment of the CPI's efforts and labour unity. The shooting of Catholic barman, Dan O'Boyle, in November 1933, the first sectarian killing since 1922, inflamed underlying animosities, as did the furore surrounding the Silver Jubilee of King George V in May 1935, Orange parades on 12 July and the inflammatory behaviour of senior Unionist figures. The summer months of 1935 saw the worst violence in Belfast since the 1920-22 period, from which even the marginal CPI was not insulated. Stirred back into action, the UPL mobilised its supporters against 'disloyal' Catholics, the CPI and the perceived communist threat to Protestant jobs and the Union. On 14 June, after two Protestants were wounded in an exchange of gunfire, the UPL orchestrated a riot that led to attacks on Catholic-owned shops and the Socialist Party's ILP Hall at York Street. The UPL was also to the fore in breaking up INUM meetings and trashing the CPI's Belfast office.[18] The *Irish Workers' Voice* blamed James Craig and Dawson Bates for inciting the violence and encouraged united front action, including the formation of a workers' defence force, to defend labour groups from attack.[19]

The conditions for rebuilding the party were inauspicious. The transformation of Fianna Fáil into a catch-all party, based on its success in developing state enterprises, increasing industrial employment, slum clearances and the provision of social housing, and limited agricultural reforms, further limited the CPI's options in the sphere of electoral politics. The Coal-Cattle Pact (1935) with Britain signalled a move away from tillage and agricultural employment in favour of maintaining the privileged position of the rancher class. However, de Valera's Machiavellian approach to welfarism — conferring benefits gradually — allowed him to keep up appearances in the impoverished west of Ireland and paint Fianna Fáil as the party of the working class majority, thus squeezing the political space open to potential rivals on the left. The Unionist Party, with its stentorian appeals to religious prejudice, Craig's unrestrained populism and the widespread use of repression, maintained its dominance of northern politics in spite of its handling of the economic recession. Paradoxically, the weak state of the CPI and its bleak prospects, for which the Comintern and CPGB apportioned most of the blame to Murray, helped to preserve his place at the head of the Irish movement. Pat Devine's brief stint in Dublin notwithstanding, the absence of an alternative leadership meant that Murray would be tasked with using the remnants of the CPI's base in Dublin and Belfast to save the party from extinction.

Opening up the united front

In January 1935, with working-class parties facing violent suppression and defeat internationally, particularly in Germany, the CPI returned to Rathmines Hall under the auspices of the Labour League Against Fascism. Among the main speakers were Murray, O'Donnell and the literary scholar, A.J. Leventhal, a Dublin-born Jew. Ernst Toller, the German dissident writer and outspoken critic of Hitler, had also been listed to speak but the Irish authorities prevented him from entering the country, and there was a large police presence at the meeting to enforce the ban.[20] At the same time, Billy McCullough addressed an ILDL meeting in Belfast and outlined the Unionist administration's use of repressive measures against political activists. He affirmed his disagreement with the IRA's policies and methods whilst explaining that they shared common cause in resisting the state's undemocratic means of curbing political dissent. He related the imprisonment without charge of three alleged IRA volunteers to the exclusion orders served upon Murray, Harry Pollitt and Tom Mann.[21] Together, these fronts represented two sides of the same coin: on the one hand, raising awareness of the threat posed by international fascism; on the other, bringing to the fore a campaign to secure basic civil and political freedoms at home.

Murray's difficulties with the CPGB did not prevent him from addressing its thirteenth annual congress in February, where he informed delegates that the Anglo-Irish Treaty had merely replaced 'British imperialist slavery' with 'British imperialist-imposed freedom' and a new type of slavery for the Irish working class and peasantry. He argued that the national democratic revolution would not be complete until the 'running sore' of partition was removed and the island reunited,[22] and assured that 'rebellions and revolutions of the future will not be for the benefit of capitalists but for the establishment of the rule of the workers'.[23]

Throughout his political career, Murray vacillated between a 'stageist' view of the national question and a two-pronged approach in which social struggles were of equal and immediate importance – something closer to Connolly's analysis. At this particular juncture, we can only be sure that Murray did not see an explicitly national focus precluding class-struggling activities, or vice versa.

Admitting in the company of his CPGB comrades that the CPI was 'not a strong Party' was an exercise in stating the obvious. It was important nonetheless for Murray to spell out, at the earliest opportunity since the Rathmines split, the need for the Irish party to continue responding to local conditions. He explained that the CPI had begun working to establish a strong presence in the Belfast and Dublin trades councils; re-engage with the trade unions; reassert leadership of the unemployed movements; and regain the confidence of 'important' republican elements. Just as in October 1932 he was realistic about the CPI's prospects, so now he believed the party could only have an impact and grow by accepting the less prestigious role of 'a factor in the political and economic struggles of the masses'.[24] Whereas he remained keen to encourage and facilitate the political transformation of IRA members with socialist inclinations, pushing them in the direction of the Republican Congress, Pat Devine was not impressed with the CPI's open displays of republicanism under Murray's leadership. However, both agreed that there was an urgent need to put the party in a position to influence the various movements that had emerged in recent months.[25] The ECCI came close to backing Devine's position whilst reminding the Irish group of Moscow's infallibility in all matters of policy.[26]

On 2 March 1935, the Dublin tramway and bus workers went on strike against wage cuts, handing the CPI an opportunity to influence a section of the trade union movement in the face of divisions and Labour Party hostility to its public overtures. Accordingly, the party committed a six-man cell to the organisation of striking workers and the publication of *Unity*, a bulletin whose purpose was to update and instil confidence in the striking workers while influencing the strike committee to hold out for a successful outcome.[27] The CPI's official newspaper also gave the strike extensive coverage. Murray commissioned a series of articles devoted to a discussion on the party's relationship with the two trade unions involved and the strike's implications for the issue of trade union unity. His article, the fourth in the series, warned against the tendency to criticise union leaders without offering an alternative, an offence committed too often by the CPI. But in charting the path forward, he continued, the movement would need to harness the energy of militant shop stewards and officials like those involved in the strike. Naturally, his party was prepared to give those militant activists a political home.[28]

One interesting aspect of the CPI's involvement in the strike is its focus on inter-generational duties, particularly in assuming the mantle from Larkin and Connolly to confront the Murphy empire.[29] Like his father before him, Murphy junior helped to create the conditions for conflict by employing the use of scab labour and strike-breakers, at an estimated cost of £2,000 per each of the dispute's thirteen weeks.[30] In response to the CPI's growing influence over the strike committee, elements sympathetic to Murphy began to distribute the *Eyeopener*, a source of anti-communist propaganda, in the workplace and around the DUTC picket line. At the risk of exposing the CPI to further undesirable attention from the conservative press and DUTC mercenaries, Murray continued to challenge 'Lombard Murphy's lies' over the course of the year. This demonstrated the party's need to reconnect with and recruit from the shop stewards' movement as well as a genuine, ideological commitment to tackling the power of the commercial class in Dublin.

The IRA had intervened violently in strikes involving its members, for example, during a dispute between O'Mara's bacon shops and the Commercial Employees Union (CEU) of which Mick Fitzpatrick was an official.[31] And when, on 20 March, the government sent in Free State Army trucks to provide public transportation in place of the dormant trams and buses, the leadership sanctioned action by its Dublin Brigade to disrupt what it regarded as strikebreaking and a 'definite challenge to all workers'. The organisation began sniping the tyres of army lorries and devised plans to mine tram depots.[32] In response, Moscow instructed the CPGB to support the CPI's endeavours and encourage 'joint solidarity' with supportive IRA units.[33] In the ensuing round-up operation, gardaí arrested forty-four republicans and socialists in the Dublin area, including Tom Barry, Peadar O'Donnell and members of the ICA, which had been reconstituted around the time of the Republican Congress.[34] The IRA leadership was forced to go on the run for the first time since Fianna Fáil came to power and, by the time the strike ended on 18 May, CPI headquarters had been raided five times.[35] During one raid of Connolly House, following a tip-off by a resigned member of the CPI that there were plans to 'do in' Seán Lemass and William O'Brien, the ITGWU leader, Larkin junior was arrested and nine improvised batons confiscated.[36] Imitating the dictatorial example of the Cumann na nGaedheal administration, the government reintroduced military tribunals and ensured that uncooperative prisoners received harsh sentences. Roddy Connolly, one of those arrested, commented sardonically that this reaction ought to be taken as Fianna Fáil's contribution to the upcoming Jubilee celebrations.[37]

Recognising once more the convergence between labour and republican grievances, particularly in relation to the arbitrary detention of political activists, Murray told one protest meeting that the arrests were a cynical attempt by the government to prevent cooperation between the two movements and to take off the streets those in a position to help the workers win the strike.[38] A follow-up meeting demanded the release of 'our Republican comrades' and a rejection by the tramway workers of the latest terms offered by DUTC. However, the meeting had to be abandoned when, despite the pleas of a priest in the vicinity, a hostile crowd of about 250 appeared, chanting: 'We want no communism in Dublin.' Pat Devine was dislodged from the makeshift platform and Murray was on the receiving end of similar treatment when he attempted to protest against the interference and the violence that had broken out. A riot ensued, resulting in a police baton charge on the attacking crowd. Eight people suffered minor injuries and two others, including Daniel Layde of the CPI and INUM, had to be taken to hospital for treatment.[39]

The strike eventually closed with a ballot vote of 2,112 for and 605 against the settlement offered by DUTC. The *Workers' Voice* published a list of the eleven wage increases won and declared a partial victory for trade union militancy and organised labour in Dublin.[40] The CPI also claimed the credit for organising a successful rent strike in Belfast, while communist trade unionists were closely involved in strikes of the shipyard welders and pipe coverers, and at Mackie's foundry, in the city. Along with its leading role in the unemployed workers' movement, these struggles for 'homes, wages and bread' put the party on a stronger footing among the industrial working class in the north-east. 'The result of our activity', Murray told a meeting of the CPI central committee, 'has prevented the capitalists from filching from the unemployed masses the gains of the great mass battles of October, 1932, in Belfast'. On this basis, he advocated an extension of agitation and propaganda, and anticipated the formation of new party units if 'every member plunges into the political and economic battles now ahead'.[41]

These predictions of gains for the CPI were dampened by the reality of slow, unsatisfactory progress in the aftermath of the tramway strike. From 2,000 in December 1934, weekly circulation of the *Workers' Voice* had risen to 2,200 by May 1935, and this growth came almost exclusively in the key cities of Dublin and Belfast. Membership figures added up to a disappointing 150 and clerical pressure had begun to tell on a number of party activists.[42] At a meeting with the Anglo-American secretariat in July, Murray explained that the strike had generated only fleeting harmony within the trade union movement and earned the CPI limited support beyond its own milieu. He advised the Comintern that although the party remained committed to working with militant shop stewards and activists in the interest of building a strong trade union movement, it was necessary to view republicans as its most reliable allies. Despite everything that had followed the Rathmines split, he was adamant that O'Donnell had been a positive influence, a champion of left unity, and that the Republican Congress had proved 'a very valuable ally in the struggle against the fascists and against the church, and for the development of a mass movement in Dublin'. A united front of the industrial working class solely through conventional labour channels had 'no possibility, and would just be an ideal'. The survival and eventual growth of the CPI therefore depended on its supporters rallying around the positive aspects of the Republican Congress model and promoting the formation of Congress groups across the island.[43]

By extension, this enthusiasm for maintaining a working relationship with republicans entailed his taking up of republican concerns. Discussing the arrest of IRA leader, Mick Fitzpatrick, Murray stated that the Fianna Fáil policy of imprisoning republicans without charge or trial 'did not give them the right' to hold Wolfe Tone commemorations, and that instead 'the Republican Party of Ireland [the CPI/Republican Congress] would celebrate it' at Bodenstown.[44] Murray's anti-imperialism also came to the fore in his criticisms of Britain's war preparations and of de Valera's ambiguous response to them which, he argued, left open the possibility of Ireland's acquiescence in any future British mobilisation. In the context of a mounting international war threat, the British naval bases in Cobh, Berehaven and Lough Swilly ports undermined the gradual process of dismantling the Treaty settlement and threatened to entangle Irish workers in the conquest of other nations.[45] This analysis placed the CPI firmly within the sphere of left republicanism. However, events at Bodenstown demonstrated most clearly that a broader communist-republican alliance was out of the question. After Seán MacBride prohibited all non-IRA groups from carrying their own banners, the IRA clashed with the communist/Republican Congress contingent, seizing and tearing up a red flag belonging to the CPI.[46] It is also notable that, during the tram strike, Tom Barry had protested at the decision to try him alongside CPI members, Christy Clarke and Jack Nalty, making an anti-communist speech in court.[47] Despite the CPI's public reaffirmation of its anti-imperialist republicanism, the chances of recruiting from or working with the IRA had not improved.

With Pat Devine in tow, Murray travelled to Moscow for the seventh congress of the Comintern, which ran from 25 July to 20 August 1935. His invitation and attendance represented a rare high point in a political career blighted by successive disappointments. Standing at about 5ft 6in, with dark hair quiffed and parted on the left side, a roundish face, ruddy complexion and discoloured teeth, dressed in an old greyish suit, Murray would have looked every bit the hardened political activist as he approached the rostrum. Typical of the contributions of delegates from peripheral parties, his long-winded congress speech was of minor significance, though he did admit to the CPI's 'sectarian and opportunist' errors and stated that he had continued to explore links with the republican movement regardless of international directives.[48] Of greater consequence to the Irish party were the main resolutions. After much prevarication and misdirection in the form of a lengthy ECCI report – a distorted history of recent international developments – delegates unanimously endorsed a resolution that finally acknowledged the 'fiendishness of German fascism and the danger of a new war'. Social democrats and reformists were now potential revolutionaries, 'struggling hand in hand with the communists against fascism and for the interests of the toiling masses'. To this end, Comintern affiliated parties were encouraged to form 'people's fronts'. It also resolved 'to proceed, in deciding any question, from the concrete situation and specific conditions obtaining in each particular country, and as a rule to avoid direct intervention in internal organisational matters of the communist parties'. The ECCI conceded that 'the mechanical application' of 'stereotyped methods' on the basis of the Soviet experience had proved no substitute for 'concrete Marxist analysis'.[49] This represented a victory for national specificity, and a number of peripheral and West European parties, particularly the French and Spanish, joined the CPI in breathing a collective sigh of relief. The decisions of the seventh congress removed some of the external caveats that had previously hindered the CPI's work with the Labour parties and the wider republican movement and its capacity to develop tactics suited to local conditions.

93

In the aftermath of the 1935 congress, the CPI moved to spell out and ratify the terms of the people's front approach. The Irish delegation submitted a series of proposals with the objective of a 'Workers' and Farmers' Republic' at their core, which elicited a positive response. They intended to approach the Labour Party and farmers' representatives and to encourage the Republican Congress to repair its broken relationship with the IRA. Through these connections, the party aimed to build a 'united front of labour and republican Ireland', involving opposition to the growing threat of fascism; exposing Fianna Fáil's complicity in British imperialist war plans; campaigning for the repeal of repressive legislation and a restoration of civil liberties; and more direct agitation on the national question.[50] The party membership officially endorsed these 'new' policies at a national conference in October, though, in reality, this only served to update campaigns that were already underway.[51] Roddy Connolly, in attendance as an observer, explained that the CPI had damaged relations with the Labour Party during its 'class against class' phase and was now in danger of replacing it with blatant opportunism. Murray conceded that the communists had displayed both traits and that much work needed to be done by party members towards the objective of labour unity.[52] Murray kept his distance from the ICA and instructed party members to do the same, for in the context of an assault on left and right opposition figures in the Soviet Union, his left sectarian tendencies led to the conclusion that it was a 'Trotskyite' plot to undermine the communist movement. However, he valued Connolly's counsel and recognised that he had, within the Labour Party, a supporter who enjoyed a measure of influence across the movement.

Of the three strands of the people's front strategy, anti-fascism was arguably the most dynamic. On its own initiative and through the Labour League Against Fascism and War, the CPI was the first party to take up the plight of Abyssinia (Ethiopia), which had been invaded by Mussolini's Italy and was on the precipice of all-out war with the nascent and hungry fascist power. *Workers' Voice* editorials devoted to anti-fascist and anti-war themes began to grow in number, and Murray's participation in a campaign that recruited former British soldiers confirmed that his concerns extended beyond narrow nationalist interests. At the same time, he did not pass up an opportunity to weave criticisms of imperialism into an analysis of fascism. At an anti-war meeting in December, he singled out Italian fascism as the 'worst form possible' while taking issue with the Hoare-Laval Pact, which looked like bringing an end to Italo-Abyssinian hostilities but would also, Murray believed, enable the French and British to divide a section of Abyssinia between them. This, Murray argued, was tantamount to imperialist manipulation of an occupied nation's misfortune and desperate need for international assistance. Here he articulated a critique of fascist and imperialist forces that had invested in the same issue.[53] Increasingly, he would compare the situation to 1914, when militarism grew, weak countries suffered invasion and the ruling classes duped even the socialist parties of Europe into supporting an imperialist war. Fascism represented a new threat, but one that could manifest itself in imperialist aggression. The growing strength of both forces would necessitate labour resistance on a global scale and with greater tenacity than in 1914.[54]

Communist-organised meetings in the last few months of 1935 and first half of 1936 allowed anti-fascist, anti-imperialist and class-struggling campaigns to run concurrently. All three struggles, in Murray's view, would necessarily involve the republican and labour movements working together. In August, an IRA Army convention succumbed to Seán MacBride's persistence and approved the formation of an abstentionist republican party, offering Murray at least a flickering hope that a tactical united front could be facilitated.[55] Murray said as much when welcoming the announcement in private and urging the Dublin district committee to keep an open mind on this latest tentative attempt at politicisation of the IRA.[56] MacBride's support for the striking bus and tramway workers was enough for Murray to forgive the antics of his men at Bodenstown, though he was still 'bitterly disliked by Congress supporters such as George Gilmore'.[57] Although the IRA's commitment to abstentionism precluded any tangible cooperation in the sphere of constitutional politics, Murray nevertheless suggested that a republican-labour alliance contest the 1936 Dublin Corporation elections.[58] MacBride's party, Cumann Poblachta na hÉireann, failed to capture the public's imagination with its vague regurgitation of Fianna Fáil's programme of the early 1930s. Moreover, the IRA's impetuous armed campaign, which prompted de Valera to proscribe the organisation in June, continued to render cooperation distinctly uninviting for a movement that aspired to represent the Protestant working class and socialists with aversions to political violence.[59] In the event, Murray and Larkin junior withdrew from the election and the communists lent ambiguous support to Frank Ryan and George Gilmore, the Congress candidates, who left a negligible impression on the electorate.[60]

Depressed economic conditions – rising unemployment, falling living standards and high levels of emigration to Britain in particular – meant that the CPI's class-struggling activities corresponded with a shift to the left by

Labour on material if not social issues.[61] Signalling his intention to seize upon and exploit this leftism while it persisted, Murray began to identify areas of mutual concern such as the Widows and Orphans Bill, which sat at the heart of a Labour-Fianna Fáil agreement in September 1933. In *The Irish Revolt: 1916 and After*, a Connollyist critique of the national revolution and its outcomes, he made nostalgic references to 'the uprise [sic] of the modern Trade Union movement' in 1907 (the arrival of Larkin in Belfast) and 'the joining of the forces of [political] Socialism and industrial labour'. Significantly, he encouraged moves toward a 'united Labour movement joined to all that is virile in the national cause'.[62] After the *Irish Times* attacked the Labour Party's break with Fianna Fáil and adoption of socialist republican rhetoric, Murray came to its defence: 'It is sincerely hoped that all that the "Irish Times" fears about the future course of Labour Policy will be justified!'[63] The problem was that this rhetoric had its limits and the Labour leadership remained hostile to any formal association with communism. When, after much deliberation, the CPI decided to support Labour Party candidates in the local Dublin elections, the latter responded with a statement denying any connection between the two parties.[64] Catholic anti-communism and the legacy of left sectarianism continued to weigh heavily on the Labour leadership.

Clerical opposition to the continued presence of the CPI in Dublin manifested itself at a public meeting in January 1936, which the CPI and Republican Congress had arranged for the visit of Harry Pollitt. After the Catholic Young Mens' Society (CYMS) disrupted Pollitt's address, Murray and Seán Nolan wrote to the *Irish Independent* to question whether the activities of a Catholic mob brandishing weapons could be reconciled with the fundamental principles of Christianity and to berate John A. Costello, a prominent Fine Gael TD and Blueshirt supporter, for attempting to make light of the attack.[65] When the Church issued its Lenten pastorals, containing all the familiar denunciations of communism and left republicanism, the *Irish Workers' Voice* responded in kind by quoting prominent members of the clergy to suggest that they were 'Against Everybody But Empire'.[66] CYMS attacks on the party continued, including at a parade to Glasnevin, where the IRA failed to intervene. These events then culminated in a particularly violent encounter on Easter Monday night, when a crowd of around 5,000 gathered at College Green to prevent William Gallacher from addressing a CPI-organised rally. In the absence of a platform, Peadar O'Donnell climbed a lamppost and attempted to address the crowd from a safe distance, but was soon pelted with bottles and other missiles, including a potato with razor blades inserted into it. He was taken into police custody for his own safety, while the hostile crowd wrecked the premises of the Republican Congress and tried to do the same to the CPI's new offices.[67] When the crowd dispersed and O'Donnell finally made it home, he found Gallacher and Murray 'with a tray in front of a blazing fire, having something to eat. And I had been dying for them down the town'.[68]

The CPI's main achievement of the period was consolidation at a low level in Dublin, with mixed fortunes in Belfast. Minutes of the party's Dublin district committee reveal that Murray inherited much of the spadework after Pat Devine's return to Britain. In the prevailing economic climate, leading national communist figures struggled to fulfil their party duties. Jim Prendergast, who would soon depart to fight with the International Brigades in Spain, briefly severed contact with the party as he contemplated emigration to England. The party launched disciplinary proceedings against Seán Nolan and Jim Larkin junior, both members of the CPI central committee, for missing consecutive meetings, with the latter explaining that circumstances had forced him to work long and difficult hours. On the occasions that members were absent from meetings, Murray invariably visited their homes to 'have a talk'. Not even his closest friends were exempt from the stringent disciplinary procedures put in place to rein in the worst offenders. Murray was also charged with the thankless task of trying to ensure the survival of weak party units such the York Street section, which had applied to the Dublin committee for permission to liquidate.[69] Eoghan Ó Duinnín (Eugene Downing) recalled only twenty or thirty genuine party activists in Dublin at the time.[70] In Belfast, meanwhile, the sectarian strife of mid-1935 affected the CPI negatively without engulfing it. The labour movement agreed on 'non-party' candidates for the local elections of May and June 1936, creating new possibilities for a rapprochement with the NILP.[71]

It appeared that the CPI would struggle to rouse a large section of the working class into action on the three overlapping facets of its people's front. Although the party continued to call for the release of republican prisoners such as Michael Conway, a Tipperary man sentenced to death by a military tribunal,[72] there were no clear avenues for cooperation with a marginalised organisation that was anti-establishment but remained wedded to the use of violence as a principle, not a tactic. On the subject of fascism, Catholic Ireland's natural affinity with Italy made it difficult for the Irish working class to rail against its actions in Abyssinia, which appeared to many distant from and irrelevant to the problems of home. When the *Irish Workers' Voice* ceased publication due to financial difficulties and red scare pressures on printers, Murray launched the *Worker*, a four-paged bulletin whose purpose was to meet Lenin's demand that revolutionary parties issue a weekly organ. The paper focused the party's gaze on trade union matters as a means of promoting broad labour unity, welcoming such moves as the decision of Dublin Trades Council to approve the affiliation of WUI members.[73] However, the CPI was on the periphery of major discussions regarding the future of the trade union movement nationally, specifically those initiated by the ITUC with the aim of achieving a more cohesive form of trade unionism. Circumstances thus denied the CPI a platform for leftist cooperation and the opportunity to assume a leadership role until the Spanish Civil War broke out in mid-July.

The Spanish Civil War

In line with traditional, grand narrative accounts of the Spanish Civil War and Moscow's response to it, two historians of Irish communism hold that Murray performed a volte-face on Spain in accordance with Comintern support for the Spanish bourgeois-democratic government.[74] It is unarguable that Murray shoehorned a rather crude class-based analysis into his reflections on the generals' coup, mainly because the commercial and particularly the landowning class provided a backbone for right nationalism, because there were obvious qualitative similarities between the social relations pertaining in Spain and Ireland, and because of the similar role adopted by the conservative media in both countries. Reports of growing industrial unrest in places such as Málaga, documented in letters to Murray, encouraged his belief in the revolutionary potential of the conflict. These views were reflected in the *Worker*, which continued to relate events in 'Madrid and Barcelona (the Dublin and Belfast of Spain)' to the struggles of the Irish working class throughout 1936.[75]

Consistent with the CPI's class-struggling activities, Murray claimed that Franco's rebellion represented 'a conspiracy of militarists, landlords and bankers', an 'uprising of the rich against the poor', but he also recognised that the working class, peasantry and middle classes all had a stake in protecting bourgeois democracy.[76] It would, therefore, be a mistake to regard his analysis as reductive. Rather, the importance of safeguarding the gains of the French, not the Bolshevik, Revolution would gain prominence in parallel with the escalation of the Spanish conflict and the growing strength of anti-democratic forces. Furthermore, the chronology and content of Murray's earliest intervention suggests two things: that domestic politics had a significant bearing on his assessment; and that he anticipated the decision of Stalin, the CPSU politburo and the ECCI to begin providing the Spanish Republic with arms, advisors, military personnel and logistical support in late September. On 10 August, the day that Eoin O'Duffy used the *Irish Independent* to announce the formation of an Irish Brigade to assist Franco, Murray responded with an appeal for Irish workers to rally to the cause of the Spanish government. In a speech worth reproducing at some length, Murray also gave a strong indication that he would sponsor the use of force to counter fascism at home and abroad:

> I warn the workers not to be misled into believing that this [is] a religious issue in Spain. It is no more a religious issue than was the Irish Land War, the struggle for Home Rule, the fight for complete independence, but what did the aristocracy of this country say the fight was about? Religion of course!
>
> O'Duffy and Lombard Murphy and other kindred spirits are calling for Irishmen to go and join this army of ruffians! Was there ever such a combination of hypocrites and traitors! But the Irish people who have seen these gentlemen at work in their own country, have seen their country partitioned by the introduction of religious issues into politics, and seen the Republic of Ireland betrayed by these supporters of Franco and his Riff [sic] army will not be deceived into throwing their lot against the Spanish people.
>
> The gallant Spanish people are not only fighting against the traitors within Spain but against the enemies of liberty throughout all Europe, Ireland included. This makes the Spanish question indeed a question for the friends of freedom in every land. Are we in Ireland to stand aside and allow this crime against the people of Spain to be carried out before our eyes? If we did, we would be traitors to the best traditions of our race, to the men who gave their lives for the cause of freedom in this country. What would Wolfe Tone, John Mitchel, or James Connolly and Pearse say if they could speak to us to-day! They would be behind their brother Republicans in the Spanish fight. They would be against the Murphys, the Churchills and O'Duffys. They would have nothing but contempt for the treason to Republicanism of de Valera and his newspaper [the *Irish Press*], who are also behind the criminal Fascist gang in Spain.
>
> I ask every Irish man and woman to answer the question. What are you doing? Have you raised your voice on the side of the heroic Spanish people?

Have you protested against the shameful attitude of de Valera's newspaper, against the foul campaign of Murphy's bloodstained 'Independent', against the criminal attempt of the Fascist O'Duffy to raise a brigade of Irishmen to attack the Spanish Republic? It is the sacred duty of every man and woman in their trade unions and political parties, to demand that their leaders give the people a lead in support of justice. We must demand that a United Front of Labour and Republicanism be formed in this country in support of the Spanish people and that financial assistance be organised for the sufferers of this Fascist rebellion. By doing so we will be a step forward to the social and national emancipation of our own nation, to the smashing of coercion, the opening of the jails and the clearing away of would-be Fascists in both Northern and Southern Ireland.[77]

Whilst it is important to exercise caution in interpreting Murray's words, it is significant that Robert Stradling, an historian of Irish involvement in the Spanish Civil War, argues that the speech pre-empted the initiative launched by the French Communist Party (Parti Communiste Français) (PCF), 'the germinal action of the International Brigades'.[78] Furthermore, his use of distinctly Irish reference points for republicanism, and his strong focus on the continuing struggle against the forces that subverted the revolutionary upsurge of 1909-23, both challenge the monocausal, Moscow-inspired explanation for his response to the onset of the Spanish Civil War.[79]

Over the summer months, events in Spain increasingly shaped the nature of relations between the Irish left and right. In August, the Fine Gael TD, Paddy Belton, founded the Irish Christian Front (ICF) to drum up support for Franco, while the *Irish Independent* reprised its role as a leading purveyor of hyperbolic anti-communism. The clergy supported an ICF fundraising effort that raised over £43,000 for 'suffering Catholics' in Spain and Cardinal Joseph MacRory liaised with a Spanish aristocrat to prepare the ground for the arrival of O'Duffy's Irish Brigade.[80] Murray's public attacks on Francoist elements served to retain the gaze of conservative Ireland on his activities. *Irish Independent* readers provided a glimpse of the hostility he could expect to face on the streets. In a letter to the editor, 'One of the old columns' wrote:

Will you tell me who is Sean Murray, anyhow? What did he do during 1920 and 1921 against the British Empire in this country? Let him give his national record. If he is so fond of the Spanish Government why doesn't he go out to Spain and fight for them, and (good riddance) bring his 'Dublin Communists' with him?[81]

Another, 'An Irish priest', speculated on his mass attendance and observation of the sacraments, and encouraged him to 'join the Orangemen' of the North or to form a 'Brigade for Degenerate Irishmen' with Peadar O'Donnell.[82] Francis Noone of the ICF and 'League of the Crusaders' recalled listening to Murray, 'one of those misguided (willingly or otherwise) instruments utilised by Stalin', and argued that 'a battalion of St. Patricks will be needed to get rid of the poisonous vipers who are attempting to instill the venom of class hatred and anti-God into the minds of the Irish workers and workless'.[83] Even the mainstream press came under immense pressure to adopt a more compliant anti-communist line, with one senior member of the clergy condemning the *Irish Times* for daring to recognise the legitimacy of the Spanish government and therefore placing itself in the 'strange company' of Murray and O'Donnell.[84] It followed that the focus on Murray's activities would only intensify and, indeed, at an ICF meeting on 30 August, one speaker identified him as an enemy of Catholicism before encouraging the 15,000 people in attendance to be vigilant about his movements.[85] In response, the Young Communist League, operating under the auspices of the Kevin Barry Youth Movement and wearing uniforms composed of a green shirt with a shamrock embroidered on the collar and flannel pants, would be mobilised, drilled and, with members of Na Fianna Éireann, encouraged to disrupt ICF and Fine Gael public meetings.[86]

One Irishman who went to Spain was Bill Scott, a twenty-eight year old Dublin bricklayer and CPI member. Having made his way to Catalonia via London, where he had been searching for work, Scott was, by September, fighting with the Tom Mann Centuria, a unit which later joined with the Thälmann Battalion of the XII International Brigade.[87] Scott was, by all accounts, the first Irishman to enlist in defence of the Spanish Republic and, in a moving letter to Murray in November, he stressed the urgency of others following suit: 'Victory is certain if Irishmen will follow the lesson of their Spanish brothers and sisters who are standing solid in the trenches beating back the might of the fascist states of Europe.'[88] The first organised group of International Brigade volunteers, the majority former IRA men, left Ireland on 11 December under the command of Frank Ryan. Peadar O'Donnell had been caught up in the action whilst holidaying in Spain and agreed with Ryan that the CPI/Republican

Congress ought to commit no more than 145 of its members.[89] According to the most recent estimate, at least 263 volunteers of Irish descent served in the fight against Franco and/or lent their support to the social revolution that had broken out in pockets of Spain.[90] Many had radical Irish republican, socialist or trade unionist backgrounds.[91] O'Duffy's Irish Brigade was 800-strong and vastly outnumbered volunteers on the Republican side, but returned to Ireland in June 1937 in disgrace, plagued by reports of drunkenness, indiscipline and internal divisions.[92] Brendan Behan famously quipped that O'Duffy's army 'achieved the remarkable military feat of coming home with more men than they went out with'.[93] By contrast, members of the International Brigades rarely made their way home without having completed 'a reasonable tour of duty'.[94]

The Marxist historian, Eric Hobsbawm, has rightly claimed that 'the wrong side won' the Spanish conflict, a defeat compounded by the loss of some of the Irish and international Left's biggest and brightest talents to the war. But it is precisely 'due to the intellectuals, the artists and the writers who mobilized so overwhelmingly in favour of the republic, that in this instance history has not been written by the victors'.[95] Orwell's *Homage to Catalonia*, Hemingway's *For Whom the Bell Tolls*, Picasso's *Guernica*, Auden's poem 'Spain 1937', Loach's *Land and Freedom*, Alex McDade and Woody Guthrie's song 'Jarama Valley', and, from an Irish perspective, Christy Moore's 'Viva la Quinta Brigada', have ensured that 'in creating the world's memory of the Spanish Civil War, the pen, the brush and the camera wielded on behalf of the defeated have proved mightier than the sword and the power of those who won'.[96]

Although Murray did not volunteer to fight in Spain and risk suffering the same fate as Charlie Donnelly, the Dungannon poet killed in action in 1937, his role in coordinating efforts on the home front is grossly understated in existing studies of the Civil War. It is important to note that the Irish communists had a disproportionate influence on the composition of the Connolly Column, a position of authority borne out by their international ties. Jack MacGougan, the NISP leader, recalled that the CPI had a 'monopoly' on the recruitment and vetting of volunteers,[97] and it appears that Murray shared this responsibility with Bill Gannon, who had joined the CPI after a long and controversial career with the IRA and after gradually moving left.[98] A stack of letters in the possession of Desmond Greaves' literary executor, Anthony Coughlan, handed down by Murray's wife and Gannon's sister, Margaret, reveal the full import and extent of his responsibilities. Liaising closely with Frank Ryan for the duration of the war, Murray determined the order in which volunteers would travel to Spain, if at all; arranged the delivery of parcels, letters and telegrams; shared news with Harry Pollitt, his counterpart in London; dealt with unruly or problematic volunteers; and visited friends and relatives with news from the front. He received gruesome reports of Nationalist atrocities, including the murder of women and children, of the massive aerial bombardment endured by the volunteers during the Battle of the Ebro, and of the injuries suffered by those he counted as comrades. Most difficult perhaps was the task of relaying the news of deaths to the friends, families and comrades of those killed in action. According to the letters in Greaves' private papers, those published in the *Worker*, and others held by independent researchers, Murray was the first in Ireland to learn of the deaths of William Laughran, James Hillen, William Beattie, Ben Murray (all of Belfast), Kit Conway (Tipperary), Mick Kelly (Ballinasloe), Jack Nalty and Tommy Woods (Dublin), Jim Woulfe (Limerick), Frank O'Brien (Dundalk), David Walshe (Ballina), Maurice Quinlan (Waterford) and Paddy Glacken (Donegal). Although these particular letters were matter-of-fact in tone, their contents were bound to have had a lasting emotional impact on Murray and the people surrounding him.

Cognisant of the likelihood that he was sending comrades to their deaths, Murray ensured that the earliest vetting procedures took into account the age, physical and mental health of volunteers as well their military training, political acumen and importance to the working-class movement at home. The main consideration of age led him to turn away an enthusiastic twenty-one year old by the name of Bob Doyle, who responded by travelling to London and persuading Harry Pollitt to acquiesce in his request to join the International Brigades.[99] Tommy Woods, another young man from Dublin, followed a similar path after being rejected by Murray for the same reason, but unlike Doyle would not make the return journey.[100] Other CPI activists simply lied about their ages, so strong was their internationalism, their determination to assist comrades in defence of the Spanish Republic. Of the first four to volunteer for service in April 1938, all involved with the liberal socialist New Theatre Group, only two secured the approval of their general secretary. Alec Digges and the poet, Tom O'Brien, travelled to Spain, while Murray explained to Bill Clare and the playwright, Seán O hEidirsceoil, that they would serve the campaign and the party better in Dublin.[101] This mirrored the concerns O'Donnell, Ryan and Gilmore had about the future of the Republican Congress.[102]

However, as the war intensified and volunteers steadily made their way to Spain in contravention of the international Non-Intervention Agreement, an enthusiastic commitment to defend the Spanish Republican government superseded these reservations. Eoghan Ó Duinnín's fears about being refused the opportunity to fight in March 1938 were quickly dispelled as Murray performed only a rudimentary eye test before sending him on his way.[103] Nineteen-year-old Michael O'Riordan had a similar experience, finding nothing particularly exhaustive about the screening and briefing he received before setting sail for Spain.[104] This relaxation of the vetting process suggests that Murray decided to take more seriously his obligation to those party members who had already travelled undaunted by the prospect of death in Spain. He also recognised that the Spanish conflict resonated with people at home and contained some potential for bringing about a reversal of the CPI's poor fortunes. While the party lost a number of members on the battle-front, other dormant activists were brought 'back from the dead' politically after the conflict stirred their instincts of solidarity and progressive struggle.[105] It is difficult to establish the number of new recruits to the party or for how long they were retained; however, it is clear from Special Branch reports that there was a steady flow of additions to the membership roll. It is significant that someone like Paddy Byrne, Republican Congress secretary, was brought into the party's ranks at the height of the war.[106]

Murray's importance to the Irish International Brigaders is further borne out by his influence on them before, throughout and in the aftermath of the Spanish Civil War. Incited by the Lenten pastoral read at Dublin Pro-Cathedral, Bob Doyle was part of the first mob that attacked Connolly House in March 1933. After discovering to his horror that the CPI headquarters had been set alight, he paid a visit to Murray, 'an outstanding public speaker and socialist', at his makeshift office. In what turned out to be a turning point in his political journey, Doyle enquired about the work of the CPI, asking Murray to clarify his position on religion and offering the party his services and that of his gun in clashes with the Blueshirts. In response to the first question, Murray cited the example of Fr Michael O'Flanagan, a devoted anti-fascist campaigner and former Sinn Féin vice-president. To the second, he pointed out the need to organise first, and that: 'When the time comes to use arms we will have the workers trained.'[107] Doyle would later join the CPGB, even standing for election. A postcard sent to Murray during one of his many trips back to Spain, dated 18 September 1960, shows that the CPI leader was never far from his thoughts.[108]

Other recollections of Murray's influence extend as far back as childhood. Peter O'Connor, an International Brigader from Waterford, remembered him as a family friend and regular visitor to the O'Connor household. He acknowledges Murray as a formative political influence and the person who taught him 'to distinguish when reading the capitalist press or listening to the radio, the distorted views they project on trade union or working-class activities'.[109] Michael O'Riordan credited Murray with countering the 'hysterical support' for Franco in the Irish media, the Catholic Church and in Leinster House. Through his articles in the *Worker* alone, he 'gave a clear analysis of what was happening in Spain' and enabled Irish anti-fascists to stand firm.[110] His efforts also won the admiration of Jim Prendergast, who grew closer to Murray upon returning to his CPI post in Dublin and continued to correspond after moving to London. As a political educator, organiser, agitator, and propagandist, Murray's contribution on the home front was as valuable as if had been in the trenches of the International Brigades.

It would be wrong to valorise Murray's role in promoting left unity, particularly after examining his infantile attempts to justify the farcical Moscow Show Trials, which saw Bukharin, Zinoviev, Kamenev and several other Bolshevik luminaries charged with subversion and sentenced to death, and many other Comintern functionaries imprisoned in a paranoia-fuelled wave of Stalinist terror.[111] Uncritically sectarian and deferential to the Stalinist practices carried out in the name of protecting the Soviet Union from the exaggerated threats of foreign interventions, Murray described Trotsky as 'a man without principle' who had betrayed the proletariat with his theory of permanent revolution. Adopting a reformist, 'stageist' conception of the Spanish Civil War, involving the restraint of revolutionary impulses, was a legitimate position to hold. Put simply, this argument ran: first win the war and consolidate democracy, then talk about revolution. It was something else altogether to claim, as Murray did at an open branch meeting in February 1937, that Trotsky's faction was acting in direct alliance with fascism and that Lenin had allowed him 'to continue his anti-revolutionary activities when it would have served the interests of the working class of the world to put him to death'. He implied along with this that the deaths of Zinoviev and Kamenev, and the imprisonment of Radek, were justified.[112] The *Worker* publicly repeated these denunciations of 'the despicable Trotsky and his terrorist groups', which certainly sat uncomfortably with the party's attempts to court the quasi-Trotskyist NISP into an anti-fascist coalition.[113]

In spite of these left sectarian relapses, Murray informed Bill Scott with optimism that the tide had begun to change in favour of an anti-fascist front at home.[114] And something of an ad hoc popular front had transpired with the formation of various broad left groups in late 1936. These included a Dublin offshoot of the London-based Left Book Club, founded by Owen Sheehy Skeffington; the New Theatre Group and its Belfast equivalent, the Theatre Guild; the Irish Friends of the Spanish Republic; and Hanna Sheehy Skeffington's Women's Aid Committee. Murray played a pivotal role in their formation and in bringing their various expressions of progressive politics together under the one banner.[115] This very distinctive form of popular frontism, which lacked formal political expression and the support of mainstream bourgeois parties in the European sense of the term, was nonetheless reinforced on 27 March 1937 with the launch of the *Irish Democrat*, an inclusive, pro-Republican newspaper sponsored by the CPI, Republican Congress, NISP, NILP and an eclectic mix of bourgeois-liberal and socialist activists and intellectuals. Murray had seconded the resolution that conceived the *Democrat* and he shared editorial duties with Seán Nolan and Frank Ryan, who continued to write for the paper and scrutinise its editorial line from Spain.[116] Frequently abrupt and brutally honest, one letter to Murray merely said of the paper: 'Editing O.K. Printing a disgrace!!!!!!'[117]

Although contact between Moscow and Dublin had slackened, reflecting the Comintern's growing indifference to the domestic affairs of peripheral parties, its growing subordination to Stalin and the state interests of the Soviet Union led to a paradoxical interest in how the CPI interpreted the Spanish Popular Front. A policy document sent to Ireland in May thus confirmed the ECCI's retrospective endorsement of the measures taken by the Irish party to extend cooperation to 'known and proved types'.[118] The Republican Congress was the CPI's foremost ally and, despite superficial differences on matters such as religion, the shared experiences of the Irish revolutionary period and clashes with the Blueshirts 'inspired in the two groups an identical loathing' of O'Duffy and his supporters.[119] Murray's political activities overlapped with those of the Republican Congress leadership in these two important regards. Furthermore, his quite liberal attitude on the issue of private faith enabled him to share platforms and form a close bond with Fr O'Flanagan. He also helped George Gilmore to arrange the visit of Fr Ramón Laborda, a Basque nationalist and Spanish Republican supporter who assisted the *Irish Democrat* coalition in dispelling some of the myths perpetuated by the conservative media and in challenging perceptions of the Spanish Civil War as a conflict between Christianity and atheism.[120]

Gaining the widespread approval of leading Labour Party figures was a far more challenging proposition. Roddy Connolly offered his customary support, while Nora Connolly O'Brien and Michael Price put aside their differences with Murray for the benefit of the alliance that had been built up around the *Irish Democrat*. However, under William Norton's direction, the Labour Party appeared to listen deferentially to its sizeable Catholic constituency, particularly in rural areas. Spain did not figure prominently on the agenda of the party's annual conference and, worse still, the presence of Labour TD, Michael Keyes, at ICF rallies proved no obvious source of embarrassment for conference delegates. Norton preferred to concentrate on drawing parallels between fascism and communism, advancing an early version of the horseshoe theory[121] and missing the point that the Spanish Civil War was fundamentally a struggle between fascism and democracy. Norton wanted no truck with communists and went to great lengths to make that clear, even going as far as to reprimand the Catholic press for linking his party to the CPI.[122]

By contrast, Harry Midgley made a distinction between communism and fascism, characterising the former as essentially good in its aims, if not its methods, and the latter as essentially evil because it represented, among other things, an extreme manifestation of capitalism. And unlike Norton, he understood that what was at stake in Spain was the survival and consolidation of democracy. Midgley's position was complicated by his anti-Catholic sentiments, his open hostility to anti-partitionist politics, close proximity to members of the Orange Order and Unionist Party, and his volatile relationship with the CPI.[123] However, as Connal Parr has cogently argued, Midgley deserves the benefit of the doubt for taking a heroic stand in the face of *Irish News* propaganda, clashes with the Catholic Church and the incitement of nationalist politicians.[124] Despite these problems, he had little difficulty with associating his support for the Spanish Republic with the *Irish Democrat* group and, by extension, the CPI, working closely with Billy McCullough and Betty Sinclair in Belfast. The *Worker* stated that it was 'to his everlasting credit' that he had intervened on the Republican side;[125] Murray and Nolan, in the pages of the *Democrat*, dispensed with their earlier criticisms of the NILP leader in favour of comradely nudges in the direction of labour unity.

Murray discerned the growing polarisation of Irish opinion on Spain in terms of left and right wings 'embracing all organisations'.[126] Yet the compromise reached in support of the Spanish government failed to suppress existing political tensions on issues of domestic and international importance. On 28 March, only a day after the launch of the *Irish Democrat*, a special meeting convened at Peadar O'Donnell's house on the Drumcondra Road to deal with the content of the first issue. With the support of Tommy Watters, representing the CPI's Belfast group, the three NISP representatives objected to the amount of space devoted to Irish republicanism and argued with some justification that this would damage the paper's standing with northern workers. Indeed, plastered across the front page of the first issue was the headline 'Ireland Honours Patriot Dead of 1916'. It was decided at the meeting, which Murray and Ryan attended, that the paper would be treated as a workers' organ and would only pay attention to Irish republican struggles insofar as they concerned working-class politics or the united front against fascism.[127]

Rather than drop its focus on republican struggles, past and present, the *Democrat* attempted to balance reports about Armistice Day protests and anti-imperialist activities with others on the builders' strikes in Dublin and Cork and the grievances of transport workers in Belfast. The support given to the striking workers by republicans associated with the International Brigades made it difficult for Murray and Nolan to separate those issues. In fact, according to the criteria agreed by the disaffected elements within the *Democrat* coalition, these were precisely the types of campaigns that merited coverage. The editors gave the Belfast communists and NISP representatives considerable column space to discuss the pressing concerns of northern workers and to mount a defence against *Irish News* propaganda. Murray even chipped in with stinging criticisms of de Valera's constitution, which, he suggested, failed to reassure the workers in the north-east of their place in a democratic united Ireland.[128]

It was no secret that Murray's ideological sympathies lay with socialist republicanism and the establishment of a thirty-two county workers' republic. Privately, in a letter to Moscow in January 1938, he noted the NISP's 'growing estrangement' from the *Democrat* group and complained that in stating their objections to the paper's republican content the Socialists 'want it to cater for the Protestant workers exclusively'.[129] This echoed Frank Ryan's view that considerable energy had been expended in placating the NISP and its leader Victor Halley, a staunch opponent of the IRA, with little benefit to the movement.[130] And yet the evidence suggests that Murray was more diplomatic in his approach than Ryan, who placed the CPI leader under immense pressure to publish more republican and deliberately green articles. Ryan's persistence on the matter is evident from a series of letters written to Murray towards the end of 1937. 'The balance in the "Democrat" between you and me isn't very well preserved these times,' one letter reads. 'I have impressed upon Peadar the necessity for him contributing. Try and get him out of his lazy fit, in order to give more of a "native" twang to the paper!!!'[131] Although we are not privy to the other side of this exchange, it is easy to detect Ryan's growing frustration that Murray disagrees with his approach. Thus a subsequent letter is more direct and the tone ill-tempered:

> As for your failure to preserve 'balance' in the paper (which you quite airily dismiss in your letter to me) Gerald O'Reilly also comments on it, so do sit up and take notice. The way I read it is – you are just slapping the paper together, and in doing so showing how you have no deep roots among your own people ... Just at this stage when Mrs [Kathleen] Clarke is wearing more vivid green than Dev. you should always be harping on the real issues of the separatist struggle. You should always be insisting (and in your role as a dyed in the wool Republican) that the Mrs Clarkes and the Mary Macs as well as the Devs. have betrayed the struggle. Despite any murmurs (loud or low) from Belfast you should be doing this. And what about 'Antrim and Down in '98', the fighting parsons and so forth? Couldn't you get those in?[132]

If we inspect the editorial line of the *Irish Democrat* in light of Ryan's pressure on Murray, it is difficult to conclude that northern concerns did not factor into the equation or that the NISP was not accommodated.

More intractable perhaps were the ideological and strategic differences accentuated by events in Spain. Specifically, the primacy of revolution advanced by the anti-Stalinist POUM (Partido Obrero de Unificación Marxista/Workers' Party of Marxist Unification), with which the NISP was most closely aligned, collided bloodily with the communists' emphasis on protecting Spanish bourgeois democracy and the national security of the Soviet Union. In this regard, the CPI was not immune to the Stalinisation of the Comintern and its affiliated parties.[133] The context of the May Days upheaval in Catalonia, which saw the Popular Front government and its supporters clash with the radical left in an attempt to centralise the war effort, exacerbating divisions within the Republican camp, is helpful in explaining the NISP's absence from a July meeting of *Irish Democrat* affiliates. Whereas the NISP supported efforts to trigger a social revolution away from the trenches, the CPI position sketched out by Murray was that the POUM and the anarchist CNT (Confederación Nacional del Trabajo/National Confederation of Labour) were 'Trotskyite agent provocateurs' bent on destroying Spanish democracy.[134] In a similar vein, Frank Ryan wrote divisive articles describing the POUM as a 'fascist force in the rear' and took to referring disparagingly to 'Peadar's friends (the Anarchists)' in a September 1937 letter to Murray.[135] Although O'Donnell had worked closely with the POUM and anarchists during his time in Spain, he ultimately fell in behind the communist position.[135] These views lent themselves to a justification of the 'overly zealous' methods used to contain revolutionary activity, including the murderous actions of Stalin's security organs in Spain.[136] For their part, Murray and Ryan's dismissal of the POUM's socialist politics exposed a degree of immaturity. And however abstract it may have seemed, the CPI was needlessly party to what one author with communist sympathies has described as the 'savage victimisation of POUM' and its allies.[137]

Political tensions, poor sales and financial difficulties would result in the *Irish Democrat*'s expiration in December 1937, while the coalition built around it gradually lost the active support of its original affiliates. But even before those divisions became apparent, the Comintern had commented on the 'exceptional weakness of the Communist Party in membership, activity, and leadership'.[138] A May Day meeting in Moscow between Frank Mooney, the new Dublin CPI chairman, and André Marty, the Comintern's representative on Irish affairs, confirmed that the Irish popular front would now involve tactical cooperation with Fianna Fáil in order to combat the ICF and obstruct Fine Gael's electoral progress. In fact, this had been the case for some time, though it went largely unspoken and resulted in no formal alliance between the parties. More significantly, the ECCI subjected Mooney to extensive questioning on the CPI leadership, speculating that the party's lack of success reflected Murray's poor performance. One major failing was that Murray had once again ceased to forward reports to the ECCI, while contact from Dublin had hitherto been 'very unsatisfactory'. Among the questions posed about Murray's overall conduct, Mooney was asked to explain why the CPI general secretary was residing with Mrs Esther McGregor, a party member whose son Liam had attended the Lenin School and would eventually die fighting with the International Brigades in Spain. Marty concluded by informing Mooney that he took seriously reports from Pat Devine and Harry Pollitt that it would be a waste to invest financially in the CPI as long as Murray remained general secretary.[139]

Historically, the CPGB leadership's understanding of the immense challenges facing the CPI was deficient. With no appreciation for the energy-sapping work carried out by Murray to ensure the survival of the Dublin branch alone, Marty accepted the CPGB's conclusion that Ireland was not 'such a difficult proposition as Murray would have them believe'. Consequently, the ECCI sanctioned a commission of inquiry to investigate the CPI's progress under Murray, which suggests that Mooney did not see fit to correct its one-eyed interpretation of events on the ground. It was arranged for Murray and Mooney to face Pollitt, Devine and Harry Shiels in London on 10 June, and for all five to report to Moscow in August with the findings. All these factors, combined with Pollitt's discernible hostility to Murray, strongly suggest that the latter's working relationship with the Comintern had run its course and that a CPGB-orchestrated leadership coup was in the offing. Garda Special Branch noted that a change of leadership was 'practically certain' unless the inquiry produced outcomes to the immediate satisfaction of the CPGB and ECCI.[140]

One contributory factor to Murray's weakened position was the handling of July's general election campaign, which brought underlying CPI/Republican Congress tensions to the surface. Following the CPI's nomination of Bill Scott as a 'Left Wing' candidate and the production of an election manifesto, which Murray endorsed, the *Irish Democrat* came out in favour of running Frank Ryan in an effort to win the support of all republicans, democrats and anti-fascists. A CPI statement announced that it would withdraw Scott 'in order that the whole forces of the workers movement may be concentrated' towards the end of returning candidates standing on 'working class and democratic principles'.[141] In fact, party members continued to support Scott's candidacy and it was only because Murray failed to secure an advance of £100 from the CPGB for an election deposit that it could not go ahead. This was due to Murray's refusal to attend the commission of inquiry into his leadership on 10 June. Taking Pollitt's response to this as an affront, he also refused to attend the rescheduled inquiry on 24 June. Undoubtedly, this damaged his already fractured relationship with Pollitt, the CPGB and Comintern.[142]

Internally, there remained questions to be answered about Scott's withdrawal from the election and Murray's handling of it. Frank Mooney boycotted one meeting in protest, at which the CPI leader claimed that the decision came down to the failure to raise the necessary deposit. However, suspicions that Murray had not made an honest effort to push Scott's candidacy were strengthened after party members learned of a long conversation between Murray and O'Donnell on the night prior to Ryan's selection. At a special gathering of the party membership on 23 June, Murray's attempt to clarify the situation was interrupted with cries of 'get out' and 'who runs this party – is it Peadar O'Donnell'. Once calm had been restored to the meeting, Murray assured those in attendance that a full and frank discussion would follow the election. Although his account of the O'Donnell meeting as one to agree a contingency plan had proved entirely unconvincing, he managed to secure widespread support for Ryan's campaign, including the establishment of an election committee and cooperation with the Republican Congress, and stave off the immediate threat of an internal revolt in the process.[143]

Following a period of rest in Dublin, Frank Ryan had returned to Spain and knew little about his selection. At most of the snap campaign meetings held in South Dublin, speakers including O'Donnell, George Gilmore and Cora Hughes of the Congress, and Frank Mooney and Paddy Byrne of the CPI, were attacked by hostile crowds.[144] In the event, the IRA boycotted the election and Ryan received only 875 votes, losing his deposit.[145] By March 1938, just prior to his capture in Spain by Italians allied to Franco, Ryan was expressing to Murray his dissatisfaction that he had been 'left so much out in the cold' concerning the collapse of the *Democrat* coalition.[146] The Spanish Civil War had provided the CPI with a policy lifeline and the Irish left with a unique opportunity to promote the broadest form of cooperation on a single issue. While the *Democrat* group would continue to mobilise under the auspices of the Frank Ryan Release Committee from 1938 onwards, there was little doubt that, as the death of the Spanish Republic grew imminent and as de Valera dealt swiftly and effectively with the threat of Fine Gael, the prospects for maintaining a semblance of left unity would become significantly diminished. With the decline of Moscow's active interest in Ireland, Stalin's Soviet Union would become more a reference point than a direct source of practical support for the CPI. Organised socialist republicanism, meanwhile, would lie 'dormant for a generation'.[147] And while Murray had survived the period without a major revolt against his leadership, his political career now stood on shaky ground.

NOTES

1   Ernest Hemingway, *For Whom the Bell Tolls* [1940] (London, 2004), p.295.
2   Niamh Puirséil, *The Irish Labour Party, 1922-73* (Dublin, 2007), p.54.
3   Mike Milotte, *Communism in Modern Ireland: The Pursuit of the Workers' Republic since 1916*, pp.158-9.
4   Donal Ó Drisceoil, *Peadar O'Donnell* (Cork, 2001), p.90; Michael O'Riordan, *Connolly Column: The Story of the Irishmen who Fought in the Ranks of the International Brigades in the National-Revolutionary War of the Spanish People, 1936-39* (Dublin, 1979), pp.25-6.
5   Mike Cronin, 'The Blueshirts in the Irish Free State: The nature of socialist republican and government opposition', in Tim Kirk and Anthony McElligot (eds), *Opposing Fascism: Community, authority and resistance* (Cambridge, 1999).
6   Seán Cronin, *Frank Ryan: The Search for the Republic* (Dublin, 1980), p.66.
7   RGASPI, 495/89/94/56-64, Anglo-American secretariat directive to Ireland, 14 October 1934.
8   RGASPI, 495/4/318/8-11, Letter to the CP Ireland re Republican Congress, 16 November 1934.
9   RGASPI, 495/96/97-102, CPI circular, 1 December 1934.
10 Emmet O'Connor, *Reds and the Green: Ireland, Russia and the Communist Internationals, 1919-43* (Dublin, 2004), pp.205-6.
11 *United Ireland*, 2 December 1933.
12 James Hogan, *Could Ireland Become Communist? The Facts of the Case* (Dublin, 1935).
13 *United Ireland*, 27 January, 10 February 1934.
14 Ibid., 2 December 1933.
15 NAI, DJ, 2008/117/722, Frank Edwards file (January 1935).
16 NAI, DJ, JUS8/386, Garda Special Branch report, 29 January 1935.
17 Cronin, *Frank Ryan*, p.58.
18 Michael Farrell, *Northern Ireland: The Orange State* (2nd ed.) (London, 1980), pp.137-40; O'Connor, *Reds and the Green*, p.207.
19 *Irish Workers' Voice*, 22 June 1935.
20 Manus O'Riordan, 'Communism in Dublin in the 1930s: The Struggle Against Fascism', in H. Gustav Klaus (ed.), *Strong Words, Brave Deeds: The Poetry, Life and Times of Thomas O'Brien, Volunteer in the Spanish Civil War* (Dublin, 1994), pp.228-9.
21 PRONI, HA/32/1/552, RUC Special Branch report, 21 January 1935.
22 *Daily Worker*, 5 February 1935.
23 *Workers' Voice*, 9 February 1935.
24 *Daily Worker*, 5 February 1935.

25 RGASPI, 495/14/334/41-47, Letter from Pat Devine to Bob [McIlhone], 18 December 1934.

26 RGASPI, 495/4/318/8-11, 495/18/1059/1-25, The CPI and the Irish Republican Congress, 19 January 1935.

27 O'Connor, *Reds and the Green*, pp.205-6.

28 *Irish Workers' Voice*, 13 April 1935.

29 William Lombard Murphy inherited Dublin United Tramways Company (DUTC) and the Independent Newspaper Group from his father, William Martin Murphy, and was therefore an obvious target for the CPI during this period.

30 *Workers' Voice*, 18 May 1935.

31 Brian Hanley, *The IRA, 1926-36* (Dublin, 2002), p.55.

32 J. Bowyer Bell, *The Secret Army: The IRA* (Revised 3rd ed.) (Dublin, 1998), p.121; Brian Hanley, 'The IRA and Trade Unionism, 1922-72', in Francis Devine, Fintan Lane and Niamh Puirséil (eds), *Essays in Irish Labour History: A Festschrift for Elizabeth and John W. Boyle* (Sallins, 2008), p.166.

33 O'Connor, *Reds and the Green*, p.206.

34 See Brian Hanley, 'The Irish Citizen Army After 1916', *Saothar*, 28 (2003), pp.37-47, for an exploration of the ICA's re-emergence and subsequent immersion into mainstream labour politics.

35 Bowyer Bell, *The Secret Army: The IRA*, pp.121-2; Hanley, 'The IRA and Trade Unionism', p.166; Milotte, *Communism in Modern Ireland*, pp.160-1.

36 NAI, DJ, JUS8/195, Garda Special Branch report, 16 March 1935; JUS8/196, Garda Special Branch report, 2 April 1935.

37 Charlie McGuire, *Roddy Connolly and the Struggle for Socialism in Ireland* (Cork, 2008), p.157.

38 *Irish Press*, 28 March 1935.

39 *Irish Independent*, 30 March 1935; *Irish Times*, 30 March 1935.

40 *Workers' Voice*, 25 May 1935.

41 *Irish Workers' Voice*, 22 June 1935.

42 O'Connor, *Reds and the Green*, p.206.

43 RGASPI, 495/14/20/1-6, Seán Murray before the Anglo-American secretariat, 19 July 1935.

44 NAI, DJ, JUS8/386, Garda Special Branch report, 17 June 1935.

45 *Workers' Voice*, 8 June 1935.

46 UCDA, Seán MacEntee Papers, P67/534, Department of Justice Departmental Notes (1941); Seán Nolan (ed.), *Communist Party of Ireland Outline History* (Dublin, 1975), p.25.

47 Milotte, *Communism in Modern Ireland*, p.160.

48 RGASPI, 495/14/335/1-12, Seán Murray speech, seventh congress of the Comintern, 20 July - 20 August 1935.

49 Jane Degras (ed.), *The Communist International, 1919-1943: Documents, Vol. 3, 1929-1943* (London, 1971), pp.350-5.

50 RGASPI, 495/14/335/84-86, Proposals for the application of the united front in Ireland, 26 August 1935.

51 NAI, DJ, JUS8/386, CPI conference material, 12-13 October 1935; Garda Special Branch report, 13 October 1935; *Irish Workers' Voice*, 26 October 1935.

52 McGuire, *Roddy Connolly*, p.161.

53 NAI, DJ, JUS8/388, Garda Special Branch reports, 10 November, 22 December 1935.

54 Seán Murray, *The Irish Revolt: 1916 and After* (London, 1936), p.1.

55 Bowyer Bell, *The Secret Army*, p.125.

56 Dublin City Library and Archive (DCLA), CPI Seán Nolan/Geoffrey Palmer Collection, Box 6/015, Dublin district committee minutes, 24 September 1935.

57 Hanley, *The IRA*, p.194.

58 *Irish Press*, 24 September 1935.

59 Richard English, *Radicals and the Republic, Socialist Republicanism in the Irish Free State* (Oxford, 1994), pp. 237-45.

60 Cronin, *Frank Ryan*, p. 68; O'Connor, *Reds and the Green*, p.212.

61 Puirséil, *The Irish Labour Party*, pp.54-7.

62 Murray, *The Irish Revolt*, pp.12-14.

63 *Irish Workers' Voice*, 8 February 1936.

64 DCLA, CPI Nolan/Palmer Collection, Box 6/015, Dublin district committee minutes, 30 May 1936; Puirséil, *The Irish Labour Party*, p.58.

65 *Irish Independent*, 17 January 1936.

66 *Irish Workers' Voice*, 29 February 1936.

67 See O'Connor, *Reds and the Green*, p.212; *Irish Press*, 14 April 1936; *Irish Times*, 14 April 1936.

68 Ben Kiely interview with Peadar O'Donnell, 1983 (transcribed by the author).

69 CPI Nolan/Palmer Collection, Box 6/015, Dublin district committee minutes, 16 November 1935 - 13 June 1936.

70 Fearghal McGarry, *Irish Politics and the Spanish Civil War* (Cork, 1999), p.92.

71 Milotte, *Communism in Modern Ireland*, pp.165-6.

72 *Worker*, 25 July 1936.

73 Ibid., 11 July 1936.

74 Milotte, *Communism in Modern Ireland*, pp.171-3; Stephen Bowler, 'Seán Murray, 1898-1961, And the Pursuit of Stalinism in One Country', *Saothar*, 18 (1992), p.44.

75   *Worker*, 25 July 1936.

76   Ibid.

77   O'Riordan, *Connolly Column*, pp.32-3.

78   Robert Stradling, *The Irish in the Spanish Civil War, 1936-39: Crusades in Conflict* (Manchester, 1999), p.133.

79   McGarry, *Irish Politics and the Spanish Civil War*, pp.51-2.

80   *Irish Independent*, 31 August 1936.

81   Ibid., 18 August 1936.

82   Ibid., 20 August 1936.

83   Ibid.

84   *Irish Times*, 21 August 1936.

85   *Irish Independent*, 31 August 1936.

86   NAI, DJ, 2008/127/926, Communist activities general file (1937).

87   David Convery, 'Brigadistas: The History and Memory of Irish Anti-Fascists in the Spanish Civil War' (unpublished doctoral thesis, University College Cork, 2012), p.31.

88   C. Desmond Greaves Papers, Letter from Bill Scott to Murray, 26 November 1936.

89   Ó Drisceoil, *Peadar O'Donnell*, p.94; O'Connor, *Reds and the Green*, p.218.

90   I am obliged to David Convery for this information.

91   Convery, 'Brigadistas'; Peter O'Connor, 'Identity and Self-Representation in Irish Communism: The Connolly Column and the Spanish Civil War', *Socialist History*, Vol. 34 (2006), pp.39, 41.

92   McGarry, *Irish Politics and the Spanish Civil War*, pp.29, 42-7.

93   Brendan Behan, *Confessions of an Irish Rebel* (London, 1965), p.135.

94   O'Connor, 'Identity and Self-Representation in Irish Communism', p.42.

95   Eric Hobsbawm, 'War of ideas', *Guardian*, 17 February 2007.

96   Ibid.

97   Francis Devine, 'Letting Labour Lead: Jack MacGougan and the Pursuit of Unity, 1913-1958', *Saothar*, 14 (1989), p.122.

98   Gannon was part of Michael Collins' 'Squad' operative during the War of Independence and is widely believed to have been part of the three-man unit that assassinated Cumann na nGaedheal Justice Minister, Kevin O'Higgins in 1927.

99   McGarry, *Irish Politics and the Spanish Civil War*, p.54.

100 NAI, DJ, 2008/117/926, Garda Special Branch report, 12 January 1937.

101 Klaus (ed.), *Strong Words, Brave Deeds*, pp.19-20.

102 Adrian Hoar, *In Green and Red: The Lives of Frank Ryan* (Dingle, 2004), pp.151-2.

103 O'Connor, *Reds and the Green*, p.219.

104 Uinseann MacEoin (ed.), *The IRA in the Twilight Years, 1923-1948* (Dublin, 1997), p.756.

105 O'Connor, *Reds and the Green*, p.219.

106 NAI, DJ, 2008/117/926, Garda Special Branch report, 18 March 1937.

107 Bob Doyle (with Harry Owens), *Brigadista: An Irishman's Fight Against Fascism* (Dublin, 2006), p.33.

108 PRONI, Seán Murray Papers, D2162/M/5/32, Postcard from Doyle to Murray, 18 September 1960.

109 Peter O'Connor, *Soldier of Liberty: Recollections of a Socialist and Anti-Fascist Fighter* (Dublin, 1996), p.8.

110 O'Riordan, *Connolly Column*, p.29.

111 Kevin McDermott and Jeremy Agnew, *The Comintern: A History of International Communism from Lenin to Stalin* (Basingstoke, 1996), pp.142-57.

112 NAI, DJ, 2008/117/926, Garda Special Branch report, 11 February 1937.

113 *Worker*, 30 January, 6 February 1937.

114 C. Desmond Greaves Papers, Letter from Bill Scott to Murray, 7 February 1937.

115 O'Connor, *Reds and the Green*, pp.216-17; Andrée Sheehy Skeffington, *Skeff: A Life of Owen Sheehy Skeffington, 1909-1970* (Dublin, 1991), pp.83-4; John P. Swift, *John Swift: An Irish Dissident* (Dublin, 1991), p.102.

116 *Worker*, 13 March 1937; Cronin, *Frank Ryan*, pp.123, 130.

117 C. Desmond Greaves Papers, Letter from Frank Ryan to Murray, 27 June 1937.

118 RGASPI, 495/89/102/1-4, Proposals in connection with the Communist Party of Ireland, 8 May 1937.

119 Stradling, *The Irish in the Spanish Civil War*, pp.131-2.

120 Ibid., p.87; NAI, DJ, 2008/127/926, Communist activities general file (1937).

121 The horseshoe theory in political science asserts that, far from being at the opposite ends of the political spectrum, the far left and far right closely resemble each other almost to the point of converging, much like the ends of a horseshoe.

122 Puirséil, *The Irish Labour Party*, pp.57-61; Vincent Geoghegan, 'Cemeteries of Liberty: William Norton on Communism and Fascism' (document study), *Saothar*, 18 (1993), pp.106-9.

123 See Graham Walker, *The Politics of Frustration: Harry Midgley and the Failure of Labour in Northern Ireland* (Manchester, 1985), pp.85-113.

124 Connal Parr, *The Undefeated: Radical Protestants from the Spanish Civil War to the 1960s* (Belfast, 2014), pp.9-12.

125 *Worker*, 29 August 1936.

126 NAI, DJ, 2008/117/926, Garda Special Branch report, 23 February 1937; *Irish Democrat*, 27 March 1937.

127 NAI, DJ, 2008/117/926, Garda Special Branch report, 6 April 1937.

128 *Irish Democrat*, 8 May 1937.

129 O'Connor, *Reds and the Green*, p.223.

130 Cronin, *Frank Ryan*, pp.105-13.

131 C. Desmond Greaves Papers, Letter from Frank Ryan to Seán Murray, 2 September 1937.

132 C. Desmond Greaves Papers, Letter from Frank Ryan to Seán Murray, 26 October 1937.

133 Emmet O'Connor, 'From Bolshevism to Stalinism: Communism and the Comintern in Ireland', in Norman LaPorte, Kevin Morgan and Matthew Worley (eds), *Bolshevism, Stalinism and the Comintern: Perspectives on Stalinization, 1917-1953* (Basingstoke, 2008).

134 NAI, DJ, 2008/117/926, Garda Special Branch report, 25 May 1937.

135 Ó Drisceoil, *Peadar O'Donnell*, pp.94-100.

136 McDermott and Agnew, *The Comintern*, p.142.

137 E.H. Carr, *The Comintern and the Spanish Civil War* (Basingstoke, 1984), p.44.

138 RGASPI, 495/89/102/1-4, Proposals in connection with the Communist Party of Ireland, 8 May 1937.

139 O'Connor, *Reds and the Green*, p.220; NAI, DJ, 2008/117/926, Garda Special Branch report, 9 June 1937.

140 O'Connor, *Reds and the Green*, p.220; NAI, DJ, 2008/117/926, Garda Special Branch report, 9 June 1937.

141 *Irish Democrat*, 26 June 1937.

142 NAI, DJ, 2008/117/926, Garda Special Branch report, 21 June 1937.

143 Ibid., 28 June 1937.

144 Ibid., 5 July 1937.

145 Cronin, *Frank Ryan*, p.116.

146 C. Desmond Greaves Papers, Letter from Frank Ryan to Murray, 22 March 1938.

147 Adrian Grant, *Irish Socialist Republicanism, 1909-36* (Dublin, 2012), p.221.

1. Pupils of Glenaan National School with Master MacNamee, 1906. Murray is in the front row, standing on the right of the picture. His sisters, Kate and Mary, are also in the photo (Fionntán McElheran).

2. Members of the IRA Antrim Brigade at the Curragh Camp, Kildare, Autumn 1922 (Fionntán McElheran).

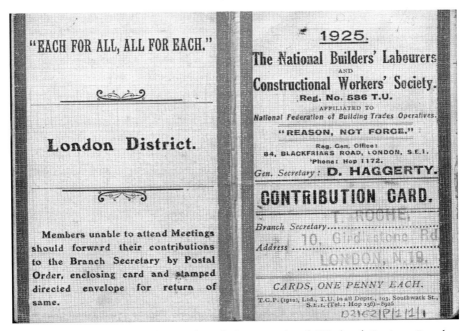

"EACH FOR ALL, ALL FOR EACH."

London District.

Members unable to attend Meetings should forward their contributions to the Branch Secretary by Postal Order, enclosing card and stamped directed envelope for return of same.

1925.

The National Builders' Labourers
AND
Constructional Workers' Society.
Reg. No. 586 T.U.
AFFILIATED TO
National Federation of Building Trades Operatives.

"REASON, NOT FORCE."

Reg. Gen. Office:
84, BLACKFRIARS ROAD, LONDON, S.E.1.
'Phone: Hop 1172.
Gen. Secretary: **D. HAGGERTY.**

CONTRIBUTION CARD.

Branch Secretary............................

Address............................

CARDS, ONE PENNY EACH.

T.C.P. (1912), Ltd., T.U. in all Depts., 103, Southwark St., S.E.1. (Tel.: Hop 156)–6925

3. National Builders', Labourers' and Constructional Workers' Society, London District branch contribution card, 1925 (CPI/PRONI).

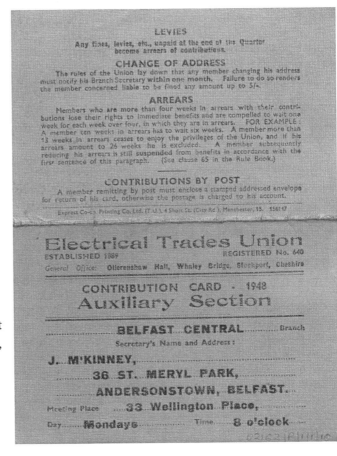

LEVIES
Any fines, levies, etc., unpaid at the end of the Quarter become arrears of contributions.

CHANGE OF ADDRESS
The rules of the Union lay down that any member changing his address must notify his Branch Secretary within one month. Failure to do so renders the member concerned liable to be fined any amount up to 5/-.

ARREARS
Members who are more than four weeks in arrears with their contributions lose their rights to immediate benefits and are compelled to wait one week for each week over four, in which they are in arrears. FOR EXAMPLE: A member ten weeks in arrears has to wait six weeks. A member more than 13 weeks in arrears ceases to enjoy the privileges of the Union, and if his arrears amount to 26 weeks he is excluded. A member subsequently reducing his arrears is still suspended from benefits in accordance with the first sentence of this paragraph. (See clause 65 in the Rule Book.)

CONTRIBUTIONS BY POST
A member remitting by post must enclose a stamped addressed envelope for return of his card, otherwise the postage is charged to his account.

Express Co-op. Printing Co. Ltd. (T.U.), 4 Short St. (City Rd.), Manchester, 15. 156117

Electrical Trades Union
ESTABLISHED 1889   REGISTERED No. 640
General Office: Ollerenshaw Hall, Whaley Bridge, Stockport, Cheshire

CONTRIBUTION CARD · 1948
Auxiliary Section

BELFAST CENTRAL   Branch
Secretary's Name and Address:

J. M'KINNEY,
36 ST. MERYL PARK,
ANDERSONSTOWN, BELFAST.

Meeting Place ...33 Wellington Place,
Day......Mondays   Time...8 o'clock

4. Electrical Trades Union, Belfast Central branch contribution card, 1948 (CPI/PRONI).

5. Seán Murray's autobiography for the Comintern, 11 August 1932 (RGASPI).

. Front page of Murray's letter to 1ingulin, a Comintern functionary, re is Russian wife, c. 1930 (RGASPI).

IReLAND'S PATh TO FReeDOM

MANIFESTO
of the
COMMUNIST PARTY
of
IRELAND

With an Introduction by
SEAN MURRAY

Price One Penny

7. *Ireland's Path to Freedom* (1933)
(Conor McCabe).

STRIKE ACTION CAN DEFEAT FASCISM

8. Irish Labour Defence League poster,
May Day 1934 (NAI, Department of
Justice, 2008/117/38).

9. Comintern profile photo (RGASPI, courtesy of Emmet O'Connor).

10. Bill Rust (CPGB and *Daily Worker*), Billy McCullough and Murray at the Hippodrome, London, for the twenty-seventh anniversary of the Bolshevik Revolution, 12 November 1944 (CPI/PRONI).

11. With Margaret outside the farmhouse at Ballybrack, 1956 (Fionntán McElheran).

12. At Nikolai Bukharin's house, Crimea, for the fortieth anniversary of the Bolshevik Revolution, 1957 (CPI/PRONI).

13. 'This is Your Life' 60th birthday celebrations at the ASW Hall, Belfast, 1958. Presentation made by Andy Barr (CPI/PRONI).

14. Visiting a factory in Bratislava, Czechoslovakia, February 1959 (CPI/PRONI).

15. Margaret Murray outside Finche's pub, London, August 1960. She is accompanied by Bill Gannon (centre left) and Jim Prendergast (centre right) (Fionntán McElheran & Jack Gannon).

16. *Irish Socialist*, June 1961 (CPI/PRONI).

17. *Ireland's Path to Socialism* (1962).

CHAPTER 4

'Pushed Upstairs'

We, the governments of Great Britain and the United States, in the name of India, Burma, Malaya, Australia, British East Africa, British Guiana, Hong Kong, Siam, Singapore, Egypt, Palestine, Canada, New Zealand, Northern Ireland, Scotland, Wales, as well as Puerto Rico, Guam, the Philippines, Hawaii, Alaska, and the Virgin Islands, hereby declare most emphatically, that this is not an imperialist war.[1]

Under the pressure of mounting constraints on his leadership, Murray threw himself back into the business of educating, organising and agitating on behalf of the CPI and its members. As well as initiating policy discussions, he somehow mustered the energy and resources to introduce the *Workers' Republic*, a short-lived 'monthly journal of left-wing opinion', in place of the *Irish Democrat*. His anti-imperialist activities grew in parallel with the disintegration of the *Democrat* coalition, while his presence alongside Maud Gonne MacBride, Cora Hughes and Peadar O'Donnell at a Liam Mellows commemoration in December 1937, though not unusual, was nonetheless symbolic of a return to socialist republicanism.[2] Anti-partitionist rhetoric, too, began to creep back into his vocabulary, for example in a pamphlet that focused on Viscount Craigavon's (James Craig) reaction to Bunreacht na hÉireann and on the Unionist government's economic policies.[3]

Whilst remaining critical of de Valera's government, Murray made a distinction between the 'popular masses within and supporting the Fianna Fáil Party' and the 'forces of the ranchers, bankers and monopolies, the sponsors of Blueshirt Fascism'. Indeed, Fianna Fáil's share of the vote in the June 1938 snap election had increased from 45.2 percent to 51.9 percent despite a fall in

Labour Party transfers, handing de Valera the first overall majority since the formation of the state. Murray acknowledged the success of the government's centre-left populist approach and therefore promoted a strong labour-republican left flank that would 'in collaboration with the Fianna Fáil backbenchers, clubs and supporters compel the Government' to fulfil its radical economic and political promises. He urged the Labour leadership to cease 'cowering before the Fascist "Red scare" propaganda of the Murphy Press' and redirect its attention to securing democratic liberties and to serving the interests of the working class.[4]

Murray pitched this contribution in the midst of yet another intervention by the CPGB, whose political bureau informed Murray and Seán Nolan that the state of the Irish party appeared 'exceptionally serious'. Positioned on the left of the debate was Rajani Palme Dutt, who had attended the Wolfe Tone Commemoration at Bodenstown as part of the CPI contingent and whose familial connection with India underlay his sympathetic, anti-colonial interpretation of the Irish national question. Whilst agreeing with Murray that the Anglo-Irish Agreement (1938) had sacrificed national unity for twenty-six county state sovereignty, his proposals for a movement against Fianna Fáil were not quite what the CPI general secretary had in mind. The analysis presented by J.R. Campbell in a brief for the Comintern, and supported by the CPGB central committee, was that Fianna Fáil could be regarded as a 'progressive, national reformist party' and that de Valera deserved credit for dismantling specific aspects of the Treaty. He complained that the CPI had not applied the line adopted at the seventh congress of the Comintern, despite 'the occasional advice given to it by the Communist Party of Great Britain', and recommended that the Irish party now seek to participate in 'a broad front of all the democratic forces to push the de Valera government to the left'. In the North, meanwhile, the Belfast branch would be encouraged to support the most progressive candidates in elections, whether green or orange, and seek to bring about reunification 'by winning a majority of people in the six counties for this purpose'.[5]

It was only because of Murray's pleas to the CPGB politburo that Harry Pollitt and William Gallacher did not see their calls for the CPI's liquidation realised. Only two weeks after securing this reprieve, the party moved quickly to consider new tactics and proposals for organisation that had emerged out of discussions with British comrades as well as internal deliberations. At a conference on 17 July, the party membership approved a number of measures to strengthen the party's numbers and influence across the island. One of the proposals agreed was the regular inspection of membership cards 'with a view to weeding out of useless and half-hearted members'. Others included the launch of a recruitment campaign, with the goal of attracting 500 new members, and the formation for the first time of a women's group, which reflected the work carried out by individuals such as Betty Sinclair, Esther McGregor and Sadie Menzies in conditions that were extremely hostile for women. Perhaps most significantly, it was decided to make it obligatory for all members to carry a trade union or Labour Party membership card, signalling an exploration of entryism as a tactic for influencing labour politics in the absence of progressive political space.[6]

While the CPI dealt with its internal affairs and worked out an independent line, some avenues to broad left cooperation remained open. Weekly lectures on subjects including fascism, *Labour in Irish History*, the history of the ICA, the life of William Thompson, and political economy, in addition to republican commemorations and Left Book Club events, continued to attract numbers of 100 and upwards. A shortage of suitable venues for meetings saw Robin (Robert) Tweedy, a party member with family connections to a profitable laundry business, offer his home at Carrickmines for a number of socials. The annual May Day parade was followed by one such event for communists, anti-fascist activists and Left Book Club members, at which Murray spoke and Roddy Connolly, Rose Burke, Molly Fitzpatrick and Seán O hEidirsceoil gave a rehearsal of Irwin Shaw's anti-war play, *Bury the Dead,* in advance of its first production at the Peacock Theatre.[7] The relationships that had survived the Spanish Civil War and collapse of the *Irish Democrat* coalition therefore provided the backbone of an emerging leftist anti-war movement.

For his part, Murray had remained cautious about the spread of fascism and the escalating threat of international war. He swiftly condemned Nazi Germany's invasion of Austria in March 1938[8] and later wrote to Hanna Sheehy Skeffington to stress the importance of an upcoming Anti-War Committee meeting: 'Then there is no knowing, by the time we may be in the cauldron of war or on the very edge of the precipice, if we can be nearer than we are at the present.'[9] Despite securing the British evacuation of the three Treaty Ports and the British government's pledge to respect the Irish state's political sovereignty, thus making neutrality in a war situation feasible, Murray argued that the Anglo-Irish Agreement represented a capitulation to Neville Chamberlain's policy of appeasement. A statement prepared for the Irish secretariat and published in the *Workers' Republic* read: 'This surrender is made to a British Government stained by the breach of every undertaking it has given to weaker nations, the aider and abettor of Fascism in Europe, the betrayer of Spain, Abyssinia and China.'[10] This view was not without its detractors. Brian O'Neill was one of three comrades to declare his opposition to the statement and reflect more positively on the economic outcomes of the Agreement, including a liberalisation of trade. However, Murray secured the support of a majority for his interpretation in the short term.[11]

Over the course of the year, he would continue to use public meetings to speak out against that 'scoundrel' Chamberlain and his policy of appeasement, which sacrificed the Czech Sudetenland to Nazi Germany and allowed for the imprisonment of thousands of German workers in concentration camps.[12] He was of course referring to the Munich Agreement, which the British and French governments had conceived as a way to avoid war at all costs. Writing in a similar vein almost sixty years later, Hobsbawm would note that 'for generations "Munich" became a synonym, in Western political discourse, for craven retreat'.[13] A proposed march to the German Legation in Dublin, agreed in Murray's absence, was postponed upon his return from a CPGB conference. However, anti-war meetings continued to attract upwards of 200 people.[14] At one such meeting, Murray warned that those who stood to gain the most from a global conflagration were profiteers in finance and the arms and munitions industries.[15] Perceptively, he interpreted the impending war as imperialist in terms of territorial annexations and the accumulation of capital by transnational interests. The working class, on the other hand, would pay the double price of deaths on the front line and higher costs of living at home.

Having been set the task of influencing the NILP and NISP from below,[16] the northern communist leadership arrived at similar conclusions. Having braved frosty labour relations in 1938 to maintain cooperation with the NILP leader Harry Midgley on the Arms for Spain Committee,[17] Betty Sinclair commented at a Belfast meeting on the necessity of preventing 'a blood bath' across Europe. Billy McCullough, meanwhile, echoed Murray's criticisms of appeasement and his comparison of conditions with those pertaining at the outbreak of the First World War. McCullough also referred to the absence of democratic norms in Northern Ireland and the use of Special Powers legislation against labour and republican activists. In his estimation, building and protecting democracy at a local and global level represented two sides of the same coin.[18] That this position echoed a motion passed at the 1938 annual conference of the ITUC indicates that the Belfast communists were not out of step with Irish labour opinion.[19] However, neither McCullough nor Sinclair advocated an international military response to the rise of German, Italian or indeed Japanese fascism outside the confines of the Spanish Civil War. Instead, they spoke vaguely of the need for 'resistance' and a boycott of goods from fascist countries.[20] There is little doubt that CPI ideologues understood the threat posed by fascism and that pacifism was no match for such an aggressive ideology. Their failure lay in overestimating the potential efficacy of non-violent methods of opposition such as boycotts, strikes, civil disobedience, economic sanctions and diplomatic measures. Like Schrodinger's cat, the party was, at that moment, both anti-fascist and pro-peace.

Although the CPI had become Stalinised and further entangled with Soviet foreign policy, the absence of a clear international response to the outbreak of war created an air of confusion around peripheral parties in particular. This left room for improvisation, which Murray was only too happy to exploit. Addressing a public meeting of around 100 people, he argued that the labour movement ought to press for Northern Ireland's withdrawal from Chamberlain's appeasement policy and instead support an all-island anti-war campaign. To this end, he advocated a tactical alliance with the Irish government, the 'Old IRA', and contemporary republican and anti-imperialist organisations to pressurise the British government into ceasing support for the Unionist state.[21] Ireland had not yet entered a state of 'emergency' or declared neutrality, but Murray felt he had identified a route to the coalescence of anti-war and anti-fascist opinion across the island. But although the Stormont government's appetite for conscription in Northern Ireland appeared to vindicate this approach in theory, it was hardly a realistic prospect in practice.

At another public meeting held to protest against the recent imprisonment of republicans in the North, Murray questioned Fianna Fáil's silence on the issue and took his anti-imperialist rhetoric even further in claiming that de Valera was misguided in thinking it would be possible to coax Unionists into a united Ireland. With Jim Prendergast's support and with potentially dangerous consequences, he proposed a march of all anti-partitionist parties into Northern Ireland to 'subdue' those opposed to Irish reunification.[22] This occurred against the backdrop of the 1938 Stormont election, which Craigavon fought on the issue of partition in order to overshadow the attempts of progressive candidates to draw attention to the Unionist government's mismanagement of the economy. However, it could also be described simply as senseless and irresponsible, ill-timed in the context of an IRA split that saw militarists assume control of the organisation's Army Council. Under the leadership of Seán Russell, the IRA started planning its 'war' against Britain, despite the absence of public support for an armed campaign. Murray and Prendergast's impetuous statements lent a certain legitimacy, however inadvertent, to the IRA's plans and brought them close to a variant of republicanism that was out of step with public opinion.

February 1939 brought yet another challenge to Murray's leadership. J.R. Campbell was at the forefront of these efforts, noting that Murray 'has shown neither the political leadership nor organising ability' and mooting Billy McCullough, 'the leading comrade' in Belfast, as a possible replacement. This pessimistic assessment chimed with a report delivered by Bill Clare, who pointed to a high turnover in membership and pervasive demoralisation that extended even to Murray. On this occasion, the latter survived only after the CPGB deemed McCullough unsuitable due to his lack of attention to the national question and, more importantly, because his transfer to Dublin had the potential of weakening the British party's influence in the NUR, where he held the position of branch secretary in Belfast. Murray was, however, taken off the Comintern payroll while the search for a new general secretary got underway.[23]

In his review for the Comintern, Campbell correctly noted that leading comrades had been critical of Murray. Tommy Watters, whom he referred to, had described Murray's policy of coaxing elements of Fianna Fáil into a united front against war as 'just another blunder added to the long list of many to the credit of the Party Leaders'. Similarly, Robin Tweedy challenged Murray to produce a financial report that had been promised for over a year and to justify his leadership with evidence that the party had experienced a net influx of members.[24] However, whether through duplicity or poor intelligence, Campbell was wrong to suggest that other comrades had offered 'no defence, or a half-hearted defence' of Murray.[25] The proceedings of special meetings convened to discuss changes to policy and organisation seriously undermine Campbell's account of events. Among those who lent their support to a policy change in Murray's favour were Bill Scott, Seán Nolan and Frank Mooney. Pat Dooley, a CPGB representative visiting Dublin in connection with the ban on the *Daily Worker*, also spoke in Murray's defence while dismissing Watters' criticisms as 'absolute defeatism' and a product of his bad health. After Murray concluded with assurances that a tactical alliance did not mean a compromise of principles, Nolan put his motion for a change in policy to the delegates in attendance, which they ratified by a convincing margin of sixty votes to twenty-three. Murray also reminded members that the responsibility for changing the party leadership rested with them. What followed was his uncomplicated election to the national committee, which now formally replaced the unrepresentative central committee and restored to the northern comrades greater input into the running of the party. It can therefore be stated with some confidence that Murray enjoyed the support of the majority of party members, particularly in the important city of Dublin.[26]

The ambiguities of anti-fascism and anti-imperialism

For the greater part of 1939, the CPI adopted an amalgam of ideas that barely resembled one particular political viewpoint. The party supported Irish neutrality in its early stages and congratulated the Fianna Fáil government for helping to prevent the introduction of conscription to the North.[27] The party remained explicitly anti-imperialist and continued to call for the release of political prisoners, coupling civil liberties agitation in the North with a focus on the imprisonment of southern republicans under the Offences Against the State Act (1939). However, when the IRA bombing campaign began in earnest, the CPI leadership endeavoured to distance itself from the former's methods. Two editorials from the short-lived *Workers' Bulletin*, penned by Murray, were clearest in this regard. The first suggested that the IRA leadership come round to the position that like Tone, Mitchel, Lalor, Pearse and Connolly, 'we are not only Separatists but Republicans and Democrats'.[28] The second distinguished between British imperialism and democracy, claiming that the armed campaign would only serve to 'drive a wedge' between Irish workers and their counterparts in Britain.[29] Proceeding in a similar vein, an early issue of the *Irish Workers' Weekly* reproduced a quote from Connolly to condemn the IRA's actions: 'Tone's present day professed followers constantly trample upon and repudiate every one of his principles.'[30] Ideological ambiguities persisted, but the party had moved closer to a position of supporting British democracy against fascism.

The CPI proceeded haphazardly towards a coherent analysis of a complicated and unpredictable series of events. Its tenuous yet enduring connection with the Soviet Union exacerbated the problems encountered on this journey. When Murray launched the *Irish Workers' Weekly* on 29 April 1939, it led with the ambiguous declaration that 'we cannot be neutral against fascism, for peace and against war'.[31] He made a point of countering Nazi propaganda while maintaining staunch opposition to conscription[32] and on 5 August published a speech under the headline 'Nazis can never be our allies'. Occupying the place of an editorial, Murray's speech relayed the message that only the 'reactionary forces' of Chamberlain and Craigavon would entertain an accord with Hitler, but also indicated that the party's preference was for a 'Peace Pact' between the Soviet Union and the democratic states of Europe, Britain included.[33] The Molotov-Ribbentrop Pact therefore came as a great shock to the CPI membership, particularly to those warming to the idea of a more proactive international response to Nazism. Nevertheless, the CPI duly revised its line. The *Irish Workers' Weekly* now asserted, with irony-free disregard for the fate of Poland, Finland and other vulnerable countries in the Baltic region, that the 'Soviet Union's policy strengthens peace', providing excerpts from a Stalin speech for the benefit of members who might have thought about questioning the new gospel.[34]

As the CPI's official history concedes, the fluidity of the situation generated 'some confusion among Party members in the North and it took much discussion to convince members of the correctness of the Party's position'.[35] Although there were local variations in attitudes to the war, it is most accurate to characterise the leadership and grassroots as united under a cloud of ambiguity. The publication of a contradictory manifesto failed to alleviate this confusion in the party ranks. Signed by Seán Murray and Billy McCullough on behalf of the CPI national committee, it presented the defence of Ireland as a priority while describing the use of emergency powers legislation as 'dangerous to popular freedom'. Arguably, these views could be reconciled. A more stark inconsistency was to be found in its criticisms of the 'non-interventionist' leaders of Britain and France on the one hand, and support for the Irish government's policy of 'military non-participation' on the other. In the absence of clear direction from Moscow, the party rowed back to the misguided position of advocating a people's victory over fascism across Europe.[36]

Following the Molotov-Ribbentrop Pact, Stalin laid out instructions for Comintern-affiliated parties to interpret the war singularly as a territorial carve-up between capitalist countries, not in terms of a struggle between bourgeois democracy and fascism: 'the division of capitalist countries into fascist and democratic has lost its former sense'.[37] This shift provided the CPI with an international reference point and the clarity to proceed with a consistent, though not entirely appropriate, critique of British foreign policy as imperialism. The distinction between British imperialism and democracy receded as the national committee reverted to calling for action to 'withdraw the six counties out of the imperialist war'.[38] Murray devoted additional column space in the *Irish Workers' Weekly* to 'the freedom of small nations' and sanctioned a greater focus on radical republican history. He reworked one of Connolly's slogans to utter 'We serve neither Churchill nor Hitler, but Ireland!'[39] and ensured that references to Lenin and the 1914-1918 imperialist war were aplenty. This rhetoric mirrored the active anti-imperialism of the Indian Communist Party.[40]

Anti-imperialist analyses of the war did appear to gain added credence after Churchill came to power in May 1940 and with the survival of French imperialism under German auspices in the form of the Vichy puppet-regime. Of course, the British and French governments had demonstrated little enthusiasm for European democracy during the Spanish Civil War. Furthermore, Churchill and members of his war ministry were unashamed imperialists who showed no intention of exporting democracy to the colonies. Just as the US only entered the war when its interests in the Pacific were at stake, Britain's ruling elite was largely motivated to protect its Asian and North African territories. Few would argue that the Allies intervened solely out of concern for the horrors inflicted upon the Chinese people or the Jewish population of Nazi-occupied Europe. It is also significant that, in September 1941, Churchill reneged on the Atlantic Charter, which contained provisions regarding the self-determination of occupied nations in the post-war dispensation, and instead, signalled his intention to retain control of British colonies.[41] In this respect, anti-imperialism formed part of a legitimate response to the war. It became a problem, however, when criticisms of Britain and France began to overshadow the CPI's anti-fascist propaganda, which had hitherto been consistent and incisive.

Throughout the early war period, the CPI coupled political opposition to the war with support for striking workers in a variety of sectors across the island, including the staple industries of north-east Ulster. These strikes related to low pay, the introduction of time-work rates of pay in place of piece-work rates, the use of scabs and non-union labour, and the stealthy introduction of dilution, which broke down complex tasks into more simple jobs that could be performed by low-paid, unskilled workers. Party publications regularly juxtaposed the drive for profits with the comparatively low wages and poor working conditions endured by employees. In late 1939, the Belfast group organised a rally to oppose Northern Ireland's involvement in a British war effort initiated primarily 'for the fruits of Empire'.[42] A 'Resolution from North' even reported some success in winning a section of NILP supporters over to an anti-war position. The Belfast comrades observed that the 'whole economic life' of the northern working class had been 'subordinated to the interests of the British war aims', and that this 'completely justifies the line put forward by the National Committee in opposition to the war'.[43]

In lieu of a Northern Ireland equivalent to the Joint Advisory Council at Westminster, and due to Stormont's refusal to engage with the ITUC on account of its headquarters being in Dublin, trades councils occasionally functioned as general negotiating bodies for northern workers. In early 1940, Belfast Trades Council organised an industrial conference to discuss the organisation and performance of the wartime economy. The sixty-one delegates in attendance, including Betty Sinclair and Billy McCullough, reached a consensus: the war was one between rival capitalist powers; wage increases had failed to keep pace with the rise in living costs; and high levels of unemployment combined with low benefits served the Westminster and Stormont governments' purpose of driving the working class into the armed forces. With unemployment sitting at 20 percent in the province and thousands of workers travelling to Britain in search of war work, the conference delegates agreed to present their concerns to the Northern Ireland Prime Minister, threatening a mass rally on the problem of unemployment.[44] Craigavon eventually met the deputation with reassurances about price controls and future war contracts for the North, thus staving off threats of coordinated trade union action.[45] Yet the Belfast communists' principled political defiance and tradition of militant economism offset any inclination to commit to the British war effort. This attitude was sustained by the infallibility of Soviet foreign policy and the fact that the six counties were, in the words of one Unionist minister, 'only half in the war'.[46]

There was no contradiction in resisting the drive for profits while maintaining resolute opposition to fascism. However, the party's intense focus on the imperialist features of the war led it in the direction of articulating a fundamentally Irish republican variant of anti-imperialism. Tommy Watters made this point inadvertently at a special meeting convened in December 1939 to discuss the party's approach to the war. He accepted an anti-imperialist interpretation – 'Our fight will assume the same forms as the fight in the last war' – and conceded that anti-imperialist rhetoric would sit easily with republicans and northern nationalists. But he also warned that continued attempts to tie the issue to Irish reunification would 'not place us in a very favourable light' in Protestant working-class communities.[47] McCullough expressed reservations about pressing for anti-war motions in northern unions, while Rajani Palme Dutt claimed that East Belfast members were least amenable to anti-war sentiments.[48] In response to Watters' concerns, several members, including Murray, argued that the key was to popularise the slogan 'withdraw the six counties from the imperialist war' by connecting it to material issues.[49] The ascendant Belfast group was ostensibly making some progress on this front through the trade union movement, though it had to be wary of allowing its message to be tainted with green.

One concern that republican and labour activists did share in common was the use of censorship and coercive legislation by the Unionist and Fianna Fáil governments. Having been imprisoned on dubious charges in 1933, the veteran Belfast communist, Val Morahan, was well acquainted with the notorious Special Powers Act. In July 1940, he found himself on the wrong side of the authorities once again, sentenced to two and a half years in jail for possession of a CPI manifesto and copies of *Red Hand*, which had replaced the suppressed *Irish Workers' Weekly* in the North.[50] The less prominent figure of James Hughes was then detained and questioned by police for being in possession of the commemorative Easter 1940 issue of the *Workers' Weekly*, but escaped a prison term despite refusing to inform on his comrades.[51] This harassment preceded the arrest and imprisonment of McCullough and Sinclair in October. Charged with spreading sedition through the publication of an article by Belfast IRA man, Seán MacBrádaigh (Jack Brady), they received reduced sentences of four months and two months respectively.[52] To compound these difficulties, the Ministry of Home Affairs banned the *Red Hand* in August, showing scant regard for the context in which the communists elected to publish the views of prominent IRA members. Stormont's overriding concern was to stifle all forms of political dissent, and national emergency conditions provided the state with the pretext for doing so.

Consequently, the CPI identified with the contemporary experience of republicans, who were being imprisoned at a rate disproportionate to the threat posed by the IRA. It was entirely consistent for the communists to view civil rights and the repeal of the Special Powers Act as part of their remit. This had been a central pillar of Irish communist thinking since the early 1930s. Yet it was imprudent to stray into the IRA's domain at a time when the organisation had taken a militarist and right-wing turn. In early 1940, the CPI joined the chorus demanding the release of Peter Barnes and James McCormack, two IRA men awaiting execution for a Coventry bombing in which five people died. The protests in the South were widespread, bringing together labour activists, republicans, Fianna Fáil representatives and members of the clergy. North of the border, the campaign was strongest in Derry and nationalist parts of Belfast, where communists and republicans united in clashes with the RUC. While these appeals for clemency were unsuccessful, the communists welcomed the Irish government's commutation in July of the death sentence handed to IRA volunteer, Tómas MacCurtain, who had killed a garda in Cork, as a 'people's victory'.[53] Far from this convergence representing any sort of calculation about what role the IRA could fulfil for the Soviet Union, the CPI leadership assessed its merits against the labour movement's temporally longer campaign for civil and political liberties. It would be remiss, however, to ignore the likelihood that any association with armed republicanism, especially in its contemporary guise, would have unnerved the predominantly Protestant shipyard communists that made up an increasing percentage of the party's support base.

Due to his republican background, and following his 1934 speaking tour of workers' organisations in New York, Murray acted as primary point of contact for Irish-American labourists seeking information on the fate of IRA men sentenced to death.[54] There is nothing particularly sinister about this. Of greater significance is the rhetoric promoted by CPI publications and the implications stemming from it. As one labour historian has noted, there is little doubt that the repeated invocation of Connolly, Lenin and the 1914-1918 war was designed to recreate the atmosphere of the Easter Rising and the feeling that 'England's difficulty is Ireland's opportunity'.[55] Even when one accounts for censorship in the South, which tended to filter through nationalist and pro-neutrality sentiments at the expense of radical anti-fascism, Murray is guilty of treading a fine line between anti-imperialism and anti-Britishness using CPI organs.[56] Yet, although the Irish communists occupied political ground usually reserved for explicitly republican actors, it would be a mistake to conflate this with support for the IRA campaign. Rather, the CPI's main theoretician attempted to challenge the thinking of IRA militarists and present the case for a radical democratic alternative.

Mike Milotte draws attention to the aforementioned MacBrádaigh article in his pioneering study of Irish communism, but fails to note the contributions preceding or succeeding it.[57] This omission suppresses the fact that the CPI only published MacBrádaigh's article as part of a debate with Murray, and could mislead readers into believing that the communists drifted towards some sort of dalliance with Nazi Germany. Matt Treacy attempts a more systematic analysis, underlining the hypocrisy involved in opposing Hitler while remaining quiet on the Soviet Union's treatment of Poland. This is a valid criticism, even if his use of the term 'totalitarian', a relic of the Cold War, is conceptually problematic in the light of post-Cold War debates within political science. However, Treacy's work is most problematic in two ways. Firstly, he combines a single Michael O'Riordan letter with extrapolation and speculation to overstate the direct links between the CPI and IRA during the period in question. Secondly, he commits the more flagrant error of misinterpreting the evidence and attributing issues of the CPI paper to the wrong year, thus placing the offending MacBrádaigh article and the arrest of McCullough and Sinclair in 1939. Moreover, he cites the very same issue of the *Irish Workers' Voice/Red Hand* as 10 August 1939 *and* 1940 (the correct year) separately, just five pages apart.[58] At best, this renders his critique ahistorical and largely irrelevant to the discussion at hand; at worst, it raises serious questions about his use of sources in general. Nevertheless, it is instructive to examine the Murray-MacBrádaigh debate and introduce a number of important nuances to existing narratives.

To take the polemic in full, Murray initially took issue with the IRA's response to George Bernard Shaw's appeal for the organisation to abandon its armed struggle for Irish reunification in favour of combating Hitler and Mussolini. With the Battle of Britain raging, this IRA statement encouraged nationalist Ireland to welcome German troops to their shores as an army of liberation. Reiterating his view of the war as essentially imperialist and leaving no room for equivocation on British adventurism or the complicity of Vichy France, Murray made a subtle moral, if not political, distinction between British imperialism and its fascist variant. He criticised the IRA leadership for distorting Irish republican history and for their admiration of the same forces responsible for the 'slaying' of Spanish democracy. Shaw at least understood the key issue at stake, Murray continued, whereas the IRA was effectively asking the Irish people to 'hitch their fortunes' to those propagating 'the theory of the superior race, the doctrine of overlordship and dependence'.[59]

MacBrádaigh's one-eyed traditionalist rejoinder claimed that the German's attack on Britain presented the 'opportune time' for republicanism to advance its cause and that, much like the British government, the IRA 'cannot afford to have scruples' in such circumstances. Significantly, his response contained the passage that landed McCullough and Sinclair in jail: 'Like Pearse and Connolly in 1916, we must look to the possibility of foreign aid for our cause.' He also argued naively that, upon accepting Nazi aid, the republican movement would be in a position to resist the importation of 'foreign social systems' to Ireland.[60] Murray replied scornfully that the IRA ought to consider the implications of setting such a dangerous course. To facilitate a German landing would be to transform Ireland into 'a battlefield for the two contending imperialist powers'. Instead of taking this risk, he encouraged IRA members to reassess their 'lack of faith in revolutionary democracy' and participate in ongoing protests against the war while the conditions for revolution matured.[61]

In this period of strong anti-imperialist discourse, the CPI general secretary avoided Shaw's invitation to support the British war effort. Such were the ambiguities involved in committing oneself to the line laid down by Moscow. However, it is important to acknowledge the significance of Murray challenging the IRA publicly, particularly as it earned him death threats from the organisation and the threat of the CPI offices being bombed for distributing 'pro-British and anti-German propaganda'.[62] Ultimately, he and his party colleagues were under no illusions about the futility of the IRA bombing campaign in Britain. They were increasingly cognisant of the damage caused to radical democratic republicanism by the armed struggle and of the limits to drawing parallels with the events of 1914-1918. Only Stalin and his apparatchiks stood in the way of a return to the anti-fascism of the Spanish Civil War years.

Murray's debate with MacBrádaigh proceeded in parallel with the Battle of Britain, which raged between July and October of that year. Throughout these months, CPI adopted the construction of air raid shelters as an economic and defence priority across Ireland while, quite distastefully, celebrating the small victories of Irish neutrality. Food prices, job creation and unemployment assistance remained at the forefront of its concerns, with the national committee warning that the island was on the verge of a 'hungry forties' in the absence of government intervention. To their credit, contributors to CPI organs understood the class bias to rationing basic goods and services: the policy kept the working class in a perpetual state of survival and fealty to the state, while the better off could always afford to circumvent such measures. The party came out strongly against conscription when it was considered again for Northern Ireland in mid-1941 and much anger was vaunted at Harry Midgley, the communists' erstwhile ally against fascism, for joining Unionist establishment figures at a 'recruiting rally' for the British war effort at the Ulster Hall.[63] Additionally, with the bourgeois concept of national interest framed in thirty-two county terms well into 1941, CPI literature continued to argue for the exclusion of Northern Ireland from British military planning. How this could be reconciled with the party's stance on industrial development and employment creation in the North is one question the party's policy experts failed to address in substantive detail.

Belfast's own traumatic encounter with the Luftwaffe began in April 1941 and lasted almost two months, costing nearly 1,000 lives and causing untold damage to the city's housing and infrastructure. The CPI lauded the efforts of emergency services during the Blitz, including those despatched north by the Irish government, and noted the indiscriminate power of the Nazi bombs, incendiaries and high explosives in creating 'a feeling of friendship between Catholic and Protestant'. More dubious, however, was the claim that this catastrophe demonstrated the necessity of all-island neutrality.[64] This failed to comprehend the potent emotive and symbolic importance of the German air raids in drawing large sections of the Northern Irish public closer to their counterparts in British industrial cities such as Birmingham, Coventry and Glasgow, all of whom were deeply affected by the Blitz. The irreversible reality of the so-called 'people's war'[65] and the virtual evaporation of non-violent opposition in Britain presented a profound challenge to supporters of neutrality in the North.

This situation of flux presented the Irish communist movement with either the most opportune or inopportune time to effect a leadership change. Despite enjoying widespread support within the party, Murray was beset with considerable personal difficulties that weakened his capacity to resist another challenge to his position. In December 1940, he applied for a Military Service Pension and was granted £28.17.9 per annum. That this was the first time he applied for the award since its introduction in 1934 suggests that his financial circumstances had diminished considerably as a result of his removal from the Comintern payroll.[66] Another problem was that he had 'went on the booze at the time of the outbreak of World War 2', in the words of Desmond Greaves, and was informed by Jim Prendergast that he had to pull himself together or else resign office.[67] By March 1941, the *Workers' Weekly* had begun referring to Tommy Watters as CPI general secretary, without a single mention of Murray's ten years' service to the party he had helped found.[68] He lost editorial control of the party paper and therefore one of the main outlets for communicating his ideas. One consolation was that he had received a letter from the CPUSA's fifth assembly district, New York, announcing its intention to form a Seán Murray

Branch in honour of his 'brilliant and courageous leadership of the struggle of the Irish people for true freedom and well-being'.[69] The other came in the summer of 1941, when he and his long-term partner, Margaret, married in a low-key civil ceremony.[70]

By the time Nazi Germany launched its invasion of the USSR in the early hours of 22 June 1941, the new *Irish Workers' Weekly* editorial team (Nolan and Watters) had already commissioned an embarrassing article that downplayed the likelihood of such an attack. What is even more remarkable is that the issue made it to print and into circulation.[71] Once news of Operation Barbarossa filtered through, the party performed the necessary volte-face, placing its faith in Stalin and, consequently, the British war effort. This is but one classic demonstration of the lasting influence of the Soviet Union on the policies and tactics of West European parties, despite the gradual winding down of the Comintern. Even accounting for his polemicism and hyperbolic tendencies, Orwell was not far off the mark when he wrote: 'Immediately after hearing the 8 o'clock news bulletin on the morning of 22 June 1941, he [the communist] had to start believing once again that Nazism was the most hideous evil the world had ever seen.'[72]

While relieving all residual pressure on the northern branches to conform to anti-imperialism, the CPI's u-turn presented the southern comrades with an acute political dilemma. After some deliberation and another intervention by the CPGB, the Dublin branch voted narrowly on 10 July 1941 to 'suspend independent activity and to apply the forces of the branch to working in the Labour and trade union organisations'. Young Jim Larkin advised against dissolution, despite the fact that he had gradually drifted out of the party since around 1937, and his youngest brother Barney led the opposition.[73] This dissolution had the effect of making communism's official structures less visible across the twenty-six counties and leaving the northern groups to keep the flag flying publicly.

Northern communism and the war effort

The Soviet Union's entry into the war made communist cooperation with the British war effort almost inevitable. Near hysterical denunciations of communism were prevalent in Britain and Ireland throughout the 1930s. These now gave way to murmurs of disapproval as the Red Army's potentially decisive role in defeating Hitler became widely recognised. Even the Catholic nationalist *Irish News* reported favourably on the Soviet Union's mobilisation against Nazi

Germany.[74] Locally, Harry Midgley's surprisingly emphatic victory over the Unionist candidate in a December 1941 by-election in Willowfield, East Belfast, demonstrated that northern Protestants were not immune to the general leftward shift of public opinion across the UK. Midgley made a point of emphasising his position on the constitutional status of Northern Ireland, but also won support by exposing the increasingly unpopular Stormont administration on its inadequate war preparations and response to the Blitz; its mismanagement of the economy; and its reluctance to investigate allegations of corruption in the running of a sanatorium in Whiteabbey.[75] Significant also in terms of pervading attitudes towards socialists was the spate of IRA attacks in the North and Britain which, along with obvious wartime security threats, consumed the attention of the Ministry of Home Affairs and RUC. The authorities no longer listed communist activities amongst their priorities. Consequently, Special Branch was conspicuously absent from meetings organised by the various labour groups in Belfast, except when they related to strike activity.

It became clear that Murray would benefit from these changed circumstances when he received word from Billy McCullough in October that Dawson Bates had revoked the exclusion order served upon him in 1933. This was partly a result of the efforts of Jack Beattie, who had petitioned the government and convinced the long-serving Minister of Home Affairs that Murray posed no subversive threat to the northern state.[76] Presented with this newly available option, the choice was between remaining in Dublin and joining a local Labour Party branch, or returning to the North, where a prominent role with the Communist Party (Northern Ireland) was by no means guaranteed.[77] Facing a bleak political future in Dublin, Murray elected to move to Belfast in order to be closer to his ailing parents. He and Margaret initially lodged with Betty Sinclair at 46 Hooker Street, stayed briefly with Jack Mulvenna (formerly of the ICA) in Andersonstown, West Belfast, and later with Michael McInerney who, on his return from England, took up a position with the party and rented a house on the Limestone Road from a comrade in the RAF. By 1944, they were living on his parents' farm at Ballybrack, with Seán assuming some of his father's farming duties in the absence of gainful employment in the city.

Because paid offices with the party were unsustainable in the long term, Murray was compelled to take up employment where he could find it. Cuttings from the *Belfast Telegraph* and *Irish News* in his private papers paint a picture of desperation, with dozens of unskilled, low paid jobs highlighted in pen. Records show that he spent two months working as a barman in the Empire Theatre, Belfast, and had a brief stint with a clothing manufacturer in the city. Incidentally, the war industries provided the greatest hope of steady employment for Murray, a Catholic small farmer with no recent experience of industrial work. He spent some time building air raid shelters before the party helped to find him a job as an 'electrician's helper' in Harland and Wolff's shipyard, where he remained until around 1948.[78] Alternating between Belfast and Cushendall until both of his parents passed away, he then sublet the farm to a distant relative and put the money towards obtaining a house at 32 Lincoln Avenue, Belfast, which was to be his final address. The farmhouse at Ballybrack lay vacant for months at a time, although Murray allowed friends to use it as a holiday home on a number of occasions.[79] One veteran communist also recalled the house being used for party meetings and weekend retreats – 'Seán was still on good terms with republicans in Cushendall, so a group of us used to go up there when we wanted to get out of Belfast'[80] – although Murray would ask comrades not to mention his work as a labourer to relatives or neighbours.[81]

Politically, the early 1940s were the least active years of Murray's long career. Elevated to the position of CPNI general secretary, Billy McCullough would come to dominate the Belfast movement during the war period, ably assisted by Betty Sinclair, who assumed the responsibilities of district organiser and treasurer. Murray remained popular with communists across the island but found that there was no clearly defined role reserved for him within the new party structures. In light of his age, precarious financial situation and variable yet mentally and physically draining working pattern, it was perhaps natural for him to make way for younger cadres with fresh ideas. He would have been left with little time or energy to attend party meetings and demonstrations, and scarce opportunities to draft Marxist tracts. Nor would his drinking habits have done him any favours. These factors combine to offer one possible explanation for the decline in Murray's influence, eliciting the words widely attributed to Oscar Wilde: 'The trouble with socialism is that it takes up too many evenings.'

An alternative narrative reads that ideology lay behind Murray's demotion – that he was deliberately frozen out of the CPNI's decision-making processes for fundamentally political reasons, or 'pushed upstairs' as one stalwart of the Irish left has described it.[82] Years later, Murray's closest comrade, Peadar O'Donnell, would offer the most detailed assessment of his demotion:

He was crucified by the situation in Dublin but there was no excuse at all for the wastage of Seán by the people in Belfast, who failed to recognise, not only in his work, but his genius: in Belfast he was wasted by his own comrades. The Communist Party of Northern Ireland has a crime to expiate…

It is a verdict on the stature of the Movement that he was not appreciated. I do hope it did not mean that it was the subjective weakness caused by the Northern environment and pressures, that it was not because he was of Catholic background from the Glens of Antrim that influenced his comrades. But probably it was the era of the organiser, the entrepreneur, the propaganda merchant, and age that displayed near contempt for the man of original thinking. If only they knew, the one man Ireland needed then, and now, was the man of original and analytical thinking. Seán was that man but none appreciated it. But if the reason was subjective, then we are perceiving in the movement a version of the weakness that held back the working class movement both North and South at all moments of crisis…

If I could recognise and appreciate his gifts, what excuse is there for people who worked so closely with him, and in the same cause, to fail to open the way for his fulfilment and the advance of the working class. They should have appreciated him even though he was 'soft', self-effacing like Liam Mellows or Paddy Rutledge (one of the very few really progressive men on the Anti-Treaty side in 1922). But, perhaps, it is a rare gift that enables one to appreciate the intelligence or even genius of others. Perhaps Belfast was not fully aware of the treasure it ignored. I was never a member of the Communist Party but I very nearly joined in 1942 so I could 'kick up murder' about Seán.[83]

It would be unhelpful to attribute Murray's isolation to his Catholic upbringing, principally because everyone connected with the CPNI knew of his avowed atheism and non-sectarianism. His proximity to left republicanism does, however, offer one valuable explanation for his relationship with a party that sought to establish itself in Protestant working-class constituencies. It was also the case that several contemporaries regarded him as 'deadwood' precisely because of his handling of party affairs in the South.[84] Similarly, one Belfast activist has offered an anecdote to explain how Murray was simply 'out of touch' with developments in the industrial North. On the first day of his employment in the shipyards, the story runs, Murray was dressed in his 'political agitator's clothing' – an overcoat, soft velvet hat, and a tie. Seeing this, and wishing to save him from embarrassment, a friendly party member took him aside: "For God's sake take that off! Somebody'll think you're a gaffer!"[85] Of course, there is every chance that this story is apocryphal. Even so, it adds to the view that Murray's years of relative detachment from the Belfast movement and association with recent communist failures in the South weakened his status in the North. The reasons for his demise were therefore personal, financial, practical and political.

An early indication that the CPNI intended to pursue a pro-war discourse came with the party's first manifesto. Launched in October 1941, it stated: 'A victory for the Soviet Union and its allies among the enslaved nations of the Continent, including Germany and the Anglo-American peoples would be a triumph for the cause of national liberty everywhere and would advance the movement for Ireland's complete freedom.'[86] Here the debate continued to be framed uncomfortably in terms of the duality of imperialism and fascism, the argument being that a Soviet Union victory would weaken both. By 1942, however, McCullough had signalled his intention to break from the CPI's legacy, declaring that neutrality was 'a matter of grave concern to democratic opinion' and that neutral Ireland now found itself 'out of step with the rest of progressive mankind'.[87] McCullough and Sinclair worked to convince the Irish labour movement to fall in behind the communist position by moving anti-fascist resolutions at successive ITUC conferences in 1942 and 1943. The first resolution failed to receive the necessary support, though ITUC delegates passed the second in dubious circumstances.[88]

In October 1942, as Northern Ireland began to experience significant increases in industrial output and a fall in unemployment, the CPI held its first national conference since the dissolution of the Dublin branch. In the ensuing report, McCullough intimated that explicitly northern and British concerns would determine the CPNI's trajectory thereafter. For example, he argued that calls for the resignation of the inept Andrews government represented 'sheer opportunism'. This reluctance to criticise what was a most sectarian and incompetent form of Unionism reflected the expectation that Stormont would throw in its lot with Britain and the Soviet Union. It was also a populist nod to the Protestant working class, upon whose support the pro-war push largely depended. The conference report promoted the opening of a second front, championed by Stalin in the international arena, and preached a doctrine of maximum production in the war industries. Significantly, McCullough instructed party members to avoid strike action in their quest for better pay and working conditions: 'A strike, no matter under what circumstances it takes place, cannot be supported by our party.'[89] The foremost concern was the Allies' successful prosecution of the war and the Soviet Union's survival. A problematic side effect of this approach was that it entangled the CPNI's interests with those of the Unionist Party.

Running from 1942 to 1946, the CPNI's weekly newspaper, *Unity*, adopted a pro-war, maximum production position under the editorship of P.J. Musgrove. However, it was McCullough, the party chairman, who regularly occupied the front pages. The newspaper provided ample column space for converts to McCullough's thinking to parrot the pro-war position. In addition, sycophantic references to the Red Army and its commander-in-chief grew apace.[90] The Christmas 1942 issue of *Unity* ran with the front-page headline 'Salute to Stalin' and proceeded in reiterating the main themes of the day. The accompanying editorial repeated the call for the opening of a second front and stressed the importance of cooperation between the labour movement and Minister of Production in order to 'do away with unemployment in the year 1943, increase our production 100% and give the soldiers of the democratic nations the weapons for victory'.[91] This, as the Red Army decisively repulsed the German relief attack at Stalingrad while obliterating the Italian Eighth Army on the Don River.

The CPNI's association with the Soviet Union certainly had a hand in strengthening its political position. The Red Army's historic victory at Stalingrad and the Comintern's dissolution ensured that Stalin became an acceptable and essential ally in the West, winning *Time* magazine's 'Man of the Year' award for the second time in 1943. Ironically, his first award in 1940 was for securing the Molotov-Ribbentrop Pact. Hostility to communism in the mainstream British press receded, allowing communist parties on both sides of the Irish Sea to function with renewed confidence. The CPGB's support for the Allied war effort and patriotic flag waving occasioned an influx of new members, with membership figures more than doubling between 1941 and 1943.[92] The year 1943 also marked the height of the (numerically less significant) CPNI's influence over the decade. The party boasted 1,000 members, which prompted a reorganisation of its two Belfast branches into four – North, South, East and West – and the formation of smaller district groups in rural areas.[93] Its new recruits were predominantly Protestant and probably of a Unionist disposition, allured by the party's newfound British nationalism and commitment to the ambiguous notion of the 'people's war'.

This progress came during what was an exceptional period of activism in the Belfast metal trades. The war years witnessed an upsurge in trade union membership and the renaissance of Belfast shop stewardism as an organised movement.[94] In search of parity with British wage rates and conditions, workers in the North's key industries were inclined to see mass action as a measure of first resort. This attitude was reinforced by the ineptitude of Shorts & Harland directors, whom civil servants accused of failing to cope with the rapid expansion in production and thus earning the company a reputation for inefficiency, and the intransigence of management at Harland & Wolff, who were prone to locking out for the whole day workers who arrived slightly late.[95] Between 1941 and 1945, Northern Ireland recorded 523 strike days per 1,000 employees, compared with the UK average of 153.[96] This militancy put the CPNI leadership in a bind as to how to respond to escalating demands from below for industrial action.

Industrial unrest during the war years took the form of notable strikes by bakers, bus transport workers, carters, dockers, riveters, linen workers and engineering apprentices, among other occupations. Chris Loughlin has taken the important step of casting some light on the October 1942 strikes in Mackie's engineering plant and a Shorts dispersal unit, which involved a combined total of 10,000 workers and set a precedent for subsequent disputes.[97] These strikes were strongly opposed by CPI leaders, who drafted in the CPGB general secretary Harry Pollitt to encourage a return to work.[98] In the aftermath of these events, Malachy Gray, a 'Falls Road red', used his column in *Unity* to praise the setting up of shop stewards' movement and to call for a 'new perspective in workshops'. This involved the coordination of workers' through joint production committees and the attainment of trade union unity around the goal of increased production.[99] Joint production committees offered the pretence of democratic control of production, but often served the disciplinary purpose of warding off industrial action. The CPNI's approach to industrial relations resonated with that of the NILP leadership, but not with the radical anti-war position of smaller leftist groups such as the Revolutionary Socialist League.[100]

Wartime legislation made union activities difficult and unofficial strikes illegal. This caveat notwithstanding, a number of historians with Trotskyist sympathies have accused the communists of going to extraordinary lengths to stifle the threat of mass action in the aircraft and shipbuilding industries, particularly during an unofficial strike for a pay rise at Harland & Wolff in early 1944.[101] This was Northern Ireland's largest and most significant dispute of the war period, occurring almost in parallel with major coal mining and munitions strikes in Britain. So significant were the strikes, especially in the context of the Allies opening a second front, that Boyd Black has identified them as the likely catalyst for the introduction of The Defence (General) Regulations 1AA Order, which prohibited the instigation or incitement of stoppages in industries considered essential to the war effort.[102] McCullough had announced brazenly in a 1943 pamphlet that 'the working class welcomes the opportunity to make sacrifices in order to smash fascism',[103] and, true to his words, the party response offered little support to those involved, even after the initial strike of 1,200 engineers spread to over 30,000 men in sympathetic action. McCullough pressed for cooperation with the government to bring about a resolution and,[104] after a deputation of Confederation Trades met with Jack Beattie,[105] wrote to the Northern Ireland Prime Minister Basil Brooke, all MPs, the Lord Mayor and various public bodies to suggest the organisation of a conference to reach a settlement. Gray, meanwhile, used his influence as a shipyard convenor to curb the strikers' demand for the unconditional release of five imprisoned shop stewards.[106] To confirm the CPNI's shift in the direction of CPGB and Labour Party thinking, *Unity* reproduced an article by J.R. Campbell condemning 'unnecessary strikes' in the Allied countries as the work of 'Trotskyist saboteurs'.[107] That this was a blatant display of left sectarianism is clear because the numerically insignificant Trotskyist groupings had no real bearing on the outcome of the Belfast strike. Similar to coal mining and other important industries in Britain, the workers' organic demands for improvements in wages and conditions determined their militancy to a greater degree than the tactics of any particular leftist party.[108]

CPNI members were prominent in the wartime industries, enough to rival the presence of NILP trade unionists. However, Black makes the important point that three major Belfast strikes recorded victories between 1942 and 1945 despite the communists' best efforts to limit the scale of industrial action.[109] The official CPI history concedes that the policy of opposing strikes as a principle caused some consternation in the ranks of younger party members cutting their teeth in the shop stewards' movement.[110] One such member was the late Andy Boyd, an organiser with the Amalgamated Engineering Union (AEU), who diverged subtly from the party leadership's position by placing an emphasis on the 'fight' for gains and juxtaposing the pursuit of full employment with the struggle for wage increases.[111] Boyd would later complain that Billy McCullough 'doubted it was keeping with the war effort to oppose the Unionists'.[112] The actions of the CPNI under McCullough's influence would appear to support this particular claim.

Although Murray was now an industrial trade unionist, his role was that of a rank-and-file member and one whose views carried little weight. His CPNI duties in the shipyards extended only as far as selling hammer and sickle badges and distributing party literature. One useful gauge for establishing the degree of his influence during the war is the number and dispersal of his articles for *Unity*, which amount to fewer than a dozen between November 1942 and the end of 1945. This figure is staggeringly low for such a prolific writer. Furthermore, three of these articles are merely abridged versions of lectures he delivered to party supporters, and all but two appear after the opening of the second front on 6 June, D-Day, which put the outcome of the war in Europe beyond doubt. The available sources give no clue as to Murray's thoughts on the editorial line; however, a series of rather bizarre letters from his old mentor, Jack White, point to a pervading culture of censorship within the party. White had returned to Ireland after the Spanish Civil War espousing a strange blend of anarchism, pacifism and mysticism. The expiry of his own exclusion order had enabled him to return to Ballycastle and reconnect with his fellow County Antrim native after some years apart. They discussed a range of subjects including spiritualism, dialectical materialism, the lectures of Professor Robert Corkey, a Presbyterian minister and Unionist politician, White's 1945 election campaign, and the 'death' of Murray's father. White also wrote on his opposition to the war, the CPNI's support for it, and the difficulty he had encountered in having his critical views published in *Unity*, likening his treatment in discussion with Sinclair and Musgrove to an experience with the OGPU, the Soviet secret police responsible for administrating the gulags.[113] It is unclear whether Murray represented his concerns to the leadership or was simply complicit in batting them away. Either way, his influence on the editorial line was negligible for most of the war period.

Outside Belfast, Murray did play a bit part in the communists' efforts to influence the Labour Party from within. A 1944 inquiry into the communist infiltration of Labour, instigated by William O'Brien as part of a personal vendetta against Jim Larkin, placed Murray in its Fairview branch, North Dublin. If he was, it is difficult to see him contributing a great deal to the branch's activities.[114] However, it is clear from his attendance at meetings of the CPI national leadership that both he and Larkin junior, now officially with the Labour Party, were aware of and involved with the party's adoption of entryism.[115] CPI Dublin district committee minutes reveal the extent to which the tactic was pursued after the formal dissolution of the party in the South.[116] Niamh Puirséil claims that entryism led to a 'Larkinite/communist element' gaining control over Dublin Labour branches whose new members included recruits from Fianna Fáil, Fine Gael and the IRA.[117] Matt Treacy demonstrates that its execution was relatively successful in terms of the selection and performance of election candidates, and that Murray was even confident of encouraging the Labour Party to adopt a pro-Soviet stance as policy.[118]

Plausibly, republican communists such as Murray would not have been as comfortable with the CPNI's easy cohabitation with the Unionist regime. Neil Redfearn has written of the CPGB that, following the Soviet Union's entry into the war, anti-colonialism 'was subordinated to the anti-fascist cause, while antifascism was increasingly conflated with the British national interest'.[119] This was true of the CPNI's crudest pro-war policies in many respects because they entailed uncritical support for the Stormont government. Despite resigning from the NILP in protest at the election of Jack Beattie as party leader, Harry Midgley enjoyed the support of *Unity* when he formed the Commonwealth Labour Party (CLP) and entered Basil Brooke's cabinet as a token left minister.[120] McCullough's apologia for Unionism, *But Victory Sooner*, commended the government's commitment to the war effort and strongly indicated that his party would support the formation of a Unionist-Labour coalition at Stormont to mirror the Tory-dominated national government at Westminster.[121] Murray did support the war effort and appealed for 'all constitutional issues such as Partition to be left until the Hitler Fascist menace is destroyed'.[122] But although there is, in one of his speeches, the hint of a distinction between Brooke's 'anti-populist' politics and the 'populist' Andrews administration,[123] there is nothing anywhere to suggest that he was in favour of organised labour cooperating with what he regarded as a local manifestation of Toryism.[124]

In its determination for Northern Ireland to see out the war in alliance with the Soviet Union, the CPNI discarded some of the movement's most fundamental policies. From 1941, this blinkered approach involved giving the Unionist government a free pass on the use of repressive legislation. Despite helping to set up a reprieve committee for six republicans sentenced to death for the killing of an RUC man,[125] the CPNI dropped its principled opposition to the Special Powers Act and adopted a robust attitude towards those interned for 'pro-Nazi activities' i.e. IRA volunteers.[126] This, we can be sure, did not have Murray's blessing. Since the early 1930s, he and his comrades had suffered at the hands of the Special Powers Act and placed democratic reform at the forefront of their programmes. The CPNI's hasty support for the government can only be described as politically utilitarian. It detracted from communists' history of campaigning for civil and political liberties and undermined their claim to consistency on such an important issue.

Around mid-1943, however, the party's analysis of the northern political environment did show signs of acquiring greater sophistication. Now situated within the loosely defined social democratic camp, the communists started working publicly to court the NILP, which had continued to gain popular support after Midgley's departure. The Soviet Union's efforts in defeating Hitler brought the CPNI and NILP closer on one important level. A path to political rapprochement then appeared to open with the publication of the Beveridge Report, which, pending the results of the 1945 Westminster elections, signalled the introduction of welfarism to Britain. Economically, Northern Ireland fared pretty well in the war years, yet there was an underlying feeling that the region continued to lag behind the rest of the UK. The poor state of Northern Ireland's health service and acute shortages in housing left the Stormont government open to criticism. The NILP's success in confronting these 'bread and butter' issues helped the communists overcome their inhibitions for adopting a similar approach. Health, housing, education and gender equality (taken up by Betty Sinclair in particular) gradually became the watchwords of CPNI publications.

The Unionists' second by-election defeat to a NILP candidate in as many years highlighted the opportunities to capitalise on working-class disenchantment with the Stormont government. The victory of Jack Beattie, who enjoyed a positive working relationship with the communists, came shortly after the publication of the Beveridge Report and spelled the end of Andrews' premiership. For the CPNI, the penny dropped that parity between Britain and Northern Ireland in the provision of social security would soften the blow dealt to employment prospects in the province by the impending post-war drop in production. Envisaging a Labour-led Britain after the next general election, delegates to the CPI's 1943 annual conference approved another change in course. The party was now prepared to help a united labour movement to 'become the fighting opposition to win the legitimate demands of the people'.[127] This marked an orientation away from what one author has described as the party's 'collaborationist' approach towards

Unionism.[128] McCullough called not only for an alliance with the NILP but also for the Nationalist Party to end abstentionism and adopt a policy of full political participation on social issues such as the housing crisis. In return, the communists would support a campaign to end gerrymandering and discrimination against Catholics.[129] Moreover, far from demonstrating great enthusiasm for 'Empire',[130] McCullough criticised Britain's role in India and lambasted the Tories for their 'out-dated imperialist' attitudes on Ireland.[131] Opportunist this shift may have been, but it moved with the prevailing domestic and international winds and represented a political break with Unionism.

Globally, the balance of power relations within capitalism had begun to shift in labour's favour, signalling to the capitalist class the necessity of some sort of compromise. The Beveridge Report and Roosevelt's New Deal represented efforts to save capitalism from itself whilst restoring democratic control of aspects of the economy and staving off the threat of social revolution. In this context, the CPNI and NILP proposals for post-war reconstruction and political reform, and support for social democracy as a system, began to converge. With both parties drawing most of their support from British-based trade unions, there were ostensibly few obstacles to cooperation at grassroots level. After the CPGB applied unsuccessfully for affiliation to the British Labour Party in 1943, the Communist Party of Ireland national committee made a similar public overture to the NILP. Interestingly, the term 'united front' re-entered the communist vocabulary in mid-1943, signalling a retreat from national-popular frontism. McCullough assured the NILP secretary, Jack Dorricott, in an open letter that his members were 'fully prepared to accept all the obligations of being affiliated to the Labour Party, and loyally to carry out all decisions reached at its Annual Conference'.[132] The NILP executive committee responded almost immediately that it would not be advising its members to support affiliation, rendering the prospect of a merger highly unlikely.[133] Undeterred, the communists devoted much attention to the endorsement given to their proposal by Belfast Trades Council, individual unions and a number of NILP branches.[134] At the NILP conference in October, a number of prominent union figures demonstrated enthusiasm for labour unity. Jimmy Morrow, a leading figure with the shop stewards' movement and influential AEU organiser, argued that CPNI members would bring some energy to the movement, while a NUR delegate said the communists ought to be rewarded for their groundwork on behalf of the NILP.[135] Ultimately, NILP trade unionists voted overwhelmingly to reject the application.[136]

Throughout 1944, the CPNI continued to promote the united front, albeit with slightly less conviction, and made renewed calls for the creation of an informal alliance in opposition to the Unionist Party as the 1945 elections approached. In the Stormont election, McCullough campaigned against Lord Glentoran in Bloomfield, East Belfast, promising 'to keep step with Britain and the new world'.[137] He received 5,802 votes, Betty Sinclair 4,130 in Cromac, and Sid Maitland 2,524 in West Down. There was some evidence of labour cooperation in Bloomfield and Cromac, where the NILP decided not to stand against McCullough and Sinclair, leaving a straight fight between the Unionist and CPNI candidates. Those standing on a 'labour' or 'socialist' platform, including the CLP, received a combined vote of nearly 126,000, while the Unionist candidates mustered a total of around 178,000. The Unionists won six fewer seats than in 1938, which seemed to represent a significant advance for class politics in the North.[138] Yet these figures only translated into five seats for the labour movement and no gains for the CPNI. The failure of the two most prominent northern communists to make a greater impact in their mainly Protestant constituencies did not bode well for the party's fortunes in less propitious conditions.

Returning to the fold

Just as Murray looked like fading quickly into obscurity, circumstances handed him another chance to make a mark on communist politics. The end of the war exposed the ephemeral nature of the CPI's growth spurt. RUC Special Branch reported a rapid decline in public support, mounting financial difficulties and the spread of disaffection through the party ranks, leading to the disintegration of McCullough's authority in particular. One unsuccessful attempt to unseat McCullough and Sinclair in favour of Murray and Michael McInerney led to the resignation of a faction led by Robert Moore.[139] By the close of the party's conference in early 1945, however, Murray had been appointed to the executive committee, to the political committee and as CPNI chairman, a position he would keep until the end of the decade. At this stage, he was one of six paid communist officers in Ireland. The others included Betty Sinclair, Billy McCullough, Michael McInerney, Seán Nolan, and probably one other southern cadre.[140] But with the party failing, these remunerated positions were allowed to expire naturally. Betty Sinclair moved to Bristol to manage the CPGB bookshop for eighteen months. McCullough secured a job as district secretary of the National Association of Theatrical and Kine Employees in Belfast. And after failing to secure a leadership position for himself, McInerney moved to Dublin, joined the Irish Labour Party and secured casual employment with the *Irish Times* before becoming its political correspondent. Murray, meanwhile, picked up a wage for editing *Unity* until the end of 1946 and enhanced his income by writing commissioned articles for left-wing organs thereafter.[141]

It is recalled that the dearth of Murray's contributions to *Unity* and writing more generally were broadly commensurate with his actual influence during the war period. Similarly, then, the paper's editorial line under his stewardship in 1945 and 1946 is an accurate indicator of his return to the fore. That Murray published the following letter from Peadar O'Donnell said as much:

> *Unity* is growing up under your Editorship. It is good to think that the Republican tradition, which gave the Irish struggle for independence its place in the vanguard of all oppressed peoples struggling to be free, should, through you, be incorporated into the fight against reaction in the Six Counties to-day. It seems a long cry now back to those days when, at the crossroads in the fight for the Republic, the great body of the movement was swept leftwards by the hold of the tradition in the mass of the Irish people; carrying you and me with it in its stormy tide … Good luck to you in your work to give life and meaning to what Mellows taught.[142]

Murray was keen to promote republican and radical nationalist solutions to the problems facing Northern Ireland. In one editorial, he promoted the slogan 'the ownership of Ireland by the people of Ireland', a nod to the 1916 Proclamation, and suggested that the labour movement revisit Mellows' 'Notes from Mountjoy', a radical political programme heavily influenced by the communist movement.[143] On the centenary of Thomas Davis' death, Murray related the contemporary conditions of squalor and housing shortages in Ulster to the Young Ireland struggle against famine and evictions.[144] More shrewdly, he commissioned Andy Boyd, a leading member of the predominantly Protestant AEU to write an article extolling Michael Davitt's example in creating an island-wide struggle for housing rights and better living conditions.[145] Finally, Murray visited the northern Protestant origins of republicanism in a lengthy and positive review of T.A. Jackson's *Ireland Her Own*, a general history popular with Irish Marxists but full of nationalist assumptions and outdated even for its time.[146] These articles demonstrate Murray's genuine desire to bring socialist republicanism to the CPNI membership but also expose the limits of his intellect and the power of ideology, not to mention a degree of wishful thinking.

Murray found opportunities to develop as a researcher and writer during this period, though he had to balance this with a return to activism and organising. His efforts at poetry, though tongue-in-cheek, were of a poor standard and cringeworthy. Take for instance this quatrain poking fun at Midgley's transformation into a Unionist establishment politician:

> If you want a good Government job
> Don't serve your time to the plumbing
> The way that lies best to that haven of rest
> is to put on your Sash and go "Drumming".[147]

Thankfully, pieces like these more often than not remained scribbles in his notebooks and failed to make it to publication. To take another example, probably written during or in the immediate aftermath of the Second World War:

> There was a fellow like you and me
> Who went to France in the infantry
> And kept the Germans from the Sea
> And died, thank God, not an O.B.E.[148]

But to give Murray some credit for his creative writing, these handwritten poems sit alongside typescripts of more sophisticated short stories that address subjects including social relations in the Glens of Antrim during the land wars. One, entitled 'The Gamekeeper and the Poacher', follows the misfortunate adventures of Alic Jameson, a 'boozer' drawn into a poaching scheme hatched by two friends. The land on which they ply their trade is owned by a Lord Osborne and guarded by Andy Thompson, a gamekeeper and Jameson's father-in-law. Eventually caught in the act by Thompson, who faces the dilemma of whether to report his son-in-law, Jameson and his two accomplices wind up in Crumlin Road Gaol. Rejected by the BBC on the grounds that it was too long, the story was never amended or resubmitted for consideration.[149]

Other works in progress included studies of Marxist political economy, based on information painstakingly harvested from local and national newspapers. One notable example is 'Belfast Bullion', which details the high levels of British investment in the Northern Ireland financial industry and in Harland & Wolff. A description of monopoly capitalism in motion, it shines a light on the dominance of five English banks and a handful of influential directors over these sectors of the Northern Ireland economy.[150] It is rather more unfortunate that articles such as these, which sit in Murray's private papers, remained undeveloped and unpublished. They demonstrate his understanding of and ability to apply the concepts of Marxist economics with reference to Northern Ireland, and, given his obvious theoretical debt to Lenin's seminal work, show that he was capable of going beyond the fundamentally Irish republican conception of British foreign policy as imperialism.

Murray's prose, more stylistically impressive and suitable for publication than his poetry and fiction, found a wider intellectual readership thanks in part to Peadar O'Donnell, who had taken over as editor of *The Bell*. Probably the most important literary journal produced in twentieth century Ireland, *The Bell* gave an outlet for writers such as Flann O'Brien, Jack B. Yeats, Louis Macneice, John Hewitt, George Bernard Shaw, Brendan Behan and Patrick Kavanagh, to name but a few. It is uncertain whether another editor would have solicited his contributions. O'Donnell did, however, thereby ensuring that Murray's name sits uneasily alongside the pantheon of literary greats. In addition to the pieces he wrote on international affairs, amended and published under O'Donnell's name, Murray contributed a number of articles and at least two book reviews in his own right.[151] One piece, 'Robinson Crusoe Politics', went for the jugular of big house Unionism, attacking its cooperation with the Tories in a recent County Down by-election and the presence of a Conservative minister at the Unionist Party annual conference. This intervention in the political affairs of the North was, he argued, a continuation of Home Rule crisis when the Tories used 'Unionist Ulster as a battering ram' against their opponents in Westminster. But rather than dismissing Unionist ideology as inherently reactionary, he recognised its 'socially homogenous' character, with the industrialists liaising with shopkeepers, lawyers, the professional middle class and the working-class UULA contingent whom the CPNI aspired to represent.[152]

Because he was a republican communist, Murray's contemptuous treatment of Unionist and Tory parties throughout the period under discussion was predictable and at the same time contradictory. Ideologically committed to a thirty-two county socialist republic, there was a profound irony in his loyalty to the emerging British social democratic and welfare state. The Stormont government did anticipate measures such as the National Insurance Act (Northern Ireland), which provided financial assistance for the sick, unemployed, the retired, widows and orphans, women on maternity, and those incurring the cost of funerals. However, as Murray's editorials for *Unity* noted, there were forces within the Unionist administration fiercely opposed to the introduction of the socialistic post-war settlement to the North, including the bill that laid the foundations for the creation of the National Health Service.[153] Murray described the opposition of senior Unionist figures to parity with Britain as the 'ourselves alone' approach, a play on words that drew unwelcome comparisons with Sinn Féin. This often led to further, more probing criticisms of the Unionist Party's raison d'etre. On the unveiling of the statue of James Craig at Stormont, he chipped in with a jibe at the two most celebrated Unionist leaders' achievements:

> The net result of the labours of the two noble lords [Carson and Craig] now in bronze at Stormont, was to give one part of Ireland a Republic and the other the very Home Rule against which they had fought all their lives.

It is highly unlikely that Murray's writings featured high on the Unionist Party's agenda. However, they may have had some influence in the shipyards, where the CPNI's presence was strongest. There he would have interacted with members of the UULA and others 'far removed from the privileged circles', the very people who by continuing to vote Tory by proxy were likely to 'imperil the very causes they are seeking to uphold'.[154]

Even though Murray had articulated a strong case against Unionist rule, unemployment, emigration, demoralisation and dwindling membership figures prevented the CPNI from building on its strong tradition of mobilisation around single issues. The transition from a wartime to peacetime economy did breed resistance against attacks on jobs, wages and conditions. In this context, the shops stewards' movement came to the fore and leading shop stewards, communists included, became union officials or executive members. Malachy Gray, who kept office in the Amalgamated Transport and General Workers' Union (ATGWU) until 1949, when the union introduced a ban on communists holding positions, recalled fighting redundancies and participating in demonstrations for the 'Right to Work'.[155] Betty Sinclair returned in 1947 to take up the post of Belfast Trades Council secretary, a position she held until her death in 1981.[156] In the same year, a three-week strike by 5,000 workers at Shorts aircraft factory secured the reinstatement of Andy Barr, a communist shop steward in the Sheetmetal Workers' Union, and Andy Holmes, a NILP member who sat in council with Barr in the works committee.[157] However, these years witnessed nothing on the scale of the outdoor relief strikes or even the wartime strikes. Furthermore, Brooke's success in winning the argument within his party ensured that British welfarism was extended to the North and his resumption of populist rhetoric all had the effect of further reducing the CPNI's political role to that of an insignificant observer.

The CPNI's integration into British labour structures, along with the Comintern's dissolution, meant greater interaction with the British party. In his capacity as CPNI chairman, Murray travelled back and forth to King Street for meetings and attended no fewer than five congresses in Scotland and England between 1945 and the end of the decade. In February 1947, with Britain, France and other major powers facing the growing threat of decolonisation, and with Irish nationalist sentiments finding expression in the work of groups such as the Anti-Partition League (APL) and the Friends of Ireland at Westminster, he accompanied Barr and McCullough at a conference of communist parties within the British Empire. Typically, the conference produced no tangible outcomes in terms of CPNI activity. However, Murray's speech gives an insight into his thinking on the national question. He spoke of events in India and of how the partition of Ireland was a 'classical example of how such a problem should not be solved'. With the border removed, he continued, 'the road to socialism will be open to the Irish people'.[158] McCullough's speech and a party statement, while confirming support for Irish reunification in principle, were enveloped in qualifications and contingencies that reflected the rapidly changing environment and ongoing debates within the labour movement.[159]

Of greater significance than the CPGB link, in terms of CPNI tactics and Northern Ireland more generally, was the CPI connection with the Connolly Association, whose lineage can be traced back to the London branch of the Republican Congress. Murray first attended the Connolly Association's annual conference in 1944 and availed of opportunities to discuss Irish matters with Greaves, Jimmy Shields, Pat Clancy and others during his visits to England. Matt Treacy, in a polemical work tainted with conspiracy theories, has shown how Murray's party and Greaves' organisation toed and froed on the national question before settling on a position that placed the onus on the British labour movement for ending partition.[160] At the same time, the Belfast communists vowed to use what influence they had to 'lessen the oppression in the Six Counties, and open the way to a fuller democracy' i.e. campaign for democratic reform of the northern state. Proposals towards this objective included: a return to the Government of Ireland Act and proportional representation, which would end gerrymandering and give northern Catholics a political voice; the introduction of 'one man, one vote'; and repeal of the Special Powers Act.[161] The party, therefore, continued to move away from Unionism but not necessarily towards a form of politics aimed at countering the integrative effects of the British social democratic and welfare state.

Murray's response to the Republic of Ireland Act (1948) lays bare his frustration at a lack of progress towards Irish reunification but also, significantly, a sense of resignation that the constitutional status of Northern Ireland would be settled for another generation. John A. Costello, Taoiseach of Ireland's first inter-party government, announced the legislation whilst on a speaking tour of Canada in September, much to the surprise and displeasure of his partners in government. It proposed to repeal the External Relations Act of 1936, withdraw Éire from the Commonwealth and declare a republic.[162] Loyal to the Soviet Union and the 'socialist democracies' of Eastern Europe, Murray feared that withdrawal from the Commonwealth would result in the South being exploited by a US-led 'Western bloc' through economic integration, NATO membership and, ultimately, the establishment of US defence bases. Although the latter two claims proved unfounded, his analysis was prescient in dealing with the national question. Firstly, he recognised that while the 'move has the advantage of outflanking de Valera's party' in the short term, it would have the unintended effect of leaving future Irish governments impotent on northern affairs. Secondly, he observed that it cleared the way for Attlee's government to fall in behind Brooke and consolidate partition.[163] Under pressure from the Northern Ireland Prime Minister, and wary of a Conservative intervention on the matter, British Labour responded sympathetically to Unionist concerns and published the Ireland Bill on 3 May 1949. The resulting Ireland Act affirmed that 'in no event will Northern Ireland or any part thereof cease to be part ... of the United Kingdom without the consent of the Parliament of Northern Ireland'. Whilst representing an abdication of Britain's responsibility for the Northern Ireland problem, it gave added legal protection to the political aspirations of Ulster Unionism and reinforced the conditions for the separate political development of the two states of Ireland.

In spite of his attempts to adapt to post-war realities, Murray's statement, oft repeated in Irish socialist circles – 'You can ignore the national question, but the national question will never ignore you' – had indeed come back to haunt him.[164] It was clear from the outset that the February 1949 'chapel-gates' election, so called because APL collections were held at chapel gates in the South, would be fought on the border. Having begun to adopt a more critical attitude towards the Stormont government, the NILP came under sustained pressure from the Unionist press to express an official preference on the pressing political question of the day. Consequently, the prospect of attempting to challenge Unionist hegemony on Brooke's terms sent pro-Union and agnostic NILPers scrambling to cement their links with British Labour. When the NILP finally endorsed the constitutional status quo, this was at the expense of party unity. Individual members drifted out of the party and the leadership expelled the West Belfast branch for convening a conference in opposition to its declaration.[165] Most of the dissenters, including the whole West Belfast branch, gravitated towards the remaining anti-partitionists in Stormont – Frank Hanna, who had just resigned from the NILP, and Harry Diamond of the Socialist Republican Party – and Jack Beattie. They soon coalesced around the Irish Labour Party, which sanctioned the establishment of northern branches in response to the Ireland Act and the NILP split.[166]

The CPNI fielded only one candidate for the Stormont election. Billy McCullough returned to Bloomfield to campaign on matters of economic reform; against the deindustrialisation of Belfast; for heavier taxation of big business and increased state investment; and for trade agreements between Northern Ireland and the Soviet Union.[167] We cannot find him guilty of 'refusing to confront' the fraught issue of partition.[168] It is truer to say his message was ambiguous and yet consistent with the party's approach in the years that followed the war. On the one hand, McCullough's election statement advanced economic arguments in favour of Irish reunification.[169] On the other, he instructed canvassers to downplay the issue on the doorsteps and concentrate on emphasising the link with social democratic Britain.[170] However, in the context of a return to the sectarian politics, this proved no match for the Unionist Party's ability to

> merge welfarism with populism with greater ease. Welfare benefits were presented as the fruit of the British connection and Catholics stigmatised as two-faced intransigents for accepting the benefits while continuing to reject the legitimacy of the state.[171]

In a bitterly fought election, the Unionist propaganda machine went to work and loyalist mobs were deployed against labour candidates such as Jack Beattie, who took to wearing a steel helmet for the duration of the campaign.[172] Although the NILP fielded only nine candidates, one of these, Tom Boyd, stood in Bloomfield and mustered enough support to beat McCullough into third place. The CPNI general secretary's paltry 623 votes were 5,000 fewer than in 1945, revealing a remarkable decline in support and the importance of objective conditions in shaping the fortunes of a marginal party.

In June 1948, the CPNI reported that only thirty-one of its sixty members in East Belfast, of which Murray was secretary, were paying their dues. Even fewer attended meetings regularly.[173] The 1951 Belfast Corporation elections yielded only 715 votes for the shipyard worker, Jimmy Graham, and 482 for Eddie Menzies, a founding member of the CPI and stalwart of its East Belfast branch. The CPNI had accumulated members and sympathisers rapidly due to its association with the victorious Red Army as well as its positive engagement with the Beveridge proposals and the declining appeal of pinkish Unionism. However, the leadership had shown no inclination at the time to question where the party's newfound support was coming from. As the national question once again came to the fore, enabling the Unionist Party to retain its grip on the Protestant working class, and as the onset of the Cold War began to undo the advantages of maintaining a connection with the Soviet Union, the party began to haemorrhage support.

Murray inherited this situation and attempted, with the help of Billy McCullough, the Connolly Association and others, to recalibrate the party's strategy away from Unionism and its identification with the British national interest. It says something of his character and commitment to the party that another leadership spell appealed after the travails of his embattled time as CPI general secretary. Whereas he remained loyal to the concept of a communist party in one form or another, Larkin junior had begun to desert what he saw as a sinking ship and carve out a career as a radical Labour Party politician. Given the latter's familial and trade union links, it is perhaps unfair to judge Murray's progress against his. Yet, the two were of comparable intellect and talent, and had set off on their political journeys from precisely the same point at the Lenin School. Their contrasting political trajectories are a graphic illustration of the effects of specific circumstances and the *choices* made by two individuals. By 1949, young Jim was a highly popular TD for Dublin South-Central, general secretary of the WUI and president of the ITUC. Indeed, one historian notes that he is 'widely regarded as the best leader Labour never had'.[174] Murray was regarded by activists as the 'brains' of the CPNI, yet he had only just recaptured his status as a big fish in a very small pond.[175]

NOTES

1 CPUSA skit, 1939, cited in Howard Zinn, *A People's History of the United States: 1492 to the Present* (Revised ed.) (New York, 2010), p.407.

2 NAI, DJ, JUS8/459, Garda Special Branch report, 9 December 1937.

3 Seán Murray, *Craigavon in the Dock* (Belfast, 1938).

4 *Workers' Republic*, July 1938.

5 Emmet O'Connor, *Reds and the Green: Ireland, Russia and the Communist Internationals, 1919-43* (Dublin, 2004), p.224; DCLA, CPI Nolan/Palmer Collection, Box 4/016, Letter from J.R. Campbell to Belfast branch CPI, 18 October 1938.

6 NAI, DJ, 2008/117/928, Garda Special Branch report, 28 July 1938.

7 Ibid., 11 May 1938.

8 NAI, DJ, JUS8/464, Garda Special Branch report, 26 March 1938.

9 Margaret Ward, *Hanna Sheehy Skeffington: A Life* (Cork, 1997), p.334.

10 *Workers' Republic*, May 1938.

11 NAI, DJ, 2008/117/928, Garda Special Branch report, 11 May 1938.

12 Ibid., 27 September, 20 October 1938.

13 Eric Hobsbawm, *Age of Extremes: The Short Twentieth Century, 1914-1991* (London, 1995), p.146.

14 NAI, DJ, 2008/117/928, Garda Special Branch report, 27 September 1938.

15 NAI, DJ, JUS8/743, Garda Special Branch report, 25 November 1939.

16 DCLA, CPI Nolan/Palmer Collection, Box 8/077, Minutes of national meeting, 2 April 1939.

17 PRONI, HA/32/1/559, RUC Special Branch report, 25 July 1938.

18 PRONI, HA/32/1/556, RUC Special Branch report, 15 August 1938.

19 *Belfast Telegraph*, 6 August 1938.

20 PRONI, HA/32/1/556, RUC Special Branch report, 15 August 1938.

21 NAI, DJ, 2008/117/928, Garda Special Branch report, 20 October 1938.

22 Ibid., 31 July 1938.

23 O'Connor, *Reds and the Green*, p.225; Matt Treacy, *The Communist Party of Ireland 1921-2011: Vol. 1: 1921-1969* (Dublin, 2013), pp.113-15.

24 NAI, DJ, 2008/117/928, Garda Special Branch report, 17 December 1938.

25 O'Connor, *Reds and the Green*, p.225.

26 NAI, DJ, 2008/117/928, Garda Special Branch report, 17 December 1938.

27 *Irish Workers' Weekly*, 6 May 1939.

28 *Workers' Bulletin*, 1 April 1939.

29 Ibid., 15 April 1939.

30 *Irish Workers' Weekly*, 24 June 1939.

31 Ibid., 29 April 1939.

32 Ibid., 6, 27 May 1939.

33 Ibid., 5 August 1939.

34 Ibid., 26 August 1939.

35 Seán Nolan (ed.), *Communist Party of Ireland Outline History* (Dublin, 1975), p.38.

36 *Irish Workers' Weekly*, 16 September 1939.

37 Kevin McDermott and Jeremy Agnew, *The Comintern: A History of International Communism from Lenin to Stalin* (Basingstoke, 1996), p.193.

38 *Irish Workers' Weekly*, 25 November 1939.

39 Ibid., 1 June 1940.

40 Ram Shakal Singh and Champa Singh, *Indian Communism: Its role towards Indian polity* (New Dehli, 1991), pp.54-6.

41 Neta C. Crawford, *Argument and Change in World Politics: Ethics, Decolonization and Humanitarian Intervention* (Cambridge, 2002), p.297.

42 *Irish Workers' Weekly*, 16 December 1939.

43 C. Desmond Greaves Papers, Resolution from North, 27 January 1940.

44 *Irish Workers' Weekly*, 27 January 1940.

45 *Irish Times*, 5 March 1940.

46 Brian Barton, *Northern Ireland in the Second World War* (Belfast, 1995), p.24.

47 DCLA, CPI Nolan/Palmer Collection, Box 6/017, Report of branch meeting, 17 December 1939.

48 Treacy, *The Communist Party of Ireland*, p.128.

49 DCLA, CPI Nolan/Palmer Collection, Box 6/017, Report of branch meeting, 17 December 1939.

50 *Irish Times*, 23 July 1940.

51 *Irish Workers' Weekly*, 30 March 1940.

52 *Irish Times*, 12, 19 October 1940.

53 Treacy, *The Communist Party of Ireland*, pp.130-1.

54 Donal Ó Drisceoil, *Censorship in Ireland, 1939-1945: Neutrality, Politics and Society* (Cork, 1996), p.87.

55 O'Connor, *Reds and the Green*, p.229.

56 Ó Drisceoil, *Censorship in Ireland*, pp.95-129.

57 Mike Milotte, *Communism in Modern Ireland: The Pursuit of the Workers' Republic since 1916* (Dublin, 1984), p.185.

58 Treacy, *The Communist Party of Ireland*, pp.126-30.

59 *Irish Workers' Weekly*, 10 August 1940.

60 Ibid., 24 August 1940.

61 Ibid., 31 August 1940.

62 NAUK, KV2/1185, Metropolitan Police Special Branch memo, July 1944.

63 *Irish Workers' Weekly*, 20 July 1940.

64 Ibid., 26 April 1941.

65 Angus Calder, *The People's War: Britain, 1939-1945* (London, 1969).

66 C. Desmond Greaves Papers, Military service certificate, 18 December 1940; Letter from Department of Defence, 19 December 1940; Award of Military Service Pension, 28 December 1940.

67 Anthony Coughlan (ed.), *Insight, Ideas, Politics: The Table Talk of C. Desmond Greaves, 1960-1988* (unpublished, 2012), p.117.

68 *Irish Workers' Weekly*, 8, 15 March, 1941.

69 PRONI, Seán Murray Papers, D2162/M/4, Letter from the CPUSA fifth district, New York, 3 January 1939.

70 C. Desmond Greaves Papers, Letter from Bill Gannon to Murray, 7 August 1941.

71 *Irish Workers' Weekly*, 22 June 1941.

72 George Orwell, 'The Prevention of Literature', in *Shooting an Elephant and Other Essays* (London, 2009), p.217.

73 O'Connor, *Reds and the Green*, p.231.

74 *Irish News*, 1 October 1941.

75 Henry Patterson, *Ireland since 1939: The Persistence of Conflict* (Dublin, 2007), pp. 39-40; Graham Walker, *The Politics of Frustration: Harry Midgley and the Failure of Labour in Northern Ireland* (Manchester, 1985), pp.124-9.

76 PRONI, Seán Murray Papers, D2162/M/5, Letter from Bill [McCullough] to Seán Murray, 1 October 1941; Letter from Ministry of Home Affairs to Jack Beattie, 8 October 1941.

77 The party refrained from using the name 'Communist Party of Northern Ireland' officially. The terms 'Communist Party, Belfast branch', 'Communist Party of Ireland', 'Irish Communist Party' and 'Communist Party' were used interchangeably. However, the party is known colloquially as the CPNI. It distinguishes the northern communists from those operating in the South, and the term's usage is preferred in the party's *Outline History* (Dublin, 1975).

78 PRONI, Seán Murray Papers, D2162/P/1/1/6,9,10, Trade union contribution cards (1942-1948).

79 I am obliged to Fiontánn McElheran for this information.

80 Author's interview with Bill Somerset, 15 June 2010.

81   Emmet O'Connor, 'John (Seán) Murray', in Keith Gildart, David Howell and
      Neville Kirk (eds), *Dictionary of Labour Biography, Vol. XI* (London, 2003), p.204.

82   Author's interview with Roy Johnston (via email), 5 June 2010.

83   Michael McInerney, *Peadar O'Donnell: Irish Social Rebel* (Dublin, 1974), pp.97-9.

84   O'Connor, 'John (Seán) Murray', p.204.

85   Author's interview with Jimmy and Edwina Stewart, 18 March 2010.

86   D.R. O'Connor Lysaght, 'The Communist Party of Ireland: A Critical History', Part
      3 (1976) http://www.workersrepublic.org/Pages/Ireland/Communism/cpihistory3.
      html (accessed 10 September 2014).

87   Terry Cradden, *Trade Unionism, Socialism and Partition* (Belfast, 1993), p.25.

88   Milotte, *Communism in Modern Ireland*, pp.194-5.

89   Billy McCullough, *Ireland's Way Forward: Report of the First National Congress of the
      CPI* (Belfast, 1942).

90   *Unity*, 2, 20 January, 26 February, 6 March 1943.

91   Ibid., 25 December 1942.

92   Neil Redfearn, 'British Communists, the British Empire and the Second World
      War, *International Labor and Working-Class History*, No. 65 (Spring 2004), p.123.

93   NAUK, KV2/1185, Note on Seán Murray (n.d.); *Unity*, 18 December 1943.

94   Phillip Ollerenshaw, 'War, Industrial Mobilisation and Society in Northern Ireland,
      1939-1945', *Contemporary European History*, Vol. 16, No. 2 (2007), p.188.

95   Barton, *Northern Ireland in the Second World War*, pp.20-1; Ollerenshaw, 'War,
      Industrial Mobilisation and Society in Northern Ireland', p.185.

96   Emmet O'Connor, *A Labour History of Ireland, 1824-2000* (Dublin, 2011), p.204.

97   Christopher J.V. Loughlin, 'Pro-Hitler or Anti-Management? War on the Industrial
      Front, Belfast, October 1942', in David Convery (ed.), *Locked Out: A Century of
      Irish Working-Class Life* (Dublin, 2013).

98   Boyd Black, 'A Triumph of Voluntarism? Industrial Relations and Strikes in
      Northern Ireland in World War Two', *Labour History Review*, Vol. 70, No. 1 (April
      2005), p.12.

99   *Unity*, 28 November 1942.

100   Walker, *The Politics of Frustration*, p.57.

101   Ciaran Crossey and James Monaghan, 'The Origins of Trotskyism in Ireland',
      Revolutionary History, Vol. 6, No. 2/3 (Summer 1996), pp.29-31; Michael Farrell,
      Northern Ireland: The Orange State (2nd ed.) (London, 1980), pp.173-5; Milotte,
      Communism in Modern Ireland, pp.204-6.

102   Black, 'A triumph of voluntarism?', pp.10-15.

103   Billy McCullough, *But Victory Sooner* (Belfast, 1943), p.12.

104   *Unity*, 16 March 1944.

105   Ibid., 30 March 1944.

106   Black, 'A triumph of voluntarism?', p.13.

107   *Unity*, 20 April 1944.

108   Keith Gildart, 'Coal Strikes on the Home Front: Miners' Militancy and Socialist Politics in the Second World War', *Twentieth Century British History*, Vol. 20, No. 2 (2009), pp.121-51; John McIlroy and Alan Campbell, 'The last chance saloon? The Independent Labour Party and miners' militancy in the Second World War revisited', *Journal of Contemporary History*, Vol. 46, No. 4 (October 2011), pp.871-96.

109   Black, 'A triumph of voluntarism', p.10.

110   Nolan (ed.), *CPI Outline History*, pp.38-9.

111   *Unity*, 16 January, 23 December 1943.

112   Letter from Andy Boyd to Emmet O'Connor, 17 December 2003.

113   PRONI, Seán Murray Papers, D2162/5/5/1-8, Letters from Jack White, 23 June 1943 - 7 April 1945.

114   Charlie McGuire, *Roddy Connolly and the Struggle for Socialism in Ireland* (Cork, 2008), pp.188-9.

115   UCDA, Seán MacEntee Papers, P67/522 (3), Revolutionary organisations in the Saorstát, January 1942 - December 1943.

116   DCLA, CPI Nolan/Palmer collection, Box 6/013, Dublin district committee minutes (1938-1944).

117   See Niamh Puirséil, *The Irish Labour Party, 1922-73* (Dublin, 2007), pp.95-114.

118   Treacy, *The Communist Party of Ireland*, pp.163-80.

119   Neil Redfearn, 'British Communists, the British Empire and the Second World War', p.117.

120   *Unity*, 8 May 1943.

121   McCullough, *But Victory Sooner*, pp.3, 10-11.

122   *Unity*, 6 February 1943.

123   Ibid., 16 November 1944; See Paul Bew, Peter Gibbon and Henry Patterson, *The State in Northern Ireland, 1971-72: Political Forces and Social Classes* (Manchester, 1979) for an elucidation of the tensions between the 'populist' and 'anti-populist' wings of the Unionist Party.

124   *Unity*, 30 November 1944.

125   Farrell, *The Orange State*, pp.165-7.

126   *Unity*, 13 March 1943.

127   Billy McCullough, *Ireland Looks to Labour* (Belfast, 1943), p.10.

128   Milotte, *Communism in Modern Ireland*, p.208.

129   McCullough, *Ireland Looks to Labour*, pp.22-3.

130 Cradden, *Trade Unionism, Socialism and Partition*, p.26; Milotte, *Communism in Modern Ireland*, p.202.

131 McCullough, *Ireland Looks to Labour*, pp.7-9, 23.

132 *Unity*, 19 June 1943.

133 Ibid., 31 July 1943.

134 Ibid., 7, 14 August, 16 October 1943.

135 Cradden, *Trade Unionism, Socialism and Partition*, pp.36-7; *Unity*, 6 November 1943.

136 Milotte, *Communism in Modern Ireland*, p.208

137 PRONI, Seán Murray Papers, D2162/A/5, CPNI election leaflet (1945).

138 Walker, *A History of the Ulster Unionist Party*, p.100.

139 NAUK, KV2/1185, Serial 91a, Extract from RUC Special Branch report, 24 July 1946; Serial 93a, Extract from RUC Special Branch report, 24 July 1946.

140 UCDA, Seán MacEntee Papers, P67/548, Department of Justice report (1947).

141 Hazel Morrissey, 'Betty Sinclair: A Woman's Fight for Socialism, 1910-1981', *Saothar*, 9, p.127.

142 *Unity*, 23 February 1946.

143 Ibid., 6 December 1945.

144 Ibid., 20 September 1945.

145 Ibid., 6 April 1946.

146 Ibid., 12 October 1946. See also the *Irish Review*, May 1948, in which Murray writes a positive review of Desmond Ryan's (ed.) *Socialism and Nationalism: A Selection from the Writings of James Connolly* (Dublin, 1948).

147 *Northern Worker (Incorporating Unity)*, Vol. 1, No.1 (November 1949).

148 PRONI, Seán Murray Papers, D2162/P/1/1/2/9, Selection of handwritten poems on scrap paper (n.d.).

149 PRONI, Seán Murray Papers, D2162/P/1/2/2/4, 'The Gamekeeper and the Poacher' (n.d.).

150 PRONI, Seán Murray Papers, D2162/C/5, 'Belfast Bullion' (c. 1946).

151 Richard English, *Radicals and the Republic: Socialist Republicanism in the Irish Free State, 1925-1937* (Oxford, 1994), p.178fn.

152 Seán Murray, 'Robinson Crusoe Politics', *The Bell*, Vol XII, No. 6 (September 1946), pp.502-8.

153 *Unity*, 30 March, 16 April, 6 July 1946.

154 Ibid., 8 November 1945.

155 Malachy Gray, 'Reminiscence: A Shop Steward Remembers', *Saothar*, 11 (1986), p.114.

156 Morrissey, 'Betty Sinclair', p.127.

157 Farrell, *The Orange State*, p.191.

158 NAUK, KV2/1185, Serial 101a, Extract from Metropolitan Police Special Branch report, 5 March 1947.

159 DCLA, CPI Nolan/Palmer Collection, Box 11/011, Communist Party special conference statement on the border, 17 November 1946; *Irish Democrat*, March 1947.

160 Treacy, *The Communist Party of Ireland*, p.194.

161 PRONI, Seán Murray Papers, D2162/F/9, Party statement on Ireland and anti-partition campaign, November 1947; D2162/M/8, Letter from Murray to the *Manchester Guardian* (1947).

162 J.J. Lee, *Ireland, 1912-1985: Politics and Society* (Cambridge, 1989), p.300.

163 PRONI, Seán Murray Papers, D2162/A/12a, Seán Murray, 'External Relations Act' (1948).

164 Author's interview with Eoin Ó Murchú, 17 May 2010. Murray's statement has obvious echoes of a famous aphorism concerning the dialectic, commonly attributed to Leon Trotsky and popularly rendered, 'you may not be interested in war but war is interested in you'.

165 Aaron Edwards, *A History of the Northern Ireland Labour Party: Democratic Socialism and Sectarianism* (Manchester, 2009), pp.36-43.

166 O'Connor, *A Labour History of Ireland*, pp.214-15.

167 *Irish Democrat*, February 1949.

168 Milotte, *Communism in Modern Ireland*, p.122.

169 *Irish Democrat*, February 1949.

170 PRONI, Seán Murray Papers, D2162/A/16, Facts for speakers and canvassers (1949).

171 Bew, Gibbon and Patterson, *Northern Ireland*, p.125.

172 Cradden, *Trade Unionism, Socialism and Partition*, p.178.

173 Milotte, *Communism in Modern Ireland*, p.112.

174 O'Connor, *A Labour History of Ireland*, p.130fn.

175 NAUK, KV2/1185, Note on Seán Murray (n.d.).

CHAPTER 5

Between Marxism-Leninism and Left Reformism

Abolition of all anti-democratic laws, an end to civil and religious discrimination, and an end to the rigging of electoral areas in the interests of the wealthy, can be accomplished by the united action of the people. The organised Labour movement is the force to lead the struggle for democracy and the rights of the individual to participate with equality in public affairs. The Communist Party has this struggle as its foremost aim.[1]

The 1950s was a decade of political turbulence and economic transformation, leading to what is commonly known as the Golden Age of Capitalism. Old empires had started to crumble, soon to be replaced by a new order dominated by American capital and the US state. The Cold War had begun in earnest, throwing into conflict two competing ideologies and economic systems. Facing economic malaise and high emigration in the South, the decline of traditional industries and problems of peripherality in the North, Ireland was neither immune from nor central to these developments. The government of Éire refused to join NATO in the interest of protecting official neutrality and its political independence, but the Marshall Plan, the Anglo-Irish Trade Agreement (1948) and the work of the Industrial Development Authority (IDA) in attracting foreign direct investment had the effect of strengthening its economic ties with Britain and accelerating its integration into the global economy. The post-war compromise and parity with Britain had similar integrative effects on Northern Ireland, though a number of political anomalies persisted. Real and alleged discrimination in housing allocation, the absence of 'one man, one vote', the role of the B Specials, the use of Special Powers legislation – all of these issues made the region a place apart from the British liberal democratic state. Added to this was the Unionist government's continued refusal to recognise the Northern Ireland Committee (NIC) of the ITUC or to follow Westminster's example in repealing the antiquated Trade Disputes Act. Ireland was, therefore, part of the Western bloc in some respects and outside of it in others.

Whereas the loyalties of West European socialists fell somewhere between 'nationalist neutralism and supra-national European Atlanticism',[2] the Irish communists continued to use the Soviet Union and the 'socialist democracies' of Eastern Europe as a reference point. One major problem for the CPNI and the newborn Irish Workers' League (IWL) in particular was that they too encountered the 'apocalyptic rhetoric' that consumed American society throughout the 1950s.[3] The imprisonment of Cardinal Mindzenty of Hungary and Cardinal Stepinac of Zagreb, an apologist for Ante Pavelić's murderous Ustasha regime, provided the headlines that contributed to the public's fear of the communist menace. A demonstration against Mindzenty's imprisonment attracted around 150,000 people, including Jim Larkin junior and Dublin Lord Mayor, John Breen, another former CPI member.[4] Such was the influence of the Church in this respect that staff at Radio Éireann refused to broadcast commentary of a soccer match between Ireland and Yugoslavia, while the Army No.1 Band was prevented from playing the obligatory pre-match national anthems.[5] Irish McCarthyism found willing purveyors of its message in the Catholic *Standard*, the *Irish Independent*, the Anglo-Unionist *Irish Times*, and in the personage of Archbishop John Charles McQuaid, who encouraged the formation of vigilance groups to monitor and actively combat 'atheistic' communist influences in the Labour Party and in the Dublin area.[6]

Archbishop McQuaid's unrivalled access to the policymaking instruments of the state gave the Church an effective veto on social and economic policy. McQuaid was central to the Mother and Child Crisis, which ended the political career of Clann na Poblachta minister, Dr Noel Browne. Developed initially by Fianna Fáil and advanced by Dr Browne, the Mother and Child Scheme proposed to introduce free maternity care for all mothers and free healthcare for all children up the age of sixteen, thus advancing the concept of universality that was central to the British welfare state. On the one hand, the Irish Medical Association strongly objected to the scheme on the grounds that free healthcare would result in a loss of earnings. But it was the Catholic hierarchy's trenchant opposition to state intervention in the areas of social security, health and education that prevented the scheme from being introduced. When the pressure mounted on Browne, neither his Clann na Poblachta colleagues nor Labour ministers came to his defence. Even the Parliamentary Labour Party, which included Roddy Connolly and Larkin junior, refused to fall in behind his radical proposals. Privately, Murray was disappointed with young Jim's 'careful evasion of the means test issue', on which the Labour leader and Tánaiste, William Norton had conceded much ground to Fine Gael.[7] But it is clear, as Browne lamented in later life, that despite their efforts the communists were 'entirely ineffective' in the face of clerical opposition.[8] In April 1951, he resigned from the cabinet at the request of Seán MacBride and was expelled from his party shortly thereafter. The affair marked a watershed in the history of Church-state relations, led quickly to the collapse of the inter-party government and revealed Labour's impotence as the weaker partner in a coalition.

Perhaps nothing expresses the scale of the challenge facing the Irish communist movement so well as the fact that its two parties represented almost no one. The enthusiastically pro-Soviet IWL was clearly hamstrung by the anti-communist atmosphere in Dublin, particularly in the context of the Korean War, 1950-53. Roy Johnston recalls encountering 'personal hostility' when selling copies of the *Irish Workers' Voice* in public and notes that party members only achieved a fraction of their target of 6,000 sales in 1950.[9] In this environment, the decision to launch a peace campaign was ill advised, because it projected onto the party an objective identification with the Soviet Union. IWL members were met with violent opposition on the streets of Dublin and managed to collect only 3,000 signatures in the twenty-six counties. In June 1951, IWL chairman, Michael O'Riordan, stood as a candidate in the general election on the back of his party's support for Browne during the Mother and Child Crisis, but received a paltry 295 votes.[10] Anti-communism also had a bearing on the CPNI's weakened state. Nationalist politicians, the *Irish News* and conservative organisations such as Maria Duce frustrated the party's efforts to organise in Catholic West Belfast and Derry.[11] Northern Ireland Prime Minister, Basil Brooke, also waxed lyrical about Ulster's vital role as a bulwark against international communism during a speaking tour of the US.[12] However, the red scare does not fully account for the CPNI's decline. The problems facing the northern communists were many, varied and, as the 1945-49 period demonstrates, of their own making.

As these factors coalesced, a conference of the Belfast district party membership on 1-2 July 1950 re-elected Murray to the executive committee and appointed him national party organiser, a position he held until his death.[13] Upon his accession to the post, the Irish movement had neither concrete organisational structures nor a coherent programme. Schooled in Marxist-Leninist methods of organisation, Murray regarded the absence of a CPNI newspaper as one telling weakness. He attempted to rectify this particular problem by setting up the weekly *Northern Worker,* but financial difficulties forced it out of circulation in November 1950 after only seven issues. In lieu of a secure CPNI publication, the party membership was encouraged to adopt the CPGB's *Daily Worker* as their official newspaper. Murray made progress in education, recommencing weekly lectures on Marxist theory and Irish history and devising lessons to equip up-and-coming party leaders with effective public speaking techniques. He also launched himself into youth work with great enthusiasm, encouraging the formation and development of the Young Workers' League (YWL), latterly the Socialist Youth League (SYL). Former members of the youth branch testify to Murray's approachable nature and to his formative influence on their politics.[14] Indeed, it is clear that he had a hand in virtually all aspects of cadre development. His papers indicate that he was ubiquitous on the party's political committee for the duration of the decade, responsible for drafting resolutions, statements and bulletins on everything pertaining to non-industrial work. RUC Special Branch described him as the 'brain behind the organisation and the person from whom the rank and file seek advice'.[15]

It is possible to discern a number of important tasks facing Murray and his comrades in leadership positions. In terms of organising, there was a pressing need to rebuild the CPNI at grassroots level, merge party work with the needs of the disenfranchised through single-issue campaigns and branch out across the North. The most obvious foundation for a rebuilding exercise was the trade union movement, where the CPNI retained a strong presence. In this sense, the party was the envy of the IWL. By 1951, Jimmy Stewart had become treasurer of Belfast Trades Council, joining Betty Sinclair in office, while Andy Barr, Jimmy Graham and Billy McCullough had all been elected to its executive committee.[16] Barr would also be elected to the NIC in 1954 and to its executive in 1956. This was despite the efforts of right-wing trade union leaders such as Arthur Deakin, general secretary of the ATGWU, who was hostile to the communists' influence and spoke of his hope that 'it will never be possible for a Communist to hold office in the union'.[17] Sam Napier, secretary of the opportunistic NILP, claimed that the communist-led Belfast Peace Council had conned 'many decent and sincere people'.[18] In spite of this, the Belfast campaign outperformed its Dublin equivalent by a significant margin, collecting 11,417 signatures by February 1952.[19] The party still carried some weight in the Belfast area, but its success in rebuilding would depend on extending its influence beyond the North's first city, reaching out to non-industrial and rural workers and the unemployed, and in achieving a balance between shop floor agitation and political activity.

At the IWL's first conference in November 1949, the apparent tension between politicism and economism was the focus of intense debate. Prior to the conference, Seán Nolan wrote to Murray, primarily to consult him on the content of the main resolution, but also to complain that the forces at the IWL's disposal were 'so limited, sectarian, or immature, it will take many headaches before any real change is effected'.[20] The conference itself amounted to a meeting of the CPI national leadership. Those in attendance echoed Nolan's assessment of the IWL and agreed that the Dublin comrades urgently needed to increase their activities in the trade union movement. Michael O'Riordan conceded that his party had suffered from 'growing pains' and recognised the importance of trade union work in attracting support. Ned Stapleton argued that the IWL could learn from the CPNI by establishing industrial and factory groups in the League. Sam Nolan added the caveat that campaigns on economic issues should be instilled with 'political consciousness'. On behalf of the CPNI delegation, Betty Sinclair accepted that trade union work 'must become political', though Billy McCullough contradicted her somewhat stating that there was room for 'a little more economism in party work'. With O'Riordan placing emphasis on Ireland's anti-imperialist tradition, McCullough stressed the importance of successful economic struggles in winning northern workers over to communist politics.[21] This position reflected the CPNI's relative strength in the shipyards and within the Belfast trade union movement, but also indicated that the hard fought lessons of 1945-49 were slow in being digested.

Discussions on the future configuration of the trade union movement ran in parallel to what McCullough regarded as the 'senseless factional struggle' within Irish communism.[22] Although its members had reservations about the Congress of Irish Unions (CIU), which had a record of anti-communism, the IWL fell in behind Jim Larkin junior to advocate 'the continued preservation of the All-Ireland character and unity of the TUC, and the fullest inter-Congress unity and action at all levels'.[23] The overriding concern for the CPNI trade union contingent was not all-island unity but gaining recognition from Stormont for the NIC or an alternative body.[24] In response to Stormont's continued refusal to negotiate with the NIC, Billy McCullough hastily proffered the establishment of an Ulster or Northern Ireland TUC as a solution.[25] This may have chimed with the NILP leadership and a number of Protestant shipyard communists. However, the proposal went against the overwhelming 90 percent of NIC members who were, by 1953, affiliated to the two Irish congresses and therefore willing to work within existing structures.[26] It threatened to undermine relations with the Irish labour movement and pigeonhole the CPNI as a party of hardline Unionist workers.

If the majority of labour activists believed in the principle of trade union unity, then CPNI trade unionists were no exception. According to a September 1951 political committee report, they were open to 'co-operation with the Irish Workers League and militant Labour men and women in the South and West'.[27] Naturally, Murray's ideological commitment to an Irish labour movement meant that he saw the gradual reorganisation of the communist movement on thirty-two county lines as one dimension of his mission to reconstitute a Marxist-Leninist party with national features. The existence of an ad hoc national committee involving senior northern figures was important in creating the conditions for exploring party political unity. To that end, he and Seán Nolan were the driving forces behind the creation of a joint council in 1952, bringing the national leadership together for regular, formal meetings. Influenced by the publication of *Britain's Road to Socialism* (1951), the CPGB's new manifesto, Murray also set about developing a potentially career-defining programme that would take account of decades of acquired knowledge and experience, reflect the domestic and international challenges facing the movement, and provide the theoretical fundamentals informing discussions on tactics and organisation.

Transitional unity

As the CPNI moved gradually towards greater cooperation with the IWL and popular support for trade union unity, Murray combined forthright socialist republicanism with measured appeals to create labour harmony on issues of common purpose. In one article, he criticised Brooke for his inflammatory statements on the constitutional question and nationalists for being 'lulled to sleep' by American Congressional platitudes on Irish reunification, such as the 1951 Fogarty resolution. One of his closest allies during the period was Jack Beattie, who regained his West Belfast seat from the Unionist candidate in the

1951 general election. Murray supported Beattie's campaign and warned against the 'antics' of the breakaway Harry Diamond-Victor Halley 'clique', which he blamed for Beattie's electoral defeat in 1950.[28] The IrLP venture had begun to fall apart at the seams after Diamond aligned himself with the Catholic Church during the Mother and Child Crisis and as Frank Hanna, vice-chairman, also moved in a more explicitly Catholic nationalist direction.[29] Openly hostile to the communists since the collapse of the *Irish Democrat* alliance, Halley had spread rumours of a CPNI takeover of the IrLP and denounced a 1950 peace conference organised by Belfast Trades Council. Murray's riposte came in the form of a *Northern Worker* editorial:

> What about the policy of neutrality, which the Irish Labour Party is committed to in the present situation? Apparently Mr Victor Halley will have none of this. The war-like military spirit of Arthur Deakin has infected him, since he became one of Deakin's boys on the E.C. of the Amalgamated Transport Union.[30]

In the context of the Cold War, the CPNI's opponents within the labour movement were vocal and numerically significant. Beattie, an anti-partitionist who was prepared to work with the British Labour whip at Westminster, was one of the few exceptions.

Beattie aside, the only leftist force capable of siphoning off the Unionist support base was openly in favour of the Union. After falling foul of the national question in 1949, the NILP gradually developed the strategy of offering a pinkish alternative to the Unionist Party in predominantly Protestant constituencies. This strategy involved holding the Stormont government to account on bread and butter issues whilst carefully avoiding its record on civil liberties. Whilst claiming that the NILP had been 'diverted from the fight for a united working class and Socialism by the pressure and intrigues of the upper class and its Unionist politicians', Murray demonstrated some residual faith in the party membership as a progressive force.[31] In contrast to its wartime position, the CPNI was confident of resisting the formation of production councils and winning NILP rank-and-file members round to an anti-government position.[32] Against the backdrop of the Tories' return to power in 1951, no greater incentive existed for labour unity in the North than to combat the imminent reversals of social democratic planning and welfare legislation. As Brooke's nine MPs formed over half of the Tories' narrow majority of seventeen at Westminster, the Unionist shift to the right was evident. The Unionist group in the Commons voted consistently with the government after 1951 and the two parties even exchanged conference delegates.[33] Yet, as the debilitating effects of the Conservative administration's deflationary policies and public expenditure controls spread to Northern Ireland, elements within the cross-class Unionist bloc began to question the wisdom of the Tory link.[34] Opportunities for political and industrial labour would open up as these tensions grew more pronounced.

Meanwhile, relations with the IWL continued to thaw. In early 1952, Murray led a delegation to the League's annual conference and, on his return to Belfast, reported that cooperation between the two groups was having 'positive results'.[35] A meeting of the joint council followed in November, producing a resolution on the unity of Ireland and setting out the direction of travel for the communist movement. The main resolution expressed principled support for the eventual ending of partition and identified gradual steps towards national policies acceptable to both parties' supporters. Articulating Murray's arguments from the late 1940s, it highlighted the penetration of British and American capital as a threat to native, export-led Irish economic development and the involvement of the six counties in NATO as an affront to peace efforts. It drew inspiration from ongoing anti-colonial struggles, which, if not led by the working class or peasantry, typically incorporated them in large numbers. The document brought into sharp focus the two parties' strategies, reaffirming the dual aims of ending the CPNI's relative abstention from politics and the IWL's detachment from trade unionism. It tasked the Belfast comrades with addressing their 'isolation' from the northern Catholic minority, recommencing work on the issue of 'democratic rights' and adopting a 'national presentation' of all political issues, and the Dublin leadership with an acceleration of trade union activity and a commitment to promote labour unity.[36]

Away from the watchful eye of the IWL, Murray could persuade the CPNI executive committee to endorse the anti-colonial aspect of the joint council resolution. As a signal of the northern party's intentions, the executive committee also agreed to bring the *Irish Workers' Voice* to Belfast. A section in the IWL paper would thereafter be devoted to northern politics and the CPNI leadership expected party branches to achieve an initial sales target of 500.[37] This contradicts the claim that the *Irish Workers' Voice* 'was not sold on the streets or in the factories of Belfast' owing to the CPNI's 'completely British orientation'.[38] The joint council's second sitting, in early 1953, revealed that the two groups had reached broad agreement on a number of issues: peace and trade relations with the Soviet Union and communist world; working-class resistance to the rearmament drive; and active opposition to the Labour Party entering into coalition with Fine Gael.[39] There was also movement from both sides on the issue of trade union unity. The IWL came to accept Murray's judgement that while the CIU was misguided in its support for wage restraint, some of its work did exhibit an understanding of the ailing Irish economy and 'a yearning for advance'.[40] Consequently, the *Irish Workers' Voice* dropped criticisms of the CIU leadership in favour of a more positive appeal for CIU-affiliated workers to demand trade union unity.[41] Internal pressure also prompted McCullough to confirm his reversal on the Ulster TUC idea, which had been taken up by right-wing NILP leaders and showed no sign of being realised. In sum, there had developed within the communist movement an appetite for 'the regular coming together of the progressive forces in the TUC Unions and those of the CIU ... to press forward the struggle for a united Trade Union Movement'.

Against this, R. Palme Dutt revealed that it was taking longer to close the gulf in political aspirations. After attending the joint council meeting as a CPGB observer, he reported that there was a reluctance in some quarters to confront the Stormont administration and its 'outright denial of democracy and civil rights'. He likened Andy Barr's pamphlet *North Ireland for Peace and Socialism* 'to what might be issued by a British Party District' and complained that no one appeared to share his view that Ireland had taken on 'a semi-colonial status' under reactionary governments.[42] Murray's report of proceedings added a number of nuances and indicated that he took Dutt's opinions on Ireland not too seriously. He observed that the CPNI had begun to seize on anti-Tory sentiments in the factories in preparation for instigating social agitation 'in the localities'. He also noted that both parties agreed on the urgent need to fend off the threat of American imperialism so that Ireland did not go the way of other West European countries in being engulfed by a world built on the dollar.[43] He drew on Stalin's speech at the nineteenth congress of the CPSU and outlined Irish labour's struggle in the following terms:

A/ Fight for independence of these Islands from American Imperialism;
B/ The defence of the Republic against the squeeze of Anglo-American Imperialism to take away its independence and use it as a tool of the war

bloc; C/ Struggle for unity of the workers of both areas as basis for the fight for a united Ireland and the development of the country towards Socialism.[44]

In continuation with the position he had begun to develop in the immediate post-war period, Murray identified the economic and military influence of the United States as a more serious threat than British imperialism. He had also moved away from the idea that Irish reunification and independence was an essential prerequisite for socialism.

In the context of inflationary pressure stemming from the rearmament drive, high unemployment, a credit squeeze that caused untold damage to the regional economies, and continued Unionist deference to Conservative policies, the CPNI stood Andy Barr against Lord Glentoran (Daniel Dixon) in the 1953 Stormont election to gauge support for the party's manifesto in its Bloomfield stomping ground. In the lead up to the election, the communists delivered fierce criticisms of the 'N. Ireland-British upper class and its Tory Governments' for subordinating the living standards of Northern Ireland citizens to the whims of 'the Billionaire Atomic War Lords'. The party coupled the usual enthusiasm for peace and trade with socialist countries with pragmatic calls for a reduction in the bank lending rate and for Keynesian state investment to compensate for the downturn in production. Interestingly, the policy document included a section that resembled a relatively coherent analysis of economic partition. It underlined the benefits of North-South cooperation on 'trade, industry and culture', slammed Brookeborough for dismissing such opportunities 'in the language of a conqueror', and proposed the mobilisation of British and Irish labour towards greater all-Ireland economic integration.[45]

A break with political Unionism, coupled with a rediscovered concern for civil rights and gerrymandering, was now central to the CPNI's programme. As election day approached, the party censured loyalist NILP leaders such as Billy Hull for defending the record of the Unionist government and particularly for denying 'there is any lack of democracy' when Derry and the border counties provided 'glaring examples' of anti-democratic practices. The CPNI instructed its canvassers to explain that the NILP's acquiescence went against all that socialists proclaimed to represent and did 'serious harm' to prospects for class unity in the North.[46] In the event, the NILP decided not to contest the Bloomfield constituency in an election characterised by general apathy, a poor turnout, and several unopposed

Unionist victories. Andy Barr doubled Billy McCullough's 1949 tally to 1,207 votes, prompting Tommy Watters to write from Manchester congratulating the party on 'a good job' and 'a surprising vote'.[47] In reality, the election told the CPNI nothing it did not already know. It was primarily an East Belfast party and lacked the wherewithal to make inroads elsewhere, including in the 'utterly confused' and congested anti-partitionist labour politics of West Belfast.[48]

These limitations did not prevent the party from challenging the Unionist government directly on social, economic and sensitive political questions. In February 1954, with a party conference looming, the leadership prepared a statement addressing Stormont's handling of inter-communal tensions. It referred to a standoff in the predominantly Catholic town of Dungiven, County Derry, which centred on a parade by local Protestants in celebration of the Queen's coronation. The RUC's decision to prevent an Orange flute band from accompanying the march sparked loyalist outrage and provided Independent Unionists with ammunition for attacking so-called 'appeasers' of nationalism in Brooke's cabinet, such as Brian Maginess, the liberal Minister for Home Affairs. The CPNI feared that events such as these enabled the Unionist Party's erstwhile supporters to force it 'back on to a more pronounced sectarian basis' and predicted that the police would soon be compelled to act as 'a partisan force'. For evidence of Stormont's capitulation, one only needed to look as far as the Flags and Emblems Act (1954), which represented an attack on nationalist rights and a victory for 'the most extreme wing of the anti-Nationalist forces' within Unionism.[49]

It is important to note that the CPNI's pronouncements, while critical of reactionary Unionism, showed no enthusiasm for mainstream nationalist politics. Murray's influence made relations with republicans less clear-cut, though there was no question of serious engagement with a movement that was numerically insignificant, narrowly focused on reuniting the national territory by force of arms and largely disinterested in social and economic issues. The IWL did count among its ranks former Curragh internees such as Michael O'Riordan, Denis Walshe and Ned Stapleton, and a small communist group continued to make its presence known at the annual Bodenstown commemorations. Communists were involved in setting up the Dublin Unemployed Association, which enjoyed the support of Tomás MacGiolla and other young republicans.[50] However, the IRA and Sinn Féin in the South were not only disconnected from socialism but actively hostile to it.[51]

However, re-engagement on the issue of civil and political liberties did lead the CPNI to take up the case of Liam Kelly, leader of the splinter republican group Saor Uladh, who had been imprisoned for sedition and, while in prison, elected to Stormont on an abstentionist ticket. The communists defended Kelly's right to voice political dissent and claimed that the Special Powers Act had been 'maintained as part of the permanent law of the state'.[52] Increasingly, and in sharp contrast to the NILP, the CPNI was articulating demands for democratic reform of the northern state. In December 1954, Murray wrote to Peter Kerrigan, CPGB industrial organiser, to spell out these demands and explain 'what is called for' within the British trade union movement. He informed Kerrigan that the CPNI planned to take action in various unions, including the AEU, the Electrical Trades Union, Amalgamated Society of Woodworkers, Sheetmetal Workers' Union, and the ATGWU. CPNI members would propose resolutions at a number of annual conferences, with the aim of achieving a coordinated and effective response:

1. Repeal of the Trades Disputes Act.
2. Stormont recognition of the NIC.
3. Calling for 'Irish Conferences in the AEU, ETU, and perhaps others'.
4. Adult suffrage in local government elections and abolition of the business vote.
5. Repeal of the Flags and Emblems Act.
6. Drawing attention to the continued use of the Special Powers Act.

Murray asked Kerrigan to ensure that the CPGB encouraged 'a strong attitude especially on the TU situation from our [CPGB] Comrades on the ECs of some of the Unions'.[53]

The dearth of papers relating to the internal workings of the aforementioned unions makes it difficult to appraise the contribution of CPNI members with any confidence. However, it is clear that the communists enjoyed a degree of influence disproportionate to their numbers. RUC intelligence reported that the CPNI trade unionists exhibited unrivalled levels of discipline, working hard to attend meetings and register their vote when important issues were at stake and when other delegates adopted an 'indifferent attitude'.[54] There is indeed a correlation between the communists' efforts, the increase in northern participation in the ITUC and the general shift in favour of trade union unity. At the close of 1955, the CPNI welcomed the news that the ITUC and CIU planned to discuss unity proposals in the new year.[55] In February 1956, the Provisional United Trade Union Organisation (PUO) briefed union officials and the NIC on its progress. The NIC received a full-time official in 1957 and the PUO later accepted that the proposed Irish Congress of Trade Unions (ICTU) constitution would have to allow for an elected NIC as a counterweight to southern Irish control of Congress. After lengthy negotiations, the merger of the two federations into the ICTU resolved the trade union movement's long-standing North-South and British-Irish divisions. Recognition from Stormont and the Trades Disputes Act would hang over the NIC and its members for some years to come. But as O'Connor notes, the merger represented a significant achievement: 'With the formation of the ICTU, Northern affiliates were more firmly embedded in an all-Ireland framework, while southerners accepted Northern realities.'[56] Larkin junior and John Conroy, ITGWU leader and first ICTU president, were the two key figures in creating the conditions for unity. Murray played no small part in ensuring that communist trade unionists committed to this process, ideologically and in practice.

De-Stalinisation?

The year 1953 witnessed the death of Stalin and the end of the Korean War. The Irish communist movement's transition from Stalinism to the Krushchev era of strategic flexibility was by no means straightforward, particularly for the IWL, which continued to suffer for its objective identification with Soviet foreign policy. To its peace campaign at the height of the Korean War, the IWL added a picket of the US Embassy in protest at the conviction and planned execution of Julius and Ethel Rosenberg for passing nuclear secrets to the Soviet Union. Under the editorship of Peadar Ward, the *Catholic Standard* carried profiles of IWL members, called for them to be ostracised in the workplace and even recommended that the authorities clamp down on the organisation. Pulpit denunciations and propaganda alone were enough to force the closure of the Ballyfermot Cooperative, which had been launched by IWL member, Joe Deasy, as a non-party political system for pooling local resources in the straitened financial climate.[57] Similarly, the Dublin Unemployed Association collapsed under the weight of anti-communism shortly after emerging in 1953. The *Standard* rejoiced at having been 'primarily responsible for driving them and their activities underground',[58] and did likewise when O'Riordan received only 375 votes as an IWL candidate for Dublin

South-West in the 1954 general election.[59] A steep decline in party membership reflected the fact that the link with the Soviet Union did more harm than good. Numbers fell from 102 in June 1952 to seventy-nine in June 1953 and fifty-nine in October 1954.[60]

In Belfast, the RUC and Ministry of Home Affairs were stirred into action by a trade union delegation to Moscow in 1954 for the May Day celebrations, organised by the CPNI under the auspices of the British-Soviet Friendship Society. Special Branch detectives were deployed to gather information on the group's activities and, in 1955, obtained documents relating to the formation of a Northern Ireland-Soviet Friendship Society, including its constitution. The authorities also noted with interest the visit of a party of schoolteachers to the Soviet Union in 1955 at the invitation of the Soviet Ministry of Education. As the CPNI effected a minor recovery, this exploratory investigation of the Northern Ireland-Soviet Friendship Society extended to include the communists. By 1960, the Ministry of Home Affairs was in possession of a door-stopping file containing the personal and political details of a number of prominent Belfast communists; membership figures for each CPNI branch; and the level of communist influence in government departments, public bodies, Northern Ireland schools and universities, and even Belfast post offices.[61]

Although Cold War antagonisms and events within the Soviet Union rapidly swept away the positive legacy of Stalingrad, there is evidence that Murray was among a large contingent that remained wedded to the Soviet myth. In 1953, at the invitation of the Czech ambassador, he had attended an event to celebrate the eighth anniversary of the liberation of Czechoslovakia by the Red Army.[62] On 14 March 1956, the anniversary of Marx's death, Murray was there to witness the unveiling of a monument over his remains at Highgate Cemetery, London. More than 300 people attended the ceremony, including the Soviet ambassador to Britain, diplomats from several socialist countries and two of Marx's great grandsons.[63] Murray and his wife, Margaret, were also actively involved with the Northern Ireland-Soviet Friendship Society. In October 1956, they were delegates to a conference at Belfast Castle that hosted three cultural representatives from the Soviet Union, and attended a subsequent concert staged by thirteen Soviet artists at the Husband Memorial Hall.[64]

Khrushchev's rise to power and attempted reforms in both domestic and foreign policy, if not welcomed enthusiastically, proved no obstacle to the Irish communist movement's identification with the Soviet project. On the fortieth anniversary of the Bolshevik Revolution, Murray returned to the Soviet Union as part of the first Irish delegation to an international communist conference since 1935, where, despite his defence of the Moscow Show Trials, his official engagements included an excursion to Bukharin's home in Crimea. He took extensive notes on the Soviet economy and visited the Stalingrad Tractor Factory, which produced equipment for the Red Army, including the T-34 tank that became famous during the Battle of Stalingrad.[65] Two years later, he travelled to Moscow for the CPSU's twenty-first congress. After meeting with the Central Council of Trade Unions and visiting the Gorki Leninskiye, formerly Lenin's dacha and now a museum housing many of his possessions, Murray made his way into Bratislava, Czechoslovakia, to study the city's political history, culture, and its industrial and agricultural economy. A notebook and a collection of photos survive from this trip, documenting a busy schedule that included a series of factory visits and political meetings.[66]

No sooner was Murray back in Ireland then he returned to Moscow for a conference of eighty-one workers' and communist parties in November/December 1960, making it three visits in quick succession and the last time he would set foot in the Soviet Union. Arriving in the summer of that year, he spent at least three months travelling across Bulgaria prior to his main engagement in Moscow. In Dimitrovgrad, a newly-built town in the south of the country that took its name from the celebrated Comintern leader, Georgi Dimitrov, he visited a chemical plant, cement plant, canning factory and paper plant, taking detailed notes on production and employment figures. This led him to the nearby town of Pazardzhik, where he was taken to see another cement plant, a power station and a large-scale cooperative farm named Kozarsko (Karl Marx). His final stop en route to Moscow was Varna, a seaside resort on the Bulgarian Black Sea Coast. Here a number of international communist leaders had convened, whether in anticipation of the Moscow conference or another meeting is not clear. Murray sought respite at the beach but also found time to meet with an Italian communist senator, among other prominent European communists.[67] When it finally came to making his first speech to an international communist gathering in twenty-five years, he affirmed his loyalty to the Soviet Union in the Sino-Soviet dispute.[68] In his words and deeds, therefore, Murray upheld the achievements of the Bolshevik Revolution and Soviet-style socialism throughout and beyond Stalin's reign. More than this, in fact, at the age of sixty-two he continued to take a keen interest in contemporary forms of Soviet economic planning and development, seeing them as containing potentially valuable lessons for Ireland. Hence the intensive study visits to factories and farms and the notebooks that survive from those trips.

It could be argued that the northern communists' association with the Soviet Union only slightly hindered their political and trade union activities. Betty Sinclair recalled anti-communism frustrating the work of Belfast Trades Council in the mid 1950s. She was the cause of a split in the labour movement during the 1955 May Day celebrations, when her presence led to a group breaking away and holding a rival non-communist meeting. Despite pulling off a small victory in persuading her comrades to invite a delegation from Leningrad to Belfast, she could not prevent the Trades Council from coming out against the invasion of Hungary.[69] Whilst the ATGWU had introduced a ban on communists holding office, other union leaderships worked in more surreptitious ways to curb the CPNI's influence. One example of this was the reversal of Sam Gardiner's election as AEU president in 1960. Following complaints about irregularities, the election was declared null and void, allowing the NILP candidate, William McDowell, to rally his supporters and reverse Gardiner's initial victory in the re-run.[70] Despite these difficult conditions, the CPNI held its ground within the trade union movement. It also worked to achieve labour unity on important issues such as the Housing Miscellaneous Provisions Bill (1956), or 'Rent Bill', which proposed to give landlords a free rein to raise the rent on their properties independent of government scrutiny. Belfast Trades Council launched a Tenants' Defence Association to oppose the Bill and, in April 1956, the CPNI was part of a deputation of opposition parties that met Dehra Parker, the unpopular Minister of Health and Local Government, to demand its withdrawal. This pressure, along with Parker's mishandling of the issue, brought underlying tensions within the Unionist Party to the surface and revealed the full extent of working-class disquiet with the government.[71]

With the CPNI suffering what Murray described as a 'lack of adequate numerical strength' and 'crippling financial poverty', the Northern Ireland-Soviet Friendship Society brought mixed fortunes for the movement.[72] It ran at a loss, depended on financial assistance from across the water and ostensibly failed to make a lasting impression on its Soviet guests. It also garnered unwelcome attention from the authorities. On the other hand, it won the party some respectability by association with such individuals as the poet, John Hewitt and attracted both new members and a core of fellow travellers from the trade unions, public sector and professions. The CPNI probably lost out financially, therefore, but gained support.[73]

Along with the Soviet Union's invasion of Hungary in 1956, which the party met with a muted response, the real litmus test for the CPNI's transcendence of Stalinism was its response to Khrushchev's secret speech given at the twentieth party congress of the CPSU in February of that year. Indeed, the CPGB's loss of around 9,000 members in two years testifies to the epochal nature of these events for communist parties operating in liberal democracies.[74] For the CPNI, they had serious implications regarding the party's moral authority for challenging the Unionist regime on political repression and the northern state's democratic deficit. Jimmy Stewart recalls that the CPNI leadership's behind-closed-doors response was not unanimously in favour of Khrushchev's repentant position, with Billy McCullough expressing his opposition in extremely colourful language.[75] The official CPNI executive committee statement was more measured, ambiguous and qualified in its tone. Aligning the party with the Italian communist leader Palmiro Togliatti, who had characterised official Soviet explanations for Stalin's excesses as inadequate, it refused to accept that the 'injustices resulting from this departure from Marxism-Leninism' were merely a result of the 'attributes of one man'. The steps taken by the CPSU towards the 'elimination of the evils attendant on the Stalin cult' were welcome, but they should account for the threats posed to the Soviet Union by fascism and now American imperialism. There was disingenuity in suggesting that the CPNI leadership, Lenin School graduates such as Murray and Sinclair in particular, were completely unaware of the crimes being committed in the name of communism. Murray's association with Pat Breslin and his justification of the Moscow Show Trials contradicts any such notion. However, the Irish communists were unlikely to have been aware of the full extent of deaths by famine, execution, and in gulags. After becoming conscious of the facts, they signalled a break with Stalin's legacy and committed to work for 'the extension of democratic liberties and the removal of restrictions on these liberties in this island'.[76]

The social achievements of the Soviet Union and its economic model continued to hold great appeal for Murray. Trade relations and economic cooperation with the socialist bloc, therefore, continued to feature prominently in the CPNI's proposals for solving Ireland's economic difficulties. However, like communist parties across the Western liberal democratic world, he had to engage seriously with the reformed variant of capitalism that had grown up in the post-war period. Consequently, the party articulated its economic preferences in the vague socialistic terms of 'ownership of the factories, land, shipyards and Banks ... by society at large'. It acknowledged the significant achievements of 'democratic socialism' and suggested that the CPNI's priority lay in protecting those gains. The CPNI advocated resistance to Tory-imposed cutbacks, proposing a house-building programme and general expansion of welfarism to aid those on the lower rungs of society. The party preached militancy in the staple industries, where significant redundancies loomed large, and committed to strengthening the NIC's bargaining position through industrial action.[77] In practice, CPNI members participated in the March 1957 engineering strikes in the Belfast area and, provoked by the sacking of shop stewards at the Du Pont factory in Derry, they led an anti-rationalisation (and anti-American) campaign against the company's management.[78]

Opposition to Toryism made strange and sometimes outright dangerous bedfellows for the Belfast communists. In 1958, for instance, Andy Barr shared a platform at a rally against shipyard redundancies with Norman Porter, the deeply sectarian Independent MP for Belfast Clifton. While an isolated incident, it indicated nonetheless that economism prevailed within the CPNI and that it had some distance to travel politically. As the 1958 Stormont election approached, the economy united Independent Unionists, the CPNI and NILP in opposition. The communists decided not to contest the election 'in the interests of working-class unity' and in support of the 'socialist principles' advocated by the NILP.[79] In the context of rising unemployment, falling living standards, a housing crisis and industrial unrest, the election carried great potential for winning labour representation in Stormont. The CPNI's decision has to be seen in that light. But while the NILP was rewarded with four seats and became the Official Opposition, the Belfast communists remained on the margins of politics and had yet to define clearly who or what they represented.

Republicanism, democratic reform and *Ireland's Path to Socialism*

As social and economic pressures bore down heavily on the two Irish states, republicanism entered into a period of political and military reorganisation. In the 1955 Westminster elections, Tom Mitchell and Phil Clarke, two IRA volunteers imprisoned for a raid on Omagh barracks, won seats in the rural constituencies of Mid-Ulster and Fermanagh-South Tyrone respectively. Sinn Féin won a total of 152,310 votes and with it a political foothold for harnessing discontent with Unionism and conservative nationalism for the purpose of social and economic change. But the party's impressive electoral showing only encouraged the mistaken belief that there was support within the northern nationalist population for a renewed offensive against the state. On 12 December 1956, the IRA launched Operation Harvest, a guerrilla venture aimed at establishing 'liberated areas' along the border. This disastrous Border Campaign has been pored over by scholars of the Irish republican left, who concur that it marked a watershed in the history of modern Irish republicanism. It not only provoked a reassessment of republican strategy, separating 'traditionalists' from 'modernisers', 'militarists' from 'politicos' and, broadly speaking, the adherents of Catholic social teaching from Marxist republicans, but also had a significant bearing on how Murray would define his politics.

The Border Campaign coincided with an increase in the activities of the Connolly Association, which had been struggling to overcome the suffocating effects of Cold War hostilities and the disruptive work of 'ultra-leftists' within its London branches. Under the leadership of Desmond Greaves, the Connolly Association escalated its campaign for Irish reunification and independence. Although he was 'not indifferent to the aims of Irish socialists', Greaves believed his main task was to convince the British labour movement to repeal the Government of Ireland Act and cease supporting the northern state.[80] A new addition to his strategy related to the concept of civil rights and the formation of an anti-Unionist government in the North. Greaves believed that a campaign for civil rights reform would help to unite Protestants and Catholics, minimise working-class sectarianism and bring about the demise of the Unionist administration. The election of progressive governments North and South, and a sympathetic Labour government in Britain, would thereby generate the conditions for the creation of a united, democratic Irish republic.[81] The main difference between the Connolly Association and the CPNI at this stage was that changes to objective political conditions had led the latter to consider democratic reform of Northern Ireland as an end in itself, not merely a tactic for destabilising the state. Greaves interpreted bourgeois democracy on thirty-two county terms; Murray and the CPNI were coming round to the position that it could be achieved in two separate states.

During the Border Campaign, the Connolly Association called for all republican internees to be brought to trial or released. This later became the demand for a general amnesty. Contrary to the claims of one author, the CPNI did, in fact, lend public support to this campaign.[82] In November 1960, a message of solidarity from Betty Sinclair and the Belfast Trades Council was read out at a Manchester Connolly Association demonstration that called for an unconditional amnesty for political prisoners. Seán Morrissey attended a corresponding rally in North London, recounting his experiences as an IRA prisoner on the *Al Rawdah* prison ship in the 1940s and urging those in attendance to support the campaign for an end to internment.[83] A crucial point of departure between the two organisations related to public attitudes towards the IRA armed struggle. Refusing to condemn republican violence, Greaves declared in an *Irish Democrat* editorial: 'If there was no British occupation of North Eastern Ireland there would be no IRA. The issue is simple as that.'[84] Seán Morrissey claims that Murray was 'totally opposed' to the IRA campaign, but for tactical reasons rather than in principle. 'If they were going to persist with violence, then they should do it properly', is how Morrissey sums up Murray's view at the time.[85] But, whatever Murray may have said privately, a statement he drafted as a CPNI response to Greaves contained a rather different message. It argued for civil and democratic rights to be addressed and for the British and Irish governments to negotiate solutions to the economic and political problems facing the two islands. Dealing with the IRA campaign, it stated unequivocally: 'The Communist Party does not advocate a policy of armed force for the solution of the national problem in this country, nor for the attainment of its own objectives of a socialist Ireland.'[86] Instead, its 'message to Republican Ireland' asserted that, 'The division of the Irish people, including the Partition of the country, would be solved in the course of the struggle for Socialism.'[87]

Because Murray's attempt to develop an Irish communist manifesto was the first in some decades, the process naturally privileged the piecemeal accumulation of material and critical input from experienced activists. Periodically, he tested his ideas on party grassroots through the various bulletins, political letters and party statements circulated by the political committee and executive committee. As early as June 1955, he had a full draft programme prepared for the eyes of his closest comrades. One of the first he consulted was William Gallacher, who had a long association with Ireland. Whilst congratulating the way in which the document set out the main problems, he suggested that Murray simplify its language and put terms like 'imperialism' into context. He also recommended that the final programme include a historical backdrop referring to Irish rebellion against forms of 'imperial tyranny and exploitation', giving emphasis to examples of cross-communal resistance in the north-east.[88] Later drafts show that Murray took on board Gallacher's advice. Tommy Watters, still involved with the Connolly Association but 'not an active spirit in it', warned against presupposing North-South cooperation and the de facto end of partition. Overall, however, he was thoroughly enthused by what he regarded as a balanced programme, an improvement on *Ireland's Path to Freedom*. Specifically, he argued that by 'making the starting point economic instead of political', Murray had adopted an appropriate framework for analysing the two states of Ireland. By focusing on material conditions and promoting democratic reform of the North, he had ensured that its 'appeal is wide enough to take in all sections of the population, especially the nationalists, without appearing as a "pure" republican document to the Prods'. Finally, Watters remarked acerbically that Murray's diagnosis and prescriptions were closer to the mark than the Connolly Association's chief ideologue: 'I imagine Desmond will get a surprise when he sees the draft, as I see in this month's "Demo" that very little can be done in Ireland until Partition is removed.'[89]

Sometime between 1955 and 1958, Murray divided his draft programme into two documents. He intended for the two documents to advance analyses and tactics reflecting the specific conditions pertaining in the two states, but also dovetail into an overarching strategy for an all-island movement. Paddy Carmody, the IWL's main theoretician, was entrusted with Murray's material and with the task of drafting a programme for the southern party in tandem with the CPNI. The two parties extended an invitation for Greaves to contribute to discussions around the details of the two programmes. He attended one joint council meeting in late 1957 but clearly disengaged from the process as time progressed, informing Seán Nolan that he 'should enter the fray only when the confusion – and there's lots of it, he believes – has been removed somewhat. And of course he thinks we're off the track altogether'.[90]

In 1957/58, the *Irish Democrat* published a debate between Paddy Carmody, writing under the pseudonym A. Raferty, and Jack Bennett, formerly of the Connolly Association and now with the CPNI. Bennett presented a version of the Greaves position, sympathetic to Sinn Féin and supportive to an anti-partition campaign. Carmody rejected the proposition that ending partition ought to be the priority and wrote that anti-partitionism would mean 'raising a division between Nationalist and Unionist workers'. He argued that the IRA campaign would only play into the hands of Ulster Unionism and, more damningly, that it was rooted in an analysis that had not adapted to the fundamental changes that had occurred since 1921: 'Both states have a political system which allows the majority of Irish people to choose their government.'[91]

Murray allowed the Bennett/Carmody debate on partition to proceed without interruption, choosing not to muddy the waters further. When in 1958 he produced 'The Irish Way to Socialism', the CPNI initiated a fraternal and democratic consultation process. Discussions at senior leadership level continued, as over the course of a weekend in mid-September, when he and Carmody presented their respective documents to a meeting of the joint council.[92] Murray solicited the views of Frank Edwards, who was impressed that he had preserved the party's 'true "Irish" character' by producing a document that was not 'a chip off the CPGB's programme'.[93] The opinions of CPNI members – branch officers, shop stewards and trade union officials, members from the women's group and the SYL – were also sought by the executive committee, which circulated a draft programme and urged everyone 'to take full part' in discussions.[94] Lance Noakes, a member of the influential Shorts branch, took the opportunity to deliver a rather perfunctory critique. His one telling point was that a programme heavily laden with references to the revolutionary British working class placed a ceiling on the CPNI's all-island ambitions and, by extension, dismissed the radical potential of the Irish labour movement as a whole.[95] Jimmy Stewart, secretary of the SYL, struck out at the suggestion that he supported Bennett's analysis and argued instead that partition would resolve itself under certain conditions: 'Through socialism'; 'Through a left-wing government in Britain'; and/or 'Through the economic interests of N.I. & Eire being brought closer together i.e. under the crisis of Capitalism in general and British Capitalism'.[96]

Bennett's 25,000-word critique of the draft CPNI programme, Murray informed Watters, had 'raised the discussion to a level not common in these parts'.[97] It was with some justification therefore that his contribution formed the subject of two full-scale debates. Bennett's main criticisms of Murray centred on his apparent neglect of the national question and a 'compromise with imperialism'. Mike Milotte is in broad agreement with Bennett and advances the simplistic, teleological argument that 'The Irish Way to Socialism' marked a continuation of the CPNI's wartime position i.e. Unionism. For Bennett, as for Milotte, the alternative lay in 'building a mass-based, all-Ireland national liberation movement under working-class leadership and embracing militant republicans who, because of their largely proletarian composition, would maintain the struggle until socialism was achieved'.[98] Whilst conceding that Bennett had offered 'many useful and telling points of criticism', Murray was scathing of his unhistorical nationalist reading of the situation:

> He failed to give any estimation of the ACTUAL situation and where 26 County Ireland just [sic] stands in regard to national independence. Is it an independent state? Has nothing happened since 1916? This is in substance the Sinn Féin position. Though even they, tactically, but not in principle, base their activities (armed ones) on the assumption that "something has happened". Politically non-recognition is based on the line that the situation is the same as 40 years ago.[99]

Like Carmody, Murray was in no doubt as to the *political* independence of the twenty-six counties. The status of the six counties was as yet undefined, and the subject of 'imperialism', complex and contested. However, Murray had dismissed irredentism and abstentionism as politically redundant.

Murray's speech to the international conference of workers' and communist parties made it explicit that he continued to draw inspiration from the 'unheard-of upsurge of national liberation movements' that had increasingly freed former colonies from the grip of imperialism. However, speaking of the classic British variant of imperialism, he argued that, although its content was similar, it was no longer as powerful or of singular importance in the Irish context:

> Imperialism has not changed its spots, it has not become more humane; it is no more pretty in appearance or substance than it was forty years ago, when it was actively engaged in armed conflict with the Irish people, fighting for their national independence ... but there has been a serious decline in its power.[100]

Understanding that traditional anti-colonial rhetoric would only take the communist movement so far in the context of political transformation and economic globalisation, Murray attempted to formulate a realistic assessment of where Ireland stood in relation to Britain and the Western world. Thus, despite Bennett's arguments to the contrary, he contended that 'the country is not a colony; the national problems (partition etc) will be solved on the way to Socialism, while every effort will be made for such partial solutions as are possible on the basis of the present situation'.[101] And the Irish communist movement moved with him in the direction of left reformism by jointly pledging to adhere to a declaration of seventeen West European communist parties, which encouraged programmatic and tactical flexibility to meet the challenge of operating in stable capitalist democracies.[102]

Murray's 1960 appearance in Moscow was his last political hurrah. After falling ill with cirrhosis of the liver in early 1961, a consequence of decades of heavy drinking, he died in the Royal Victoria Hospital, Belfast, on 25 May with his wife, Margaret, and Seán Morrissey by his bedside. Having 'developed under Murray's tutelage', Jimmy Stewart assumed responsibility for the 'Irish Way to Socialism' and made no significant amendments other than to clarify its arguments for progressive governments North and South.[103] After consulting the party membership on a third draft, the CPNI launched its manifesto, *Ireland's Path to Socialism*, at a Belfast congress in June 1962. Simultaneously, the Irish Workers' Party (IWP) published Paddy Carmody's programme, entitled *Ireland Her Own* in tribute to T.A. Jackson's history of Ireland's underdevelopment and the immortal words of James Fintan Lalor. The two programmes dealt with separate parties and separate jurisdictions, with the IWP leaning slightly more towards a cultural nationalist outlook. Ultimately, though, they kept with Murray's original intention that they read like two intersecting parts of the same manifesto.

Stephen Bowler has appraised *Ireland's Path to Socialism* as a 180-degree reversal of the 'two-stage' or 'stageist' position adopted by Murray during the 1934 Republican Congress negotiations.[104] Milotte diverges slightly in describing a 'national road' or 'dual carriageway' to socialism, which is perhaps more accurate because this takes account of the programme's Connollyist language and alludes to a distinction between tactics and strategy (ideology). Milotte is right to describe the two parties' strategies as 'gradualistic' and 'distinctly reformist', though it is not appropriate to argue that these 'had *their* roots in the class-collaborationist Popular Front'.[105] Although he has something important to say about the difficulty of reversing fundamental changes to revolutionary strategy, his analysis neglects the twists and turns of CPNI policy in the turbulent wartime and post-war years and betrays a teleological urge that does a disservice to his impeccable historical research. Matt Treacy chooses to underline the anti-imperialist and pro-republican aspects of the CPNI programme. His account is valuable in terms of understanding the environment that shaped communist attitudes towards the republican movement, particularly as the Border Campaign began to peter out and as Ireland applied to join the European Economic Community (EEC). However, he exaggerates the influence of Bennett, the Connolly Association and the CPGB without considering Murray's efforts to lead the party away from Unionism, his understanding of the transnational economic phenomenon of imperialism, or the wider consultation process undertaken in developing the programme.[106]

One striking feature of *Ireland's Path to Socialism* is that it attacked the Unionist Party on class grounds as well as its anti-democratic practices. Following on from Murray's earlier critiques of big house Unionism, it took aim at what he described as the 'political arm of the industrial, commercial and financial magnates', a local branch of the Tory Party. He condemned Unionist MPs for giving 'unqualified support' to deflationary Conservative policies in Northern Ireland and committing themselves 'to a policy of private enterprise at all costs'. Murray's programme also criticised Unionism for maintaining the link with sectarian organisations such as the Orange Order, thus serving to 'perpetuate religious divisions among the people'. The NILP received kinder treatment, praised for its essentially working-class character; for supporting redistributive policies and greater state investment; and for demanding of the government the introduction of universal suffrage, abolition of the business vote and a re-examination of electoral boundaries. But whereas grassroots members were authentically radical, socialist and non-sectarian, its parliamentary leadership was 'reformist', 'pro-Imperialist' and 'anti-Irish'. The leadership had isolated itself from large sections of the island's trade union movement, despite the fact that the overwhelming majority of NILP trade unionists were affiliated to the ICTU. It had also demonstrated short-sightedness and failed an 'acid test' by refusing to acknowledge the historical use of the Special Powers Act against the labour movement or to call for its repeal.[107]

According to *Ireland's Path to Socialism*, there was nothing inherently progressive about Irish nationalism. On the contrary, the Nationalist Party had demonstrated its commitment to conservative ideas and had failed to present the northern working class with an 'all embracing' political programme. Nationalist politicians were, therefore, only progressive from a tactical perspective, insofar as they challenged the Unionist regime on civil liberties. In terms of its attitude towards republicanism, there is little disputing Treacy's broad argument that there was a shift in tone. The final programme lauded the republican movement's consistent struggle against British imperialism and alluded to its importance in combating the imperialist plans of NATO and the EEC. But it came nowhere close to endorsing Bennett's arguments and, in fact, noted that the armed struggle had resulted in republicanism's 'divorcement from other aspects of the anti-imperialist struggle, social, economic and political'. Rather than capitulating to the republican movement, it stressed the importance of republicans joining the 'forces of the working class movement who are prepared to struggle against the Unionist Party on the economic and political level'.[108]

Authors spanning the full spectrum of leftist interpretative positions have drawn useful parallels between the contemporaneous Irish communist and republican conceptions of 'imperialism'. Approaching the subject from different angles, Milotte and Patterson reach an incongruous agreement that the communists resisted the so-called march toward progress in favour of retrogressive economic nationalism. Drawing on Milotte's research, Patterson criticises the IWP and CPNI programmes for taking issue with a Fianna Fáil 'sell-out' on the EEC, the dismantling of the Control of Manufactures Acts and the introduction of the *First Programme for Economic Expansion*. He concludes that, by adopting this critical position, they joined 1960s republicanism in a denial 'of certain massive realities upon which a "Marxism" less influenced by nationalism would have paused to reflect'.[109] A more careful reading of *Ireland Her Own* in particular finds that the two communist groups were not opposed to global economic integration as such. Rather, their concerns related to the gradual erosion of national democracy and the residual importance of political state in terms of its capacity to negotiate globalisation for the benefit of its citizens. *Ireland Her Own* conceded that 1930s economic nationalism and policies of self-sufficiency were unrealistic, but urged caution in having a wager on the foreign direct investment model as the basis for sustainable economic development. One effect of relaxing capital controls would be to surrender the political state's capacity for guaranteeing re-investment in the local economy, putting employment and domestic consumer demand in jeopardy. It suggested, whether as an alternative or as a corrective strategy, that a government priority ought to be a readjustment of the flawed policies that had, for so long, allowed the production of raw materials and development of agriculture to work in isolation from manufacturing and the productive economy.[110]

Murray, too, referenced the 'all-out efforts to attract foreign capital' in the South. Writing in a similar vein to Carmody, he discussed the double blow that taxpayer subsidies and outward capital flows had dealt to Northern Ireland. Drawing on sources including *The Economic Survey of Northern Ireland* (1957), a ground-breaking piece of research by two Queen's University Belfast economists, he observed that the efforts of the Chandos Development Council to invest in industrial diversification had been 'strangled at birth by the British credit squeeze'. The effects of the post-war slump and the underlying problems of peripherality and underdevelopment were exacerbated by Northern Ireland's integration with British capital, which saw the profits from industry and agriculture extracted from the local economy, and by the refusal of the North's 'monied interests' to invest in anything other than the ventures accumulating super-profits in the British colonies. Crucially, the Unionist Party remained ideologically and materially wedded to a British imperial project that had entered into decline and 'become a subordinate vassal of United States Dollar Imperialism'. This policy and by extension Northern Ireland's membership of the EEC would, he argued, see local linen, textile, shipping and import companies gradually pass into the hands of monopolies. More generally, the development of a common market had the potential to intensify one of the central contradictions of monopoly capitalism, namely that between 'increasing capacity to produce and the total purchasing power of the people' – the overproduction/underconsumption formulation.[111] Thus, while Sinn Féin opposed the EEC on narrow nationalist grounds, out of hostility to foreign interference in Irish affairs, Murray got there via a distinctly Marxist-Leninist analysis. As Swan notes, the republican and communist movements reached the same conclusion for reasons that were different, or even contradictory, but 'not antagonistic'.[112]

Not surprisingly, the two communist programmes were closer to traditional republican thinking on the cause of partition. British imperialism, in Murray's view, had imposed the border in order

> to rupture the life of the Irish people, bring about the present divisions in Northern Ireland, create two antagonistic states, and disunite the struggle that caused it to relinquish its political hold over the major part of the country.[113]

One would expect nothing else from the pen of a War of Independence veteran and anti-Treaty republican. It is striking how this attitude remained fixed for decades. Where he departed from the traditional republicanism of Sinn Féin, which attributed all of the island's ills to British rule, was in attaching an equal portion of the blame for underdevelopment to native bourgeois forces on both sides of the border. And regardless of how he made sense of the border's construction, it did not necessarily follow that he would see the solution to Ireland's problems solely in its removal. Demonstrating his ideological and intellectual debt to Connolly, Murray reaffirmed the ideal of an Irish socialist republic as his ultimate goal and envisaged a 'fight for national liberation and social and economic justice [which] must go hand in hand'. Crucially, though, he recognised that anti-partitionism would bring 'certain sections only' into the struggle, and, returning to the tradition of the United Irishmen, described his united Ireland as 'the people of this land, not a geographical term'.[114] This suggests that uniting the 'people', however the term is defined, took priority over territorial unification and, indeed, was now considered a prerequisite for it.

If these extracts appear ambiguous and contradictory – and they are – the sections dealing with the North offer some clarification. It is clear that Murray did not share Carmody's view that Northern Ireland had attained the status of a fully-fledged democracy. However, he was optimistic that organised labour would help bring about democratic reform of the state and described this as the CPNI's 'foremost aim'. Although it is important not to exaggerate the significance of *Ireland's Path to Socialism*, it clearly played off the work of the Connolly Association and the NCCL, perceptive and influential in its proposals for reform: repeal of the Special Powers Act and an end to 'all anti-democratic' laws; abolition of the business vote; an end to gerrymandering; disbandment of the B Specials; an end to civil and religious discrimination; and abolition of university parliamentary seats.[115] In terms of what would make it into the NILP/NIC-ICTU *Joint Memorandum on Citizens' Rights in Northern Ireland*[116] and constitute the core demands of the Northern Ireland Civil Rights Association (NICRA), only discrimination in local housing allocation fails to receive explicit attention in the CPNI programme. The subject matter of Sam Thompson's play *Over the Bridge* (1960) may have shaken the Unionist establishment to its core,[117] but Murray and Stewart deserve credit for their contribution to the labour movement's struggle for civil rights in Northern Ireland in the 1960s.

Ultimately, the achievement of political and economic democracy depended on the defeat of the Unionist Party and the election of a progressive government 'representing the majority of the people in the six counties'. Assuming extended fiscal and policy-making powers from Westminster, Stormont would, in cooperation with a progressive Dublin government and aided by a united trade union movement of 500,000 workers, advance an ambitious economic programme. It is unarguable that the 'ill-defined' programme comprised aspects of Soviet 'state socialism',[118] but it also drew on eclectic sources of inspiration ranging from social democratic capitalism to Gaelic cooperativism and infant industry protectionism. Evoking the radical British Labour Party programme of the late 1940s, it promised nationalisation of key industries and the re-introduction of strong capital controls to enable modernisation outside of the 'anarchy' of the market. Small and medium enterprises would be afforded credit from government controlled banks and given the freedom to trade competitively without the threat of being engulfed by larger commercial interests. Interestingly, Murray promoted the establishment of export-led 'home industries based on agriculture i.e. food processing, canning, leather, fertiliser plants etc ... [which] would end the present dependence on the export of live cattle, pigs and sheep'.[119] The voluntary organisation of farming along cooperative lines – a policy inspired by Murray's Connollyism and bolstered by his 1960 visit to Kozarsko – would aid this process by eliminating 'the usurious profits of the middleman', removing a barrier between the rural producer and urban consumer and, at the same time, guaranteeing the welfare of the rural population. Finally, underpinning these economic reforms was an extension of social democratic welfarism, funded by the redirection of rearmament funds secured through Northern Ireland's withdrawal from NATO. These measures included a slum clearance project, the nationalisation of 'large property holdings' and the introduction of a rent cap tied to wages; a rise in pensions; the introduction of universal healthcare and education, administered by the working class; and the extension of leisure and cultural facilities.[120]

What Murray had envisaged is perhaps best described as the possibility of building socialism in two states in advance of Socialism in One Country. He understood that, for the Irish socialist republic to become a reality and remain in existence, it would require 'measures to ensure socialist democracy in the entire state organisation'. In addition to the disbandment of partisan state units such as the B Specials, he envisaged the reorganisation of the police, judiciary and civil service 'under new leadership', and democratisation of the media.[121] The obvious problem with *Ireland's Path to Socialism* was that the transition from its strong Marxist diagnosis to its credible left social democratic programme involved an imaginative leap that presupposed a strong labour movement with a clear route to power. The NILP's parliamentary presence and the establishment of ICTU offered limited possibilities for the CPNI to exert political and economic influence. However, the party alone had to contend with serious financial difficulties and slow growth in membership figures. In 1958, it launched a fundraising drive which, in combination with individual donations, cleared its rent (£120) and rates (£50) arrears, though it still had to vacate its premises on Church Lane.[122] When the much-frequented International Bookshop closed in early 1959, the executive committee assured members 'that the ideas of Marxism can never be crushed by the mere closing of a shop'.[123] Privately, Murray admitted to Tommy Watters that the CPNI had 'gone through some hell of a period'.[124] His house at 32 Lincoln Avenue was used as a makeshift office for some four months before the party relocated to 13 Adelaide Street at the beginning of 1959. Hugh Moore made a personal loan of £35 to the party, ostensibly for rent or a deposit, and promised another £10 in due course. Crucially, the CPNI had added just 100 new members in the ten years since 1949. And of its 280 due-paying members, only forty-seven were active.[125]

Not for the first time had Murray led a process of consolidation in difficult circumstances. Politically, the CPNI had grown very slowly. Records suggest that its numerical gains were achieved almost exclusively in Protestant areas, coinciding with a strengthening of the party's position in the trade union movement. Murray did have some success as the architect of substantial cooperation between the two communist parties. By convening a joint council in 1952, he and Seán Nolan had initiated a process of dialogue that would enable the IWL/IWP and CPNI to gradually converge towards organisational unity. In conjunction with this, he ensured that the two parties produced manifestos reflecting the specific conditions of the two states of Ireland, but aspiring to the same end goal of an Irish socialist republic and promoting complementary tactics towards that end. He would have been quite satisfied to know that he had bequeathed to the movement the structures and the 'base documents' for the reconstitution of the CPI, the party he founded, in 1970.[126] *Ireland's Path to Socialism* was Marxist-Leninist in its analysis and social democratic, reformist and socialist republican in the solutions it offered. Along with *Ireland Her Own*, it carries significance for underpinning the communist movement's engagement with the left republican strain of political thought that was to emerge in the 1960s and 1970s. This type of republicanism was to depart from its traditionalist forms in a number of ways: through its non-sectarianism, secularism and serious engagement with the Protestant working class; in recognising the merits of electoral participation; and in recognising the value of reforming the two Irish states, both in principle and as part of a strategy for achieving the goal of a socialist republic. It was significant that Roy Johnston, Connolly Association graduate, leading member of the Wolfe Tone Society and later Director of Education for the IRA, would use Murray's programme 'in the context of persuading the left-republican politicisers that the CPNI was to be cultivated as a source of left-wing experience'.[127] Another legacy of *Ireland's Path to Socialism*, as noted above, was the involvement of Betty Sinclair, Edwina Stewart and other communist activists with NICRA, which produced one of the most important social movements in a generation.[128] These were tasks that Murray left unfulfilled, but which marked a continuation of his life's work.

NOTES

1   Seán Murray (with Jimmy Stewart), *Ireland's Path to Socialism* (Belfast, 1962), p.25.

2   Donald Sassoon, *One Hundred Years of Socialism: The West European Left in the Twentieth Century* (Revised Edition) (London, 2010), p.209.

3   Eric Hobsbawm, *Age of Extremes: The Short Twentieth Century, 1914-1991* (London, 1994), p.226.

4   Niamh Puirséil, *The Irish Labour Party, 1922-73* (Dublin, 2007), p.146.

5   Dermot Keogh, *Twentieth Century Ireland: Nation and State* (Dublin, 1994), pp.228-9.

6   David Connolly, 'The "Red Scare" in 1950s Dublin: Genuine or generated? The role of Archibishop McQuaid's Vigilance Committee' (unpublished MPhil thesis, Trinity College Dublin, 2011).

7   PRONI, Seán Murray Papers, D2162/K/25, Jim Larkin election manifesto, annotated by Murray (1951).

8   Noel Browne, *Against the Tide* (Dublin, 1986), p.249.

9   Roy Johnston, *Century of Endeavour: A Biographical and Autobiographical View of the Twentieth Century in Ireland* (Dublin, 2006), p.117.

10 Mike Milotte, *Communism in Modern Ireland: The Pursuit of the Workers' Republic since 1916* (Dublin, 1984), p.219.

11 Author's interview with Wilson John Haire (via email), 17 March 2011.

12 Graham Walker, *A History of the Ulster Unionist Party: Protest, Pragmatism and Pessimism* (Manchester, 2004), p.123.

13 NAUK, KV2/1185, Note on Seán Murray (n.d.); PRONI, Seán Murray Papers, D2162/G/15a – Communist Party congress, Belfast, 1-2 July 1950.

14 Author's interview with Jimmy and Edwina Stewart, 18 March 2010; Author's interview with Wilson John Haire (via email), 17 March 2011.

15 PRONI, HA/32/1/938, RUC Special Branch report, 27 February 1959.

16 PRONI, Seán Murray Papers, D2162/C/16, Belfast and District Trades' Council – A Short History: 70th Anniversary, October 1951.

17 *Irish Times*, 15 June 1950.

18 Ibid., 4 August 1950.
19 PRONI, Seán Murray Papers, D2162/J/60, 'Peace Volunteer', Issue 2, February 1952.
20 PRONI, Seán Murray Papers, D2162/M/5/10/1, Letter from Seán Nolan to Murray, 28 October 1949.
21 DCLA, CPI Nolan/Palmer Collection, Box 3/010, Irish Workers' League first annual conference, 19-20 November 1949.
22 PRONI, Seán Murray Papers, D2162/A/18, Executive committee circular, 7 March 1950.
23 DCLA, CPI Nolan/Palmer Collection, Box 3/06, Trade union resolution (c. 1950).
24 Terry Cradden, *Trade Unionism, Socialism and Partition* (Belfast, 1993), pp.200-2.
25 Ibid., pp.214-19.
26 Emmet O'Connor, *A Labour History of Ireland, 1824-2000* (Dublin, 2011), p.209.
27 PRONI, Seán Murray Papers, D2162/A/22, Political committee letter to branches, 4 September 1951.
28 *Irish Workers' Voice*, November 1950.
29 O'Connor, *A Labour History of Ireland*, p.215.
30 *Irish Times*, 14 August 1951; *Northern Worker*, November 1950.
31 Ibid., February 1950.
32 *Irish Workers' Voice*, November 1951.
33 Walker, *A History of the Ulster Unionist Party*, pp.119-20.
34 Paul Bew, Peter Gibbon and Henry Patterson, *Northern Ireland, 1921-2001: Political Forces and Social Classes* (London, 2002), pp.110-16.
35 PRONI, Seán Murray Papers, D2162/A/26, Political committee letter to branch secretaries and secretary of the YWL, 5 February 1952.
36 PRONI, Seán Murray Papers, D2162/C/22, Joint council resolution on the unity of Ireland (Draft) (c. 1952).
37 PRONI, Seán Murray Papers, D2162/I/29, 'Political Letter No. 9', 10 November 1952.
38 Milotte, *Communism in Modern Ireland*, p.221.
39 PRONI, Seán Murray Papers, D2162/G/29, Report from joint council second meeting, 31 January - 1 February 1953.
40 PRONI, Seán Murray Papers, D2162/G/26, Letter from Murray to Seán Nolan, 27 June 1952; D2162/I/29, 'Political Letter No. 9', 10 November 1952.
41 *Irish Workers' Voice*, May 1953.
42 PRONI, Seán Murray Papers, D2162/G/29, Report from joint council second meeting, 31 January - 1 February 1953.
43 Günther Stein's *The World the Dollar Built* (London, 1952) was a favourite in northern communist circles and helped to inform understandings of the nature of

post-war reconstruction and US imperialism. I am obliged to Seán Morrissey for this information.

44 PRONI, Seán Murray Papers, D2162/G/30, Joint council: Questions arising from the report of the party to the JC, 1 February 1953.

45 PRONI, Seán Murray Papers, D2162/A/31, CPNI general election leaflet, February 1953.

46 PRONI, Seán Murray Papers, D2162/A/37, 'Political Letter No. 46', 5 October 1953.

47 PRONI, Seán Murray Papers, D2162/M/5/19/1, Letter from Tom [Watters] to Murray, 18 December 1953.

48 Cradden, *Trade Unionism, Socialism and Partition*, p.204.

49 PRONI, Seán Murray Papers, D2162/G/34, CPNI draft statement, 14 February 1954. For an examination of these events, see Henry Patterson, 'Party versus Order: Ulster Unionism and the Flags and Emblems Act', *Contemporary British History*, Vol. 13, No. 4 (Winter 1999), pp.105-29.

50 Henry Patterson, *The Politics of Illusion: A Political History of the IRA* (London, 1997), p.89.

51 Brian Hanley and Scott Millar, *The Lost Revolution: The Story of the Official IRA and the Workers' Party* (Dublin, 2009), pp.3-8; Eoin Ó Broin, *Sinn Féin and the Politics of Left Republicanism* (London, 2009), pp.197-8.

52 PRONI, Seán Murray Papers, D2162/A/41, 'Northern Ireland' (1954).

53 PRONI, Seán Murray Papers, D2162/G/38, Letter to Peter Kerrigan, 11 December 1954.

54 PRONI, HA/32/1/938, RUC Special Branch report, 27 February 1959.

55 PRONI, Seán Murray Papers, D2162/A/43, 'Political Letter No. 127', 19 December 1955.

56 O'Connor, *A Labour History of Ireland*, p.212.

57 Seán Nolan (ed.), *Communist Party of Ireland Outline History* (Dublin, 1975), p.54.

58 *Catholic Standard*, 5 March 1954.

59 Ibid., 28 May 1954.

60 Johnston, *Century of Endeavour*, p.152.

61 PRONI, HA/32/1/938, Communist Party membership, British-Soviet Friendship Society (1960).

62 PRONI, Seán Murray Papers, D2162/5/17, Invitation to celebrate the liberation of Czechoslovakia (1953).

63 Denis Smyth, *Sean Murray, A Pilgrim of Hope: The Life and Times of an Irish Communist, 1898-1961* (Belfast, 1998), pp.47-8.

64 PRONI, HA/32/1/938, RUC Special Branch report, 13 November 1956.

65 PRONI, Seán Murray Papers, D2162/E/3, Seán Murray's notebook (1957).

66 PRONI, Seán Murray Papers, D2162/E/4, Seán Murray's notebook (1959).

67 PRONI, Seán Murray Papers, D2162/E/8-9, Seán Murray's notebooks (1960).

68 DCLA, CPI Nolan/Palmer Collection, Box 8/105, Seán Murray speech at international meeting of communist and workers' parties (October-November 1960).

69 Hazel Morrissey, 'Betty Sinclair: A Woman's Fight for Socialism, 1910-1981', *Saothar*, 9 (1983), p.128.

70 *Irish Times*, 7 June 1960.

71 Ibid., 13 April 1956; Nolan (ed.), *CPI Outline History*, p.39.

72 PRONI, Seán Murray Papers, D2162/C/52, Main resolution for congress (1957).

73 PRONI, HA/32/1/938, RUC Special Branch report, 13 November 1956.

74 Robert Service, *Comrades: Communism, A World History* (Basingstoke, 2007), p.315.

75 Author's interview with Jimmy and Edwina Stewart, 18 March 2010.

76 PRONI, Seán Murray Papers, D2162/G/42, CPNI executive committee statement on the twentieth congress of the CPSU and the Stalin cult of the individual (1956).

77 PRONI, Seán Murray Papers, D2162/C/52, Main resolution for congress: The Party and the Political Situation (1957).

78 *Irish Times*, 22, 23 March 1957, 2 December 1958.

79 Milotte, *Communism in Modern Ireland*, p.230; PRONI, Seán Murray papers, D2162/C/52, Main resolution for congress (1957).

80 C. Desmond Greaves, *Reminiscences of the Connolly Association* (London, 1978), pp.25-8; Author's interview with Anthony Coughlan, 10 September 2010.

81 Simon Prince, *Northern Ireland's '68: Civil Rights, Global Revolt and the Origins of the Troubles* (Dublin, 2007), pp.88-93.

82 Milotte, *Communism in Modern Ireland*, p.230.

83 *Irish Democrat*, November 1960.

84 Matt Treacy, *The Communist Party of Ireland 1921-2011: Vol. 1: 1921-1969* (Dublin, 2013), p.252.

85 Author's interview with Seán Morrissey, 12 March 2010.

86 *Irish Democrat*, February 1957.

87 PRONI, Seán Murray Papers, D2162/G/52A, Communist Party anniversary statement, 14 June 1958.

88 PRONI, Seán Murray Papers, D2162/M/5/7/2, Letter from William Gallacher to Murray, 12 June 1955.

89 PRONI, Seán Murray Papers, D2162/M/5/19/2, Letter from Tommy [Watters] to Murray, 14 June 1955.

90   PRONI, Seán Murray Papers, D2162/M/5/10/3, Letter from Sean Nolan, 27 April 1959.

91   Treacy, *The Communist Party of Ireland*, pp.255-7.

92   PRONI, Seán Murray Papers, D2162/G/64, Letter informing party members of a joint council meeting, 3 September 1958.

93   PRONI, Seán Murray Papers, D2162/5/31, Letter from Frank [Edwards], 2 June 1960.

94   PRONI, Seán Murray Papers, D2162/A/57, Executive committee letter to party members, 5 August 1958; D2162/A/63, Executive committee 'Irish Way to Socialism' circular, October 1958.

95   PRONI, Seán Murray Papers, D2162/C/47, Letter from Lance Noakes to the executive committee (c. 1958).

96   PRONI, Seán Murray Papers, D2162/5/?, Letter from Jimmy Stewart to the executive committee, 27 November 1958.

97   PRONI, Seán Murray Papers, D2162/G/80, Letter from Murray to Tommy [Watters], 9 July 1959.

98   Milotte, *Communism in Modern Ireland*, p.232.

99   PRONI, Seán Murray Papers, D2162/G/80, Letter from Murray to Tommy [Watters], 9 July 1959.

100 DCLA, CPI Nolan/Palmer Collection, Box 8/105, Seán Murray speech at international meeting of communist and workers' parties (October-November 1960).

101 PRONI, Seán Murray Papers, D2162/G/80, Letter from Murray to Tommy [Watters], 9 July 1959.

102 NAI, DFA, 5/305/55/2, Irish embassy in Italy to the Department of External Affairs, 9 January 1960.

103 Author's interview with Jimmy and Edwina Stewart, 18 March 2010.

104 Stephen Bowler, 'Seán Murray, 1898-1961, And the Pursuit of Stalinism in One Country', *Saothar*, 18 (1992), pp.49-50.

105 Milotte, *Communism in Modern Ireland*, p.233.

106 Treacy, *The Communist Party of Ireland*, pp.255-77.

107 Murray (with Stewart), *Ireland's Path to Socialism*, pp.19-22.

108 Ibid., pp.23-4.

109 Milotte, *Communism in Modern Ireland*, p.236; Patterson, *The Politics of Illusion*, p.103

110 Paddy Carmody, *Ireland Her Own* (Dublin, 1962).

111 Murray (with Stewart), *Ireland's Path to Socialism*, pp.4-10.

112 Seán Swan, *Official Irish Republicanism: 1962 to 1972* (S.I., 2008), p.100.

113 Murray (with Stewart), *Ireland's Path to Socialism*, p.28.

114 Ibid., p.38.

115 Ibid., p.25.

116 NILP & NIC-ICTU, *Joint Memorandum on Citizens' Rights in Northern Ireland* (Belfast, 1967).

117 Connal Parr, 'The pens of the defeated: John Hewitt, Sam Thompson and the Northern Ireland Labour Party', *Irish Studies Review*, DOI: 10.1080/09670882.2014.898892, pp.2-4.

118 Milotte, *Communism in Modern Ireland*, p.238.

119 These proposals chime with Conor McCabe's critique of Irish agricultural policymaking and of the fetishisation of grazing in particular, *Sins of the Father* (Dublin, 2011), pp.57-86.

120 Murray (with Stewart), *Ireland's Path to Socialism*, pp.10-18.

121 Ibid., p.27.

122 PRONI, Seán Murray Papers, D2162/G/48, Executive committee letter to party members, 14 February 1958.

123 PRONI, Seán Murray Papers, D2162/A/69, Executive committee circular, February 1959.

124 PRONI, Seán Murray Papers, D2162/G/80, Letter from Murray to Tommy [Watters], 9 July 1959.

125 PRONI, HA/32/1/938, RUC Special Branch report, 27 February 1959.

126 Nolan (ed.), *CPI Outline History*, p.43.

127 Author's interview with Roy Johnston (via email), 5 June 2010.

128 Author's interview with Jimmy and Edwina Stewart, 18 March 2010.

Epilogue

Murray's death in 1961 came as a great surprise to his many comrades in Ireland, Britain and internationally. Few were aware of the extent of his illness, or the rate at which his health had deteriorated. Indeed, several wrote to him on the week of his death to joke about his condition and discuss matters relating to party work, fully expecting him to make a swift return to the fold. Following his passing, Murray's wife, Margaret, received letters of sympathy and telegrams in large numbers, from local Irish communists, leading CPGB and Connolly Association figures, and others further afield. Elizabeth Gurley Flynn, the former Wobbly, wrote a moving tribute to Murray in the *Worker*, while Michael McInerney contributed an obituary in the *Irish Times*, and Seán Nolan in the *Irish Socialist*.[1] CPGB London district branches organised a joint memorial event in honour of his 'service to the working people and socialism'.[2] On 30 May, Murray was taken for burial at Dundonald Cemetery. A cross-section of the Irish, British and international labour movements – around 300 people – attended the funeral. A lone piper played 'Lament for the Dead', Jimmy Graham sang Connolly's 'Rebel Song', and Graham's wife, Dolly, gave a rendition of 'The Blue Hills of Antrim'. Naturally, the service concluded with 'The Internationale'.[3]

In 1985, a year before his death, the CPI published Peadar O'Donnell's *Not Yet Emmet: A Wreath on the Grave of Seán Murray*, an outline of the Irish revolutionary period and postscript to his good friend's life. In O'Donnell's analysis, between 1916 and 1923 the conditions existed briefly for a social and national revolution. However, as the forces of reaction gathered, enlisting the support of the British state, the struggle became one for 'worthwhile democracy', an anti-colonial struggle for the creation of an independent bourgeois-democratic republic. Yet the Treaty failed to yield even this gain. It deceived the people by obscuring the social forces behind its design, ushered in 'the imposition of the rule of the upper classes in Irish society' and protected the dual interests of social conservatism and comprador capitalism. This set back, by some years, the achievement of a 'workers' and farmers' government'.[4]

For an assessment of Murray's contribution to post-1916 Irish radicalism, it is appropriate to call to mind the words of O'Donnell, his closest confidant and, along with Connolly and Larkin, the person who most embodies the ideals, achievements and failures of twentieth century socialist republicanism:

> In my opinion Murray was the greatest achievement of the Republican Left … a great Fenian … In some ways, he was Connolly fully matured, fully grown up in a changing situation and therefore, was more developed, more rounded off even than his master … he had a wonderful gift of convincing everyone, particularly young people, and women, that they had something especially important to contribute to the working class movement, and he inspired young people to make a real effort.[5]

That Murray was a Fenian, a Connolly republican, is not in doubt. It was a chance encounter with Roger Casement and the events of 1916 that drew him into the ranks of Sinn Féin and the IRA, and led to his participation in the War of Independence. Throughout his political career, Murray quoted Connolly liberally and frequently channelled the legacies of radical republicans such as Tone, the Young Irelanders, Davitt and Mellows, both out of ideological commitment to their ideals and in order to colour his communist politics with Irish republicanism.

Murray's understanding of the Irish revolutionary period is significant and deserves respect because he was an active agent of radical republicanism during those years. With O'Donnell, Frank Ryan, David Fitzgerald, George Gilmore and others, he experienced the disappointment of the Treaty settlement, which carried into the second half of his career. This and a Marxism infused with Connolly's ideas informed the socialist republican dimension of his politics. Cumann na nGaedheal's consolidation of Catholic social conservatism, economic dependence on Britain and limited political autonomy formed the starting point for Murray's analysis of the Free State. The existence of the northern polity was underpinned by a powerful Unionist elite of merchants, industrialists and landed gentry, whose prosperity depended on the link with Britain, and by the informal imperialist actions of British governments. Dealing critically with the two Irish states, whose relationships with Britain were, in his view, neo-colonial, he acknowledged the limitations of regurgitating Connolly's writings in post-partition Ireland and therefore presented a variant of Connollyism that took account of contemporary conditions.

The Ireland to which Murray returned in 1930 had little in common with the vision of anti-Treaty republicans, including de Valera, who promised that his Fianna Fáil party would break Ireland's political and economic dependence on Britain. Although Murray's experiences in the intervening years complicated his views on republicanism and placed limitations on his ability to seek out communist-republican alliances, he continued to judge republican formations against two overlapping criteria. The first was the prospect of achieving democracy in anticipation of the struggle for socialism – the 'stageist' conception of the revolution. The second was the potential for achieving Connolly's social and national 'Reconquest'. If there was nothing necessarily contradictory about combining these two worldviews, particularly when they assigned the working class a leading role in the bourgeois or national revolution, there were certainly tensions in terms of how Murray applied them during the Republican Congress deliberations at Rathmines, for example. But whether he wished to draw constitutional republicanism to the left or create a leftist alternative, Murray generally responded positively to glimpses of progressivism based on one or both of these criteria and encouraged the communist and labour movements to do the same.

Murray's involvement with the Republican Congress reflected socialist republican concerns that, despite his pronouncements on building an independent and economically viable republic, de Valera would ultimately succumb to the same class interests that lay behind the Cosgrave government. In this event, the bourgeois-democratic revolution would remain incomplete. Supporters of the Price-Connolly 'Workers' Republic' resolution advanced a class-based solution that plausibly held greater appeal for workers in the industrial North. Yet this failed to appreciate the extent of the southern state's political and economic subservience to Britain. It was only in 1938 that the British government relinquished control of the Free State's ports, and in 1948 that Dublin, by a sleight of hand, broke all remaining formal political ties with London. The economic relationship was more complex and cut across constitutional matters. The overriding effect of the 1935 Coal-Cattle Pact and 1938 Anglo-Irish Trade Agreement was to strengthen Irish agriculture's dependency on the British market and aid the graziers at the expense of plans to expand tillage farming. Additionally, Fianna Fáil only established an Irish Central Bank in 1943, which allowed Dublin to control the instruments of monetary policy for the first time since the foundation of the state. These aspects of de Valera's early years in office add weight to the view that his party was reluctant to establish a fully functioning capitalist nation-state with healthy class antagonisms. Murray, therefore, based his support for O'Donnell's minority resolution on an analysis of the Free State's composition as well as an appraisal of the prospects for socialism and an ideological commitment to a 'stageist' conception of the revolution. Whether the 'Workers' and Farmers' Republic' compromise offered an opportunity to bring together greater numbers of leftist republicans and labourists, including Ulster Protestants and rural workers, is a matter of conjecture. What is clear is that Harry Pollitt prevented this option from entering into consideration.

Whereas Price's resolution was class reductionist and narrow in scope, O'Donnell's proposal was equally naïve for different reasons. The bourgeois revolution to which Murray and O'Donnell aspired included the six counties that constituted the state of Northern Ireland and, therefore, involved a number of misguided assumptions regarding the allegiances of workers in the north-east. At different stages of Murray's career, in diverse historical contexts, socialist republicanism led him to analyse and approach the Unionist working class from different angles. During the outdoor relief strike, he made an abortive attempt to encourage the IRA to put itself at the disposal of the Belfast working-class and unemployed. Unlike O'Donnell and Gilmore, he did not necessarily view these strikes as a cross-communal expression of socialist republicanism, principally because republicans did not become involved in an official capacity. Initially, he was satisfied with a place for the RWG at the heart of a historic stand by organised labour in the North, working at the same time to establish friendly relations with leftist republicans in Dublin. He only put an anti-imperialist slant on the events of 1932 when it became apparent that labour unity had faltered in the aftermath of the strikes.

Murray's confidence in independent labour's ability to achieve a socialist republic diminished in light of his practical experience. He reached the conclusion at an early stage that while cooperation with the labour involvement was desirable, republicans were the communists' most dependable allies. This was borne out by his experience of the Irish revolutionary period and by the IRA left's continued involvement in radical, working-class campaigns in Dublin and elsewhere – campaigns that social democrats in the Labour Party and NILP would not (or could not due to left sectarian tensions) bring themselves to support. In his early writings and statements, Murray often referred to the necessity of ending partition in order for labour politics to flourish across the island. A frustrating lack of progress on this front brought out the worst of his republicanism. Analysing the Second World War within an imperialist framework produced some cogent arguments relating to territorial annexations and profits in the war industries. However, CPI publications drifted towards Anglophobia and Murray foolishly made an irredentist speech that brought him dangerously close to a marginal group of IRA militarists. This undermined his and the CPI's genuine opposition to fascism and right-wing nationalism in Ireland and Europe.

None of this should lead us to the view that the CPI leader shared the 'solipsistic' trait that Richard English has identified in IRA men such as Seán Russell. Murray quickly retreated from his momentary irredentism, publicly rejected the traditional republican view that there existed an opportunity for an armed campaign in the North and in Britain, and eventually discarded comparisons between the Second World War and the 1914-1918 period. Two decades later, when confronted with the Border Campaign, he repeated these denunciations of the use of violence on the road to reunification and independence. For Murray, these campaigns did not compare with the anti-colonial struggle in which he had participated. They ignored certain political and economic realities and lacked popular support. They also set out to achieve a different type of republic than that advocated by Murray and the republican left: put simply, a thirty-two county variant of what existed in the twenty-six – a form of political independence, divorced from social upheaval, which safeguarded Gaelic Catholic conservatism.

The timing of Murray's return to Belfast afforded him a different perspective and in some respects allowed his ideas to evolve. He became (re)acquainted with the industrial, predominantly Protestant, politics of the Belfast labour movement and with British social democracy. He did not accept the logic of taking the CPNI in an explicitly Unionist direction and, crucially, rejected economism as a strategy. Nevertheless, he acknowledged the material benefits of introducing British welfarism to Northern Ireland and subsequently protecting its gains. This came to the fore as the northern economy entered into decline and Murray placed the link between the Unionist elite and Toryism at the centre of his arguments against working-class support for the Unionist Party. During the 1958 election, he deferred to the democratic socialist NILP on bread and butter issues. He incorporated this into *Ireland's Path to Socialism*, along with a Soviet communist approach to the organisation of industry and society and a Gaelic cooperativist approach to the land.

One of Connolly's major weaknesses was his inability or reluctance to undertake a serious analysis of rural Ireland. Similarly, Murray failed to take the land question seriously in the early stages of his career. Excepting symbolic references to Lalor and Davitt, for example, Murray's early writings dismissed the radical potential of sections of the peasantry and failed to comprehend social divisions and class formations on the land. Where he did write about the peasantry, he did so in a dismissive way that was typical of European Marxist thinking. This attitude is surprising, since he came from 'poor peasant' or small farming stock. O'Donnell, who came from a similar northern background, made land a key focus of his social agitation. He directed the IWFC and attempted to bring the Irish rural workers under the ambit of a European movement. Most notably, he pushed the land annuities issue to the forefront of Irish politics at a crucial juncture in Free State's history. Murray, meanwhile, prepared to launch a communist party in the two main cities, and rarely looked beyond those locales.

It is important to acknowledge that Murray eventually started treating land as a matter of importance in the early 1940s, both in his creative and political writings. He began to warn against the shock imposition of free trade on Irish agriculture, which he argued would precipitate its decline. For Murray, Irish farmers lacked not only competitiveness but a domestic market for their produce. Agriculture and industry had, for decades, sat in isolation, preventing the development of native export-led industries. Furthermore, the pre-eminence of grazing in the agricultural policies of both Irish governments benefited no one but the rancher class and British importers, the preferred buyers of Irish cattle. That this continued while small and medium farmers lacked the necessary credit to modernise made no economic sense in Murray's mind. Separated from his political prejudices, Murray's analysis of the island economy often took on a sophisticated form, particularly in the latter stage of his career. The insertion of voluntary cooperativism into the 1962 CPNI and IWL programmes may not have represented a significant advance on Murray's early analyses of rural Ireland. Above all, it underestimated the likely opposition to the measure from the small and medium farming classes. But it reflected his dual aim of reaching out at once to agricultural workers and rural republicans.

Politically, significant changes occurred in Anglo-Irish relations over the course of a decade, beginning with the introduction of the 1937 Irish Constitution and concluding with the British government's introduction of the Ireland Act (1949). These legislative measures confirmed the achievement of bourgeois-national democracy for the twenty-six counties and copper-fastened partition by enacting into law the Unionist claim to self-determination. The transnational phenomenon of imperialism was increasingly significant. It was no longer appropriate to present the relationship between Britain and Ireland as classically colonial, although the British government retained a measure of responsibility for the composition of the northern state, given that several anomalies prevented the institutionalisation of democracy.

In the final years of his life, Murray reiterated his commitment to the goal of a thirty-two county Irish socialist republic. He developed a strategy and reorganised the Irish communist movement in accordance with that ultimate objective. Yet he also took account of the substantial changes that had occurred since last developing a political programme. He envisaged a radical alliance coming to power in the South and implementing an as yet undefined socialist programme based on cross-border cooperation with a fully representative progressive government in the North, which, due to the absence of democratic norms, would conceivably take longer to gestate. Most importantly, Murray based his vision of a socialist republic on the unity of the northern working class in advance of, or in parallel with, unity of the Irish working class as a whole. This differed from the more traditional republican views expressed by Jack Bennett and Desmond Greaves. Whereas they favoured coercion in order to realise the same objective as Murray – the first, conventional IRA violence to force a decision upon the British, the second, political coercion by the British government against the Unionist population – the CPI leader explicitly recognised the importance of Protestant working-class cooperation for any socialist republican project to succeed.

Authors such as Seán Swan have made this distinction in a discussion of the 1970s republican split, placing Greaves and the Connolly Association firmly in the traditionalist camp in terms of tactics if not overall objectives.[6]

It is important to acknowledge the work that has gone before on the subject. This notwithstanding, this book posits the idea that aspects of *Ireland's Path to Socialism* anticipated aspects of Official republican thinking that would germinate over the subsequent decade. The CPNI and IWL manifestos jointly articulated a radical, democratic and non-sectarian variant of republicanism. This did not amount to a re-reading of Connolly. Rather, Murray and Carmody assessed the possibilities for labour and left-wing republicans in light of radically different political and economic circumstances than existed in Connolly's time, or during the Republican Congress period for that matter. In theory, Murray's socialist republicanism was more realistic than the traditional republican and far left alternatives on offer. A major problem, which Murray understood, was that the two communist parties did not enjoy a receptive audience, particularly at the height of the Cold War. Therefore, it is plausible to argue that Murray would have been prepared to help individuals such as Roy Johnston facilitate closer cooperation between the CPI and left republicans from the early 1960s onwards.

Socialist republicanism forms one important dimension of Murray's political make-up. And yet he owed international communist structures an equal if not greater debt of gratitude for his development as a theorist and organiser. Through his experience of British industrial radicalism, he first became acquainted with the dynamics of class relations. By virtue of this early introduction to British Marxism, first in Glasgow and later in London with the CPGB, he finds commonality with figures on the Irish republican left such as Seán McLoughlin, Roddy Connolly and indeed James Connolly. Involvement with the CPGB led him to the International Lenin School in Moscow, where he and other future leaders of peripheral communist parties became partly or fully 'Bolshevised'. The Lenin School experience equipped him with the necessary skills to establish himself as a prolific writer, pamphleteer and propagandist. A full collection of Murray's articles, editorials, lectures, speeches and party statements would be voluminous and of considerable historical value, containing in magnified form the very best and worst features of socialism and republicanism. And to be fair to Murray, his major writings from a Marxist-Leninist perspective contained acute diagnoses of the economic and political problems facing Ireland, diagnoses that have been supported by subsequent studies in political economy. Indeed, he would have had good reason to echo Che Guevara: 'It's not my fault that reality is Marxist.' It was in advancing socialist (republican) solutions to these problems that he encountered the barriers that have frustrated the Irish left for the best part of a century.

'Bolshevisation' also furnished leading party functionaries such as Murray with an understanding of the practical application of Marxist-Leninist methods of organisation, agitation and propaganda (agit-prop). Leninist revolutionary discipline and democratic centralism, instilled at a national level through individual party structures and at a global level through subordination to the Comintern, were crucial in securing the CPI's survival at difficult junctures. A number of Lenin School graduates and Comintern agents helped instil this discipline in a rump of communist activists, and Murray stands out as the individual who maintained it throughout the period in question. These same levels of commitment also ensured that the communists established a lasting and disproportionately influential presence in the trade union movement. More generally, the Comintern provided financial assistance and international networks that enabled the CPI 'to regard oneself as part of a global vanguard … It is unlikely that a revolutionary party, outside the republican tradition at least, would have survived for very long without the Comintern'.[7]

Murray entered into free association with the Comintern, which provided him with a number of career high points and earned him recognition as a leader on the international left. Early in the Irish movement's development, Murray committed to the Marxist-Leninist concept of a vanguard party. Initially, he did this to secure Moscow's backing, for there was no compromise solution that would have satisfied the Comintern hierarchy during the Third Period. Irrespective of policy differences, the main problem with the non-negotiable principle of the vanguard party was that it placed serious limitations on what the RWG/CPI could realistically achieve in cooperation with radical republican enterprises such as Saor Éire and the Republican Congress. It also restricted the movement's capacity to work productively with political expressions of organised labour on its left and right. The hostile environment fostered by powerful interests – the clergy in the South and Unionist state in the North – compounded these difficulties, making it impossible, at times, for a working-class party with a 'communist' title to organise. Murray understood this and expressed his concerns to the CPGB in the strongest possible terms. It is conceivable that he favoured the creation of a body that performed similar tasks to a communist party, but under a different title and with a broader remit to form alliances with other socialists and progressive republicans. Ultimately, these misgivings were trumped by his loyalty to the international communist project, which remained constant for the duration of his career.

Loyalty, however, did not always mean uncritical acceptance of Comintern policy. This book challenges existing interpretations of Murray's career, particularly those presented by Mike Milotte and Stephen Bowler. Furthermore, in search of the 'comprehensiveness' alluded to by C. Wright Mills,[8] it adds a number of nuances to O'Connor's discussion of relations between the Irish communist movement and the Comintern. Firstly, it is important to recall the RWG's 'class against class' experience, which saw Murray and Larkin junior levy criticisms at the left sectarianism of party leaders such as Tom Bell and express their preference for cooperation with the WUI. Murray also supported those who had attempted to draw the IRA to the left. At the same time that 'class against class' was working against the formation of alliances, he was promoting progressive republicanism in the *Workers' Voice* and helping to establish Saor Éire. Ultimately, he ensured that the RWG's Third Period lasted only a few months, not years. Secondly, in direct contravention of Comintern directives, Murray bypassed the 'united front from below', placed emphasis on the CPI's national character and sought out 'anti-imperialist' allies. This brought down the wrath of the Comintern and almost cost Murray his position at the head of the Irish movement. Crucially, however, the Comintern conceded to Murray on a number of important points, and, rather than reversing his nationally-specific policies and tactics, endorsed them retrospectively. Finally, the CPI, under his direction, adopted a position on fascism that departed from Comintern orthodoxy in rhetoric and practice, advocating the formation of a united front to combat the fascist threat. These examples, taken in conjunction with his socialist republicanism, suffice as evidence of a more autonomous and organic process of decision-making and policy formulation than Milotte, Bowler or even O'Connor have discerned.

One significant point on which it is possible to agree with O'Connor and Milotte is that CPGB leaders such as Pollitt were wholly unsympathetic to the plight of the Irish party. Murray remained on cordial terms with the British party until his death in 1961. In fact, his relationship with the CPGB seemed to improve after the dissolution of the Comintern, which coincided with his move to Belfast and reintegration into the British labour movement. However, during the Comintern era, the British party and Pollitt in particular made successive attempts to undermine Murray's position and stymie the CPI's independent development. As early as 1933, the CPGB considered removing Murray from the CPI leadership. Added to this is Pollitt's role in contributing to the Rathmines split and his attempt to orchestrate Murray's demotion in 1937. Whether due to personal animus or social imperialist ambitions – an attempt to retain a degree of influence over the trade union movement in the North – pressure on Murray's leadership almost invariably originated with Pollitt and the CPGB, not the CPI membership. As the evidence accumulates, it appears that the CPGB eventually secured Murray's removal as general secretary in 1940, and it took the best part of a decade for him to recover.

To deal with Murray's 'Stalinism', it is instructive to divide the contested term into three broadly distinct categories: Stalinist terror; Soviet foreign policy; and Stalinist theory. The first is a most uncomfortable and problematic legacy for communists internationally to confront, even to this day. The death of Pat Breslin at the hands of the regime in Kazan raises serious questions about Murray's view of the Soviet Union under Stalin. It would be difficult to argue that Murray was fully aware of the gravity of Stalin's crimes. But it is simply inconceivable that he did not learn of Breslin's fate, particularly as they were classmates at the Lenin School and Murray was friendly with Breslin's second wife, Daisy McMackin. We also recall Murray's nonsensical and bitter outburst at the height of the Spanish Civil War, which attacked the POUM on sectarian grounds and attempted to justify the Moscow Show Trials. If the worst example of Murray's republicanism is his 1939 irredentist speech, this is certainly the communist equivalent. It reflected poorly on the movement and did the CPI no favours in building bridges with the NISP. Thankfully, this left sectarianism was uncommon in his repertoire. But in light of these facts, one can understand why readers would be reluctant to accept the CPNI's penitent response to the Khrushchev speech, which he drafted.

Whilst reiterating the point that Murray anticipated aspects of the popular front and had Irish republican motives for rallying to the defence of the Spanish Republic, the CPI's involvement in the Spanish Civil War was tied to the Stalinisation of Comintern parties and Soviet foreign policy. Spanish democracy and the national security of the Soviet Union, bulwark of the global revolution, became paramount in the face of external threats. This could be justified with reference to the 'stageist' conception of the revolution. However, it also led to the CPI's painful and farcical attempts to keep step with Stalin's u-turns on the Second World War. This had the effect of further discrediting Murray at a crucial stage in his career and placing him in a weakened position upon his return to Belfast.

In terms of Stalinist theory, there is no doubt that Murray and the CPI advanced the notion of Socialism in One Country. He employed this theoretical framework, developed by Stalin and Bukharin, and ultimately had no problem defending and indeed celebrating the progress achieved in the Soviet Union. At the same time, *The Irish Case for Communism* was the most heavily Soviet-oriented of his programmes. Over the course of his career he developed his own vision for a new Ireland, culminating in *Ireland's Path to Socialism*. It is also significant that, in the final analysis, Murray readjusted his strategy to allow for the possibility of building socialism in the two Irish states before Socialism in One Country. This reflected the political changes discussed above and a re-awakening of the central Leninist principle that treats the state as the primary unit of analysis.

On a related note, one must call attention to the fact that Murray owed a greater debt to Marxist theory than contemporary socialist republicans such as Ryan, Gilmore and O'Donnell. These individuals, as with Roddy Connolly and Jim Larkin junior, were well versed in the fundamentals of Marxism and obviously familiar with Marx, Engels and Connolly's view of capitalist colonialism as a central feature of British imperialism. As a socialist republican, Murray too subscribed to this view. One could give a blow-by-blow account of his obscure and poorly-attended lectures on historical materialism, dialectics or the communist organisation of society. However, it is most instructive to focus on his understanding of imperialism as a transnational and essentially economic phenomenon. This was most evident in the latter stage of his career, as the political opportunities for resolving the national question rapidly diminished and pressure to liberalise the domestic economies gained intensity. He identified the displacement of British imperialism by the American variant and predicted the dominance and exploitation of the Irish economy by transnational capital. He held that the only defence against this threat was for labour and/or the republican left to wrest decision-making powers from the native bourgeois-bureaucratic class that acted in the interests of capital whilst feathering its own nest.

It is apparent that, despite his best efforts, Murray failed to achieve the desired communist-republican synthesis. But whatever his shortcomings, it is clear that his posthumous influence extends across the Irish republican and labour movements, including, perhaps most surprisingly, the Trotskyist Irish Workers' Group (IWG), which reprinted Murray's *The Irish Revolt* on the fiftieth anniversary of the Easter Rising, noting that 'a more detailed Marxist history of the Rebellion has not been written'.[9] Similarly, the influential Cork Workers' Club reproduced *The Irish Case for Communism, Ireland's Path to Freedom* and Murray's report to the seventh congress of the Comintern as part of its Historical Reprints Series. More importantly, Murray bequeathed to successive Irish communists and socialist republicans a fundamentally positive legacy. Firstly, he demonstrated a commitment to addressing the root causes of social injustice and fought consistently for social change in the face of clerical and secular reaction, putting his life in danger on more than one occasion. He also remained committed to the communist movement in spite of the various attempts to undermine him, setting a positive example for future generations of party activists. Secondly, he voiced opposition to fascism when it was a highly unpopular position to hold. Seeing this through, he played a key role in ensuring that the Irish communist movement actively resisted fascism and the nationalist right domestically and internationally. Thirdly, he formalised Irish communism's position on the issue of civil rights and provided the theory with which to underpin CPI involvement in the civil rights campaigns of the 1960s. Fourthly, he helped to create conditions through which the CPNI and IWL contributed to and benefited from the achievement of trade union unity in 1959. In lieu of a united communist organisation, Murray is likely to have viewed the formation of the ICTU as a vindication of the ideas he formulated in the twilight of his career. Finally, *Ireland's Path to Socialism* achieved a healthy and pragmatic balance of Marxism-Leninism, left reformism and socialist republicanism. Crucially, it recognised the Unionist working class claim to self-determination, offered a route to the reconstitution of the CPI and laid the foundations for renewed cooperation between the communist movement and left republicans. It is conceivable that, had he lived into the 1970s, he would have made a substantial contribution to the emergence of a radical republican movement based on Marxist-Leninist principles of organisation and socialist republican ideology infused with the ideals of the United Irishmen.[10]

NOTES

1 *Irish Times*, 26 May 1961; *Irish Socialist*, June 1961; *Worker*, 30 July 1961.
2 PRONI, Seán Murray Papers, D2162/I/45, Seán Murray memorial meeting – London District Communist Party, June 1961.

3 PRONI, Seán Murray Papers, D2162/I/49, Seán Murray's funeral service, 30 May 1961; Emmet O'Connor, 'John (Seán) Murray', in Keith Gildart, David Howell and Neville Kirk (eds), *Dictionary of Labour Biography, Vol. XI* (London, 2003), p.205.

4 Peadar O'Donnell, *Not Yet Emmet: A Grave on the Wreath of Seán Murray* (Dublin, 1985).

5 Michael McInerney, *Peadar O'Donnell: Irish Social Rebel* (Dublin, 1974), pp.96-8.

6 Seán Swan, *Official Irish Republicanism, 1962 to 1972* (S.I., 2008), pp.374-6.

7 Emmet O'Connor, *Reds and the Green: Ireland, Russia and the Communist Internationals* (Dublin, 2004), p.236.

8 C. Wright Mills, *The Sociological Imagination* (New York, 1959), p.245.

9 Seán Murray, *The Irish Revolt: 1916 and After* (Reprint, with an introduction by Gery Lawless) (London, 1966).

10 See Brian Hanley and Scott Millar, *The Lost Revolution: The Story of the Official IRA and the Workers' Party* (Dublin, 2009).

Bibliography

PRIMARY SOURCES

Russian State Archive for Social and Political History (Rossiiskii Gosudartsvennyi Arkhiv Sotsial'no-Politischeskoi Istorii fondi)
- 495, ECCI

National Archives of the UK (NAUK)
- Cabinet papers
- Security Service files

Public Record Office of Northern Ireland (PRONI)
- Ministry of Home Affairs
- Seán Murray Papers

Dublin City Library and Archive (DCLA)
- CPI Seán Nolan/Geoffrey Palmer Collection

Military Archives, Cathal Brugha Barracks, Dublin
- Bureau of Military History witness statements (1913-1921)
- Military service pensions collection

National Archives of Ireland (NAI)
- Department of Foreign Affairs
- Department of Justice
- Department of Taoiseach

National Library of Ireland
- Seán O'Mahony Papers
- Hanna Sheehy Skeffington Papers

Private Papers
- C. Desmond Greaves Papers (in the possession of Anthony Coughlan)
- Letters from Andy Boyd to Emmet O'Connor (in the possession of Emmet O'Connor)

Parliamentary Records
- *Acts of the Oireachtas*
- *Dáil Debates*

University College Dublin Archives (UCDA)
- Seán MacEntee Papers
- Moss Twomey Papers

Newspapers
- *An Phoblacht*
- *Daily Worker*
- *Irish Democrat*
- *Irish Democrat* (Connolly Association)
- *Irish Independent*
- *Irish News*
- *Irish Press*
- *Irish Review*
- *Irish Socialist*
- *Irish Times*
- *Irish Worker*
- *Irish Workers' Voice*
- *Irish Workers' Weekly*
- *Northern Worker*
- *Republican Congress*
- *Standard*
- *The Bell*
- *Unity*
- *Worker*

- *Workers' Bulletin*
- *Workers' Republic*
- *Workers' Voice*

INTERVIEWS

- Anthony Coughlan, 10 September 2010
- Wilson John Haire (via email), 17 March 2011
- Roy Johnston (via email), 5 June 2010
- Seán Morrissey, 12 March 2010
- Peadar O'Donnell, interviewed by Ben Kiely, 1983, transcribed by the author
- Eoin Ó Murchú, 17 May 2010
- Bill Somerset, 15 June 2010
- Jimmy and Edwina Stewart, 18 March 2010

ARTICLES, BOOKS AND PAMPHLETS

Barton, B., *Northern Ireland in the Second World War* (Belfast, 1995).

Beevor, A., *Stalingrad* (London, 1999).

Behan, B., *Confessions of an Irish Rebel* (London, 1965).

Bell, T., *The Struggle of the Unemployed in Belfast, Oct. 1932* (Cork, 1976).

Bew, P., Gibbon, P. and Patterson, H., *The State in Northern Ireland: Political Forces and Social Classes, 1921-1972* (Manchester, 1979).

— *Northern Ireland, 1921-2001: Political Forces and Social Classes* (London, 2002).

Bew, P., Hazelkorn, E. and Patterson, H., *The Dynamics of Irish Politics* (London, 1989).

Black, B., 'A Triumph of Voluntarism? Industrial Relations and Strikes in Northern Ireland in World War Two', *Labour History Review*, Vol. 70, No. 1 (April 2005), pp.5-25.

Borkenau, F., *World Communism: A History of the Communist International* (Michigan, 1962).

Bowler, S., 'Seán Murray, 1898-1961, And the Pursuit of Stalinism in One Country', *Saothar*, 18 (1993), pp.41-53.

Bowyer Bell, J., *The Secret Army: The IRA* (Revised 3rd ed.) (Dublin, 1998).

Browne, N., *Against the Tide* (Dublin, 1986).

Byrne, P., *The Republican Congress Revisited* (London, 1994).

Carmody, P., *Ireland Her Own* (Dublin, 1962).

Carr, E.H., *The Comintern & the Spanish Civil War* (Basingstoke, 1984).

— *What is History?* (2nd ed., with new introduction by Richard J. Evans) (Basingstoke, 2001).

Cohen, G. and Morgan, K., 'Stalin's Sausage Machine. British Students at the Lenin School, 1926-37', *Twentieth Century British History*, Vol. 13, No. 4 (2002), pp.327-55.

Bibliography

Connolly, J., *Ireland Upon the Dissecting Table: James Connolly on Ulster & Partition* (Cork, 1975).

Cradden, T., *Trade Unionism, Socialism and Partition* (Belfast, 1993).

Crawford, N.C., *Argument and Change in World Politics: Ethics, Decolonization and Humanitarian Intervention* (Cambridge, 2002).

Cronin, M., 'The Blueshirts in the Irish Free State: The nature of socialist republican and government opposition', in T. Kirk and A. McElligot (eds), *Opposing Fascism: Community, authority and resistance* (Cambridge, 1999).

— *The Blueshirts and Irish Politics* (Dublin, 1997).

Cronin, S., *Frank Ryan: The Search for the Republic* (Dublin, 1980).

Crossey, C. and Monaghan, J., 'The Origins of Trotskyism in Ireland', *Revolutionary History*, Vol. 6, No. 2/3 (Summer 1996), pp.4-48.

Deasy, J., 'Seán Murray: Republican and Marxist' (correspondence), *Saothar*, 19 (1994), p.13.

Degras, J. (ed.), *The Communist International, 1919-1943: Documents, Vol. 3, 1929-1943* (London, 1971).

Deutscher, I., *Stalin: A Political Biography* (London, 1964).

Devine, F., 'Letting Labour Lead: Jack MacGougan and the Pursuit of Unity, 1913-1958', *Saothar*, 14 (1989), pp.113-24.

Devlin, P., *Yes We Have No Bananas: Outdoor Relief in Belfast, 1920-39* (Belfast, 1981).

Doyle, B. (with H. Owens), *Brigadista: An Irishman's Fight Against Fascism* (Dublin, 2006).

Dunphy, R., *The Making of Fianna Fáil Power in Ireland, 1923-1948* (Oxford, 1995).

— 'Fianna Fáil and the Irish Working Class, 1926-38', in F. Lane and D. Ó Drisceoil (eds), *Politics and the Irish Working Class, 1830-1945* (Basingstoke, 2005).

Edwards, A., *A History of the Northern Ireland Labour Party: Democratic Socialism and Sectarianism* (Manchester, 2009).

English, R., *Radicals and the Republic: Socialist Republicanism in the Irish Free State, 1925-1937* (Oxford, 1994).

Fallon, D., 'Newsboys and the "Animal Gang" in 1930s Dublin', in D. Convery (ed.), *Locked Out: A Century of Working-Class Life* (Sallins, 2013).

Farrell, M., *Northern Ireland: The Orange State* (2nd ed.) (London, 1980).

Feeley, P., 'Labour and local history: The Case of Jim Gralton', *Saothar*, 14 (1989), pp.85-94.

— *The Gralton Affair: The Story of the Deportation of Jim Gralton, a Leitrim Socialist* (Dublin, 1986).

Ferriter, D., *The Transformation of Ireland, 1900-2000* (London, 2004).

Freyer, G., *Peadar O'Donnell* (Lewisberg, 1973).

Geoghegan, V., 'Cemeteries of Liberty: William Norton on Communism and Fascism' (document study), *Saothar*, 18 (1993), pp.106-9.

Gildart, K., 'Coal Strikes on the Home Front: Miners' Militancy and Socialist Politics in the Second World War', *Twentieth Century British History*, Vol. 20, No. 2 (2009), pp.121-51.

Gilmore, G., *The Irish Republican Congress* (Cork, 1979).

Girvin, B., *Between Two Worlds: Politics and Economy in Independent Ireland* (Dublin, 1989).

Gray, M., 'Reminiscence: A Shop Steward Remembers', *Saothar*, 11 (1986), p. 109-15.

Greaves, C.D., *Liam Mellows and the Irish Revolution* (London, 1971).

— *Reminiscences of the Connolly Association* (London, 1978).

— *Seán O'Casey: Politics and Art* (London, 1971).

— *The Irish Transport and General Workers' Union: The Formative Years, 1909-1923* (Dublin, 1982).

— *The Life and Times of James Connolly* (London, 1961).

Hallas, D., *The Comintern* (London, 1985).

Hamill, J., 'Saor Éire and the IRA: An Exercise in Deception?', *Saothar*, 20 (1995), pp.56-66.

Hanley, B., 'Moss Twomey, Radicalism and the IRA, 1931-1933: A Reassessment', *Saothar*, 26 (2001), pp.53-60.

— *The IRA, 1926-1936* (Dublin, 2002).

— 'The IRA and Trade Unionism, 1922-72', in F. Devine, F. Lane and N. Puirséil (eds), *Essays in Irish Labour History: A Festschrift for Elizabeth and John W. Boyle* (Sallins, 2008).

— 'The Irish Citizen Army After 1916', *Saothar*, 28 (2003), pp.37-47.

— 'The Storming of Connolly House', *History Ireland*, Vol. 7, No. 2 (Summer 1999), pp. 5-7.

— and Millar, S., *The Lost Revolution: The Story of the Official IRA and the Workers' Party* (Dublin, 2009).

Harris, M., 'Catholicism, Nationalism and the Labour Question in Belfast, 1935-1938', *Bullán*, No. 1 (1997), pp.15-32.

Haywood, H., *Black Bolshevik: Autobiography of an Afro-American Communist* (Chicago, Illinois, 1978).

Hegarty, P., *Peadar O'Donnell* (Cork, 1999).

Hemingway, E., *For Whom the Bell Tolls* [1940] (London, 2004).

Hennessey, T., *A History of Northern Ireland, 1920-1996* (Dublin, 1997).

Hoar, A., *In Green and Red: The Lives of Frank Ryan* (Dingle, 2004).

Hoare Q. and Nowell Smith, G. (eds.), *Antonio Gramsci: Selections from the Prison Notebooks* (London, 1971).

Hobsbawm, E., *Age of Extremes: The Short Twentieth Century, 1914-1991* (London, 1994).

— 'War of ideas', *Guardian*, 17 February 2007.

Hogan, J., *Could Ireland Become Communist? The Facts of the Case* (Dublin, 1935).

Hopkins, J.K., *Into the Heart of the Fire: The British in the Spanish Civil War* (Stanford, 1998).

Hopkins, S., 'French Communism, The Comintern and Class Against Class: Interpretations and Rationales', in M. Worley (ed.), *In Search of Revolution: International Communist Parties in the Third Period* (London, 2004).

Hopkinson, M., *Green Against Green: The Irish Civil War* (2nd ed.) (Dublin, 2004).

– *The Irish War of Independence* (Dublin, 2002).

Howell, D., *A Lost Left: Three Studies in Socialism and Nationalism* (Manchester, 1986).

Johnston, R., *Century of Endeavour: A Biographical and Autobiographical View of the Twentieth Century in Ireland* (Dublin, 2006).

Kennedy, K.A., Giblin, T. and McHugh, D., *The Economic Development of Ireland in the Twentieth Century* (London, 1988).

Keogh, D., *Ireland and the Vatican: The Politics and Diplomacy of Church-State Relations, 1922-1960* (Cork, 1995).

– *Twentieth Century Ireland: Nation and State* (Dublin, 1994).

Keohane, L., *Captain Jack White: Imperialism, Anarchism and the Irish Citizen Army* (Sallins, 2014).

Kostick, C., *Revolution in Ireland: Popular Militancy 1917 to 1923* (London & Chicago, 1996).

Lee, J.J., *Ireland, 1912-1985: Politics and Society* (Cambridge, 1989).

Loughlin, C.J.V., 'Pro-Hitler or Anti-Management? War on the Industrial Front, Belfast, October 1942', in D. Convery (ed.), *Locked Out: A Century of Irish Working-Class Life* (Sallins, 2013).

MacEoin, U. (ed.), *The IRA in the Twilight Years, 1923-1948* (Dublin, 1997).

McCabe, C., *Sins of the Father: Tracing the Decisions that Shaped the Irish Economy* (Dublin, 2011).

McCullough, W.H., *But Victory Sooner* (Belfast, 1943).

— *Ireland Looks to Labour* (Belfast, 1943).

— *Ireland's Way Forward*, Report of the First National Congress of the CPI (Belfast, 1942).

McDermott, K. and Agnew, J., *The Comintern: A History of International Communism from Lenin to Stalin* (Basingstoke, 1996).

McGarry, F., *Eoin O'Duffy: A Self-Made Hero* (Oxford, 2005).

— *Frank Ryan* (Dundalk, 2002).

— *Irish Politics and the Spanish Civil War* (Cork, 1999).

McGuire, C., *Roddy Connolly and the Struggle for Socialism in Ireland* (Cork, 2008).

— *Seán McLoughlin: Ireland's Forgotten Revolutionary* (Pontypool, 2011).

McIlroy, J. and Campbell, A., 'The last chance saloon? The Independent Labour Party and miners' militancy in the Second World War revisited', *Journal of Contemporary History*, Vol. 46, No. 4 (October 2011), pp.871-96.

McInerney, M., *Peadar O'Donnell: Irish Social Rebel* (Dublin, 1974).

McLoughlin, B., *Left to the Wolves: Irish Victims of Stalinist Terror* (Dublin, 2007).

— 'Proletarian Academics or Party Functionaries? Irish Communists at the International Lenin School, Moscow, 1927-37', *Saothar*, 22 (1997), pp.63-79.

— and O'Connor, E., 'Sources on Ireland and the Communist International, 1920-1943', *Saothar*, 21 (1995), pp.101-7.

Millar, S., 'Roger Casement and North Antrim', in E. Phoenix, P. O Cleireachain, E. McAuley and N. McSparran (eds), *Feis na nGleann: A Century of Gaelic Culture in the Antrim Glens* (Belfast, 2005).

Mills, C.W., *The Sociological Imagination* (New York, 1959).

Milotte, M., *Communism in Modern Ireland: The Pursuit of the Workers' Republic since 1916* (Dublin, 1984).

Morrissey, H., 'Betty Sinclair: A Woman's Fight for Socialism, 1910-1981', *Saothar*, 9 (1983), pp.121-32.

Munck, R. and Rolston, B. (with G. Moore), *Belfast in the 1930s: An Oral History* (Belfast, 1987).

Murray, P., *Oracles of God: The Roman Catholic Church and Irish Politics, 1922-37* (Dublin, 2000).

Murray, S., *Craigavon in the Dock* (Belfast, 1938).

— *Ireland's Fight for Freedom and the Irish in the USA* (New York, 1934).

— *Ireland's Path to Freedom* (Dublin, 1933).

— *The Irish Case for Communism* (Dublin, 1933).

— *The Irish Revolt: 1916 and After* (London, 1936).

— with J. Stewart, *Ireland's Path to Socialism* (Belfast, 1962).

National Council for Civil Liberties (NCCL), *The Special Powers Acts of Northern Ireland: Report of a Commission of Inquiry appointed to examine the purpose and effect of Civil Authorities (Special Powers) Acts (Northern Ireland) 1922 & 1933* (London, 1936).

Nolan, S. (ed.), *Communist Party of Ireland Outline History* (Dublin, 1975).

Ó Broin, E., *Sinn Féin and the Politics of Left Republicanism* (London, 2009).

O'Connor, E., *A Labour History of Ireland, 1824-2000* (Dublin, 2011).

— 'Bolshevising Irish Communism, 1927-31', *Irish Historical Studies*, Vol. 33, No. 132 (2003), pp.452-69.

— 'From Bolshevism to Stalinism: Communism and the Comintern in Ireland', in N. LaPorte, K. Morgan and M. Worley (eds), *Bolshevism, Stalinism and the Comintern: Perspectives on Stalinization, 1917-1953* (Basingstoke, 2008).

— 'John (Seán) Murray' in K. Gildart, D. Howell and N. Kirk (eds), *Dictionary of Labour Biography, Vol. XI* (London, 2003).

— *Reds and the Green: Ireland, Russia and the Communist Internationals, 1919-43* (Dublin, 2004).

— and McCabe, C., 'Ireland', in J. Allen, A. Campbell and J. McIlroy (eds), *Histories of Labour: National and International Perspectives* (Pontypool, 2010).

O'Connor, P., *Soldier of Liberty: Recollections of a Socialist and Anti-Fascist Fighter* (Dublin, 1996).

O'Connor, P.E., 'Identity and Self-Representation in Irish Communism: The Connolly Column and the Spanish Civil War', *Socialist History*, Vol. 34 (2006), pp. 36-61.

O'Donnell, P., *Not Yet Emmet: A Grave on the Wreath of Seán Murray* (Dublin, 1985).

Ó Drisceoil, D., *Censorship in Ireland, 1939-1945: Neutrality, Politics and Society* (Cork, 1996).

— *Peadar O'Donnell* (Cork, 2001).

O'Malley, K., 'The League Against Imperialism: British, Irish and Indian connections', *Communist History Network Newsletter*, Vol. 14 (Spring, 2003).

O'Riordan, M., 'Communism in Dublin in the 1930s: The Struggle against Fascism', in H.G. Klaus (ed.), *Strong Words, Brave Deeds: The Poetry, Life and Times of Thomas O'Brien, Volunteer in the Spanish Civil War* (Dublin, 1994).

O'Riordan, Michael, *Connolly Column: The Story of the Irishmen who Fought in the Ranks of the International Brigades in the National-Revolutionary War of the Spanish People, 1936-39* (Dublin, 1979).

Ollerenshaw, P., 'War, Industrial Mobilisation and Society in Northern Ireland, 1939-1945', *Contemporary European History*, Vol. 16, No. 2 (2007), pp.169-97.

Orwell, G., 'The Prevention of Literature', in *Shooting an Elephant and Other Essays* (London, 2009).

Parr, C., 'The pens of the defeated: John Hewitt, Sam Thompson and the Northern Ireland Labour Party', *Irish Studies Review*, DOI: 10.1080/09670882.2014.898892.

— *The Undefeated: Radical Protestants from the Spanish Civil War to the 1960s* (Belfast, 2014).

Patterson, H., *The Politics of Illusion: A Political History of the IRA* (London, 1997).

— 'Party versus Order: Ulster Unionism and the Flags and Emblems Act', *Contemporary British History*, Vol. 13, No. 4 (Winter 1999), pp.105-29.

— *Ireland since 1939: The Persistence of Conflict* (Dublin, 2007).

Prince, S., *Northern Ireland's '68: Civil Rights, Global Revolt and the Origins of The Troubles* (Dublin, 2007).

Puirséil, N., *The Irish Labour Party, 1922-73* (Dublin, 2007).

Redfearn, N., 'British Communists, the British Empire and the Second World War', *International Labor and Working-Class History*, No. 65 (Spring 2004), pp.117-35.

Sassoon, D., *One Hundred Years of Socialism: The West European Left in the Twentieth Century* (London, 1996).

Service, R., *Comrades: Communism, A World History* (Basingstoke, 2007).

Sheehy Skeffington, A., *Skeff: A Life of Owen Sheehy Skeffington, 1909-1970* (Dublin, 1991).

Singh, R.S. and Singh, C., *Indian Communism: Its role towards Indian polity* (New Delhi, 1991).

Smyth, D., *Sean Murray, A Pilgrim of Hope: The Life and Times of an Irish Communist, 1898-1961* (Belfast, 1998).

Stradling, R., *The Irish in the Spanish Civil War, 1936-39: Crusades in Conflict* (Manchester, 1999).

Stein, G., *The World the Dollar Built* (London, 1952).

Swan, S., *Official Irish Republicanism, 1962 to 1972* (S.I., 2008).

Swift, J.P., *John Swift: An Irish Dissident* (Dublin, 1991).

Thorpe, A., *The British Communist Party and Moscow, 1920-43* (Manchester, 2000).

Tosh, J., *The Pursuit of History* (5th Edition) (Harrow, 2010).

Treacy, M., *The Communist Party of Ireland 1921-2011: Vol. 1: 1921-1969* (Dublin, 2013).

Walker, G., *A History of the Ulster Unionist Party: Protest, Pragmatism and Pessimism* (Manchester, 2004).

— '"Protestantism Before Party!": The Ulster Protestant League in the 1930s', *The Historical Journal*, Vol. 28, No. 4 (1985), pp.961-7.

— *The Politics of Frustration: Harry Midgley and the Failure of Labour in Northern Ireland* (Manchester, 1985).

— 'The Northern Ireland Labour Party, 1924-45,' in F. Lane, and Ó Drisceoil, D. (eds), *Politics and the Irish Working Class, 1830-1945* (Basingstoke, 2005).

Ward, M., *Hanna Sheehy Skeffington: A Life* (Cork, 1997).

Wicks, H., *Keeping My Head: Memoirs of a British Bolshevik* (London, 1992).

Zinn, H., *A People's History of the United States: 1492 to the Present* (Revised ed.) (New York, 2010).

THESES AND UNPUBLISHED SOURCES

Connolly, D., 'The "Red Scare" in 1950s Dublin: Genuine or generated? The role of Archibishop McQuaid's Vigilance Committee' (unpublished MPhil thesis, Trinity College Dublin, 2011).

Convery, D., 'Brigadistas: The History and Memory of Irish Anti-Fascists in the Spanish Civil War' (unpublished doctoral thesis, University College Cork, 2012),

Coughlan A. (ed.), *Insight, Ideas, Politics: The Table Talk of C. Desmond Greaves, 1960-1988* (unpublished, 2012).

O'Connor Lysaght, D.R., 'The Communist Party of Ireland: A Critical History', *Arguments for a Workers' Republic*,

http://www.workersrepublic.org/Pages/Ireland/Communism/cpihistory1.html.

Index

Note: Entries for newspapers, pamphlets, journalistic articles and other publications are in italics.

Index

Index